Matters of the Heart

A WORKBOOK FOR PERSONAL TRANSFORMATION

STEVE EVANS

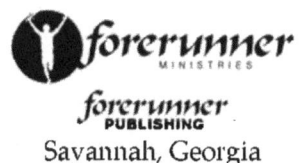

Savannah, Georgia

Matters of the Heart: A Workbook for Personal Transformation
Copyright © 2011 by Steve Evans

Distributed by Forerunner Ministries, Inc.
  Email: **steve@forerunners4him.org**
  Website: www.healingstreamsusa.org

Published by Forerunner Ministries, Inc.
ISBN-13: 978-0615597904
ISBN-10: 0615597904

Edited by Anne-Marie Evans.

All rights reserved. This book is protected by the copyright laws of the United States of America and may not be copied or reprinted for commercial gain or profit. The use of short quotations or occasional page copying for personal or group study is permitted and encouraged. Permission will be granted upon request to use this material for such teaching and ministry purposes, providing proper credit is given to its source.

Unless otherwise indicated, all Scripture quotations are from The Holy Bible, English Standard Version® (ESV®), copyright © 2001 by Crossway, a publishing ministry of Good News Publishers. Used by permission. All rights reserved.

Scripture quotations taken from the Amplified® Bible, Copyright © 1954, 1958, 1962, 1964, 1965, 1987 by The Lockman Foundation. Used by permission. (www.Lockman.org)

Scripture quotations marked (WEB) are from The World English Bible (public domain).

Scripture quotations marked (KJV) are from The Holy Bible, King James Version (public domain).

Cover and interior design by Forerunner Publishing, Savannah, Georgia. Original illustrations with captions by Steve Evans.

Cover image used with permission from iStock. Other illustrations, photos and clip art used with permission from Microsoft and Google Images.

Printed in the United States of America by CreateSpace.

TABLE OF CONTENTS

Preface   5

Acknowledgements   9

Section One: Foundations
- The Spiritual Roots of Disease   13
- Truth or Consequences   23
- The Keys to the Kingdom   33
- Kingdoms in Conflict   43
- Separation from Sin   53
- The Pathway of Temptation   63
- Recognize and Replace!   73

Section Two: Image Bearing
- Beholding the True Image   85
- Our New Identity   95
- The Father's Heart of Love   105

Section Three: Strongholds
- Strongholds   117
- Reversing the Curse (GENERATIONAL SIN)   127
- The Power of Believing (UNBELIEF)   137
- Discerning the Enemy (ACCUSATION)   147
- Freedom through Forgiving (BITTERNESS)   157
- Mending the Broken Heart (TRAUMA)   167
- Accepted in the Beloved (REJECTION)   177
- Love Thyself! (SELF-REJECTION)   187
- Godly Contentment (ENVY)   197
- Exposing the Darkness (THE OCCULT)   207
- Fear Not! (FEAR)   217
- No More Idols! (ADDICTION)   227

Section Four: The Journey Forward
- Spiritual Warfare 101 (SURRENDER)   239
- Walking in the Spirit (SUBMISSION)   249

The Way of the Cross
- Negative Emotions   263
- The Disciple's Cross   267

Appendix
- Bibliography   273
- Forerunner Ministries   275
- Forerunner Books   277
- About the Author   282

PREFACE

If you have had a taste of the marvelous peace of Christ and want to learn how to live consistently in it then this book is for you. A heavenly peace—gentle and uplifting, resplendent with hope and pregnant with possibilities for joy—is your true Inheritance in Christ. Whether you are a brand new Christian or a veteran of many campaigns, this peace is meant to be your daily, moment by moment, experience of your union with Him, even and especially, in the midst of all the cares and pressures of this life. Sadly, this peace is *the missing piece* in many Christians' experience of their faith. We have Bible studies, church services, prayer and fellowship enough to fill our days, but this peace was meant to fill our hearts.

How can it be that the peace of Christ has gone missing? Is this not the peace of which Jesus said, "Peace I leave with you, My peace I give to you; not as the world gives do I give to you" (John 14:27)? The world is famous for its take backs. Jesus, on the other hand, makes His peace *always available* to us. Peace is His perpetual gift to us, but we are not living in it: What's going on?

Consider how the world gives beauty and strength to youth for free; riches, prestige and power to those who care for nothing else. It even gives a measure of peace to anyone on top of their game—whether it is self-protection or self-promotion—so long as you can see how things are going to work out in your favor. These gifts are all too often fleeting treasures. Yet, this peace that Jesus gives is intended to be an everlasting inheritance, *our* inheritance, our *daily* inheritance.

To be sure, most Christians can enter into this peace during an anointed worship service and can touch base with this peace during moments of devoted Bible study or prayer. We even have a rock bottom sense of peace that we are headed toward heaven and that God is in control. But do we *live in this peace* as our daily delight and source of surpassing strength—no matter what comes our way? That seems to be beyond us.

Throughout the Body of Christ there are those who suffer not only from diseases of the body but from the many and varied dis-eases of the soul: stressed by anxious concerns, carrying deep pain from the past, depressed in heart and spirit or just plagued by a whole host of negative emotions which can so easily quench the simple joy of living. Rather than being released into the glorious liberty of the children of God, many believers have become captive to their inner lives at the very time when the world needs a witness of the life-changing power of the gospel. As in Isaiah's day we are a people in need of restoration.

"But this is a people plundered and looted; they are all of them trapped in holes and hidden in prisons; they have become plunder with none to rescue, spoil with none to say, 'Restore!'" Isaiah 42:22

This book grew out of a conviction that there is a real power of transformation available through faith in Christ, but that His Words of life are somehow not reaching His people in a way that they can appropriate. As a pastor I knew the frustration of preaching and pleading, "Trust the Lord and follow Him," as the great answer to life's problems and a very real means of recovering peace, yet I rarely saw the needed changes come to others. I was gently haunted by a passage in Jeremiah about speaking words that do not heal.

> **"They have healed the wound of my people lightly, saying, 'Peace, peace,' when there is no peace."** Jeremiah 6:14

I realized that others needed more, because I myself needed more. From the first moments of my new life in Christ, I had been introduced to the ministry of deliverance and have been gratefully walking in the benefits of that early release from demonic bondage ever since. But there would prove to be much more in the tangled mess of my innermost emotional life than could be addressed by simple deliverance. It was of course absolutely necessary—if I wanted freedom—to resolutely "put to death" anything that the Word or the Spirit identified as sin, lest I become enslaved to the enemy all over again. It was also essential that I learned to try my level best to trust the Lord and seek to follow Him—these two requirements of basic discipleship (along with Bible study, prayer, worship, fellowship and service) certainly bring tremendous comfort, growth and healing to those who walk in them. Basic discipleship helped me live with my pain and damaged inner life, it even helped me prune away the unwanted fruit, but it was not mending my heart or getting to the root issues that were causing me such abiding anguish.

Again and again I happily discovered that God was sending into my life two other graces that produced remarkable "results": strong revelation of truth and inner healing by His Spirit. Revelation and inner healing are therefore two goals of this series of lessons. Only the Holy Spirit can reveal truth in the way we need to receive it for its freedom-making power to liberate us; only the Spirit can do the transforming works of ministry necessary to restore our lost wholeness. However, there is much that we can do to position ourselves for grace to happen. Why else would He entreat us so often to seek Him?

These 24 lessons from Healing Streams Ministry's *Matters of the Heart* teaching series will show you how to bring your heart to God and how you can receive His Heart for you. That is the essence of the Great Exchange—our *dis*-grace for His grace—and it is always available for us to access through the faith He has given us. Where our inner state is concerned, there are two great assignments which are actually gracious invitations to experience the surpassing vitality of *new life* in Christ:

1) Restoration. Preparing our inward state to hold up under the pressures of daily life requires recovery of the natural grace that got lost along the way. For countless reasons—not least of which is getting free of the pain—we need to recover from any emotional brokenness emanating from our past. But there is another level…

2) Mastery. As we learn to manage our emotional life, we not only receive freedom from the past, but we gain the graced ability to reign with wisdom over our own emotions, making it possible to live even the most active or embattled days with deep peace and Spirit-led resourcefulness!

By a process of recovery leading to mastery we can experience our own life, no matter how damaged initially, becoming just what Jesus described to Nicodemus so long ago: weightless and free. Being "born again" is only the entry point. Those who learn this new way of yielding to His Spirit will become like leaves floating on the wind:

"Do not marvel that I said to you, 'You must be born again.' The wind blows where it wishes, and you hear its sound, but you do not know where it comes from or where it goes. So it is with everyone who is born of the Spirit." John 3:7-8

We truly can learn how to be lifted and carried by the river of peace that God is sending our way each day. Being born again ushers us into the new life; the Holy Spirit within us provides the power to live the new life. He is the River of Peace. Are you only experiencing trickles and puddles of that peace? Take these lessons to heart, learn *the way of the heart* and the peace will soon become a slender stream. Persevere and it will grown into a mighty river leading you into great adventures in company with your Lord. One Day it will carry you all the way to God's throne in heaven.

I leave it to God and the devil to provide the pop quizzes, times of testing and final exams. The Lord never tempts us at any time, but He does provide opportunities for growth. In our times of trial and struggle God is "testing" to see if we are ready and willing to take a step upwards into greater faith and faithfulness (He already knows our true spiritual condition, but do we?). Meanwhile the enemy becomes active, tempting us to come into agreement with his distorted perspective, take on his demented attitudes and walk in his destructive ways. I pray that you will learn to recognize the difference, shun the enemy and hearken to the Lord. May this become your time of learning these essential lessons of the heart and growing greatly in grace!

ACKNOWLEDGEMENTS

It takes the Light of Christ, streaming to us through the scriptures, to enlighten our darkness and lead us out into the blessed sunshine of God's new day. Enough cannot be said in praise of God's Word, for upon it hangs our whole hope of liberation and transformation. That it was our Lord's own hope for us, too, is shown by His prayer to the Father, "Sanctify them by Your truth. Your Word is truth" (John 17:17). Ultimately, every word of truth that reaches us is lovingly sent by the Father of Light, who is Himself the giver of every good gift. Yet, we cannot help but thank the ones through whom that life-giving Word comes our way.

I feel such a debt of respect and gratitude for Dr. Henry W. Wright of Be In Health®. More than anyone else that I know, Dr. Wright has boldly wedded the findings of medical science with Holy Scripture and then carried them to their logical conclusion, reaping practical applications for healing with astonishing specificity. As he has shown in his book, *A More Excellent Way,* these previously uncharted depths of the soul hold the answer to one of life's most intriguing questions: Where does disease come from? Any informed reader of this book will quickly note my dependence upon many of Dr. Wright's basic categories and insights learned during unforgettable seminar sessions at his ministry base in Thomaston, Georgia beginning in the fall of 2000.

This workbook therefore owes much of its structure to the model for ministry that I saw in Thomaston, though there are many others I have learned from along the way. François Fénelon, Bishop of Cambrais and defender of Jeanne Guyon, is at the head of my list. I wanted out of my pain so badly! It took all the considerable kindness of Fénelon to persuade me that there can be no healing of anyone's life without an entire embrace of the cross. Let all who would be truly whole drink from the fountain of his wisdom and thank God with me that people in his day wrote such extensive letters! The Bibliography for further reading at the back of this book gives a more complete list of my indebtedness.

This book itself would never have come into being were it not for the polite entreaty of my wife Eunice, who championed the idea of a workbook from the beginning and who encouraged me to devote the time to its writing. At first all I could see was *more work*, but then as the vision developed and words seemed at times to leap upon the page, I became exhilarated with the hope that people all over the world would have access to the same truths and the very prayers that helped me bring my wounded heart to God and receive mending from His own Great Heart in return. May you find in Him, dear reader, all that He truly is!

SECTION ONE

Foundations

*Keep your heart with all diligence,
For out of it is the wellspring of life.*
Proverbs 4:23 WEB

CHAPTER 1

THE SPIRITUAL ROOTS OF DISEASE

Though we begin with the body, this series of lessons is not primarily about physical health and the means to achieve it. Rather, it is about seeking emotional and spiritual health of the highest order. Finding the life that is "hidden with Christ in God" (Colossians 3:3) or entering into "the glorious liberty of the children of God" (Romans 8:21) would be excellent Biblical ways of expressing the goal. As it happens, however, modern medical science has been shown us a connection between our emotional life and the root issues of disease that gives us a practical place to begin looking at our deeper, truer need. C. S. Lewis once described pain as "God's megaphone," meaning that He gets our attention when our bodies break down.[1] So, it is in seeking to find a remedy to our illnesses that we have been drawn into a far greater understanding of the ways in which we are actually going astray from our God. The diseases of our bodies are but reflections of the dis-ease of our souls!

Three Flawed Theories

Before we look at what is actually making us sick, let's go over some cherished notions that we may still be carrying around in the back of our minds. There are three flawed theories of why we get sick. They may not be taught, but they are often caught.

1) The germ theory: As an explanation of why we get sick, this is accurate but misleading, since germs account for only part of all diseases. Nor does this theory tell us why we had the weakened immune system that allowed germs to infect us in the first place. Stressing the body by lack of sleep, poor nutrition, or lack of exercise can weaken the immune system, but are you aware that research has shown that just six minutes of a negative emotion can suppress the immune system for more than 21 hours?[2]

2) The "out of the blue" theory: This provides a graceful covering for us, since we are claiming to have no idea of any connection between our lifestyle and the disease. (Surely it is nothing we have done. It just came on us *out of the blue*!) Yet everything on earth happens by cause and effect. The real problem with this theory is that it seems to be pointing a finger at God who lives in those "blue" heavens. However, God is never the author of evil: Untainted by any shadow He is instead the Giver of "every good gift" (James 1:17). Death, disorders and disease are consequences of the Fall of man.

---

[1] C.S. Lewis, *The Problem of Pain* (New York: MacMillan Publishing Co, Inc. 1962), 93.
[2] Berk, L.S. as quoted by Art Mathias, *In His Own Image* (Anchorage, AK: Wellspring Publishing, 2003), 29

3) The punishment theory: According to this theory we sinned, so God is punishing us. But that cannot be! God punished Jesus fully and completely at the cross for our sins; it would be a breach of justice for God to punish us when the penalty has already been paid in full by Another. A further problem is that it seems to suggest that God reaches, in anger, into His bag of punishments and puts one on us without regard to the natural order.

The Mind-Body Connection

The truth is that there is a natural connection between the way that we live and the diseases that come upon us. As much as 80% or more of all incurable diseases have a mind-body connection. According to one study, stress related disorders account for 75-90% of all visits to primary care physicians.[3] Consider these connections between disease and emotional stress: high blood pressure and heart disease correlate with anger and hostility; autoimmune disorders, Multiple Sclerosis, Lupus and arthritis are associated with bitterness, resentments and self-hatred; gastrointestinal disorders such as IBS, panic attacks and heart palpitations are related to anxiety; tension and migraine headaches, along with back pain, TMJ and Fibromyalgia are all associated with repressed anger.[4] Now reflect that our science is just beginning to discover the linkages between *specific* negative emotions and *specific* physical disorders, but already these connections can be made. Imagine how fine-tuned this may one day become.

Negative emotions damage the body. When we perceive a situation to be dangerous, adrenaline and cortisol are released by our bodies to facilitate "flight or fight" responses. This is part of the General Adaptation Syndrome (G.A.S.) which gives us the extra "gas" we need to power-up for potentially life-threatening situations. The problem is that most of the "dangers" that cause stress cannot be resolved by fighting or running away! Modern life seems to be characterized by a mounting sea of stressful events and daily pressures coming at people from every conceivable direction. And yet the real culprit isn't the situations which surround us—it is the emotional reactions going off inside of us. That is why Dr. Don Colbert entitled his book on the mind-body connection *Deadly Emotions*—not "deadly situations." Stating that emotions are not confined only to the mind or heart, he describes the physiological processes by which all emotions are translated into chemical reactions which occur at both the organ level *and* the cellular level!

> Chronically elevated cortisol levels have been shown to:
>
> Impair immune function
> Reduce glucose utilization
> Increase bone loss
> Reduce muscle mass
> Inhibit skin growth
> Increase fat accumulation
> Impair memory
> Destroy brain cells
> Increase blood pressure
>
> *Deadly Emotions* p. 17

---

[3] Don Colbert, MD, *Deadly Emotions* (Nashville, TN: Thomas Nelson Publishers, 2003), p. 6.
[4] Ibid., cover.

Apparently, the "most damaging" emotions are feelings we might consider "garden variety" such as un-forgiveness, anger, worry, fear and frustration.[5] Clearly, no one with an emotional life is immune to the danger!

These negative emotions which place so much stress upon our bodies come in two forms: those that arise out of present situations and those that are "embedded" in our deepest memories. Doctors Alexander Loyd and Ben Johnson in their book, *The Healing Code*, state that embedded negative emotions are the most damaging kind, producing "physiological stress" (at a subconscious level), as opposed to "situational stress" (at the conscious level).[6] These unhealed memories are actually stored as false beliefs and negative images which form "destructive cellular memories" in the cells of our bodies![7] In terms of the mind body connection they list three "one things" which we need to know: There is one thing that can heal anything—our immune system; there is one thing that turns off the immune system—stress; there is one thing that will turn the immune system back on— healing "the issues of the heart."[8]

From the Bible's perspective there are a few "good" emotions that we might perceive as negative ones due to the way that they feel: godly fear (awe and respect for God as both holy and all-powerful); "danger fear" (in life-threatening moments); righteous anger (hating the sin, yet still loving the person); and pure grief (mourning that is uncontaminated by anger, fear, doubt or guilt). These emotions are actually very good to have even if they don't *feel* like it at the time.

From a medical point of view all other negative emotions are stressors to the body, and it is extremely evident how damaging they are to our physical health. However, from a Christian point of view they represent something that is also very damaging to our spiritual health—they are sins! Now this may seem like adding to the bad news: The negative emotions we don't like feeling in the first place are not only causing disease, they are also sins, separating us from God! Isn't this very bad news indeed? No, not at all: It is wonderful news! It shows us there is a way out, both from disease and from the entrapment of negative emotions.

If the negative emotions, causing us so much loss of peace and joy as well as health, are actually things in our personality that God has given us and wants us to have, then we are stuck with them—and the diseases they induce. However, if they are sins then He has provided a way of freedom, since Jesus died to free us from sin's power as well as from its penalty. That way of freedom will be the subject of all of the following lessons. For now let us consider the negative emotions in relationship to their polar opposite—the peace of Christ.

---

[5] Ibid., 9, 20
[6] Alexander Loyd, PhD, ND with Ben Johnson, MD, DO, NMD, *The Healing Code* (New York, NY: Grand Central Publishing, 2011), p. 44.
[7] Ibid., p. 97.
[8] Ibid., p. 20-25.

The Peace of Christ

We always have a choice how we will respond to life: Will we give in to stress, take on the negative emotions so close at hand, or will we choose to find the path of peace that comes from trusting and obeying God? God created us to live in peace with His peace. Even under the terms of the Hebrew covenant, it was possible to live with perfect peace, but there was a condition: Keeping one's mind fixed or stayed on the Lord. How does one do that? In a word—trust. Trusting God is how we "live by faith" (Romans 1:17).

You keep him in perfect peace whose mind is stayed on you, because he trusts in you. Isaiah 26:3

Peace comes to us on the basis of our actual "heart trust" in God, not the doctrinal rightness of our beliefs. Our minds judge right and wrong, but it is with our hearts that we judge who to trust. Whenever we actually release our hearts to trust God, our minds naturally become rested or stayed upon Him, until something else disturbs our rest. In the New Covenant Jesus also promises us peace and His peace goes far beyond any of the outward things that disturb us.

"Peace I leave with you; my peace I give to you. Not as the world gives do I give to you. Let not your hearts be troubled, neither let them be afraid." John 14:27

How does the world give us peace? Anyone can get peace from the world in this way: *I see the problem; I go to work on it; I begin to see the thing get better; I get peace back.* You don't have to be a believer in anything but yourself to get peace in this way. But there are real problems with getting peace this way: *I can't always make things better so I lose even more peace in the attempt; I have to wait until things look like they are getting better before peace begins to return to me; and as soon as one trouble is fixed, I may lose peace over two more things that just flared up.* This way is guaranteed to produce many seasons of significant stress over the course of a lifetime. We know it all too well—it is the way of trusting Self to be our savior.

Jesus gives believing, trusting hearts peace at the first sign of trouble—whenever we cast our cares on Him as our only Savior (Psalm 55:22; Matthew 11:28-30; 1 Peter 5:7). All of us get a daily report card on how well we are doing at trusting and obeying the Lord. In fact it is personally delivered moment by moment as the Holy Spirit reveals our actual peace levels to us. In any moment the peace of Christ is either going up, holding steady, or going down—all according to our ability to trust and follow Jesus throughout the day (Colossians 3:15).

When our hearts and minds fully trust Him with the whole of our life and that of our loved ones, we are at peace. Our bodies can then experience peace (*homeostasis* or physiological equilibrium) and all systems work in balance to maintain health. As Dr. Art Mathias of Wellsprings Ministries in Alaska likes to say, our bodies are barometers of our spiritual health.[9] Seen in this light the diseases and disorders we can't ignore are "warning bells" alerting us of our need to return to living in the peace of Christ.

The Pathway of Disease

Pay close attention to this pathway of disease for it is also the way by which mental illness, addictions and all sinful behaviors become entrenched:

1) Loss of health comes from loss of peace in the mind or heart. This is the overwhelming evidence of mainstream science.

2) Loss of peace comes through the entry of negative emotions. This is simple displacement—after an internal "tug-of-war" either the peace of Christ or stress will always win out.

3) Negative emotions draw power from unresolved issues carried from the past. These are the root causes.

4) Unresolved issues always reveal that there are broken relationships of trust and love with God, self or others. The two Great Commandments have been breached (Matthew 22:37-39). These issues are crying out to be healed, not buried.

5) Loss of peace indicates there is a sin issue to deal with. We have been turning *from* God, which is why His peace was lifted.

6) Loss of peace warns that the other kingdom is manifesting through us. We have been turning *to* the enemy, which is why unchristlike thoughts and feelings are beginning to grip us.

Just as peace, love, joy and the other savory fruit of the Spirit manifest the life of Christ and the working of God's Kingdom through us, so too do negative emotions actually manifest the "emotional life" of the enemy, coming out of our carnal or fallen nature, and advance his dark kingdom through us. *We are paying a terrible price for not living in the peace of Christ.*

NOTES/JOURNAL

___

[9] Art Mathias, PhD, *In His Own Image* (Anchorage, AK: Wellspring Ministries of Alaska, 2003), p. 43.

_____
_____
_____
_____
_____

EXERCISE

List any diseases or infirmities you may have. Now consider how they may be affected by stress. Do the symptoms seem to get better or worse when you experience times of excessive stress? Did any time of specific stress seem to be going on in your life when the disease began? Could it have been caused by a stressful event? Not all disease are directly related to stress—consider researching any that you may have to see if they are. Ask your doctor; search the web.

Disease or condition	Moods or stress emotions that may trigger or amplify it
_____	_____
_____	_____
_____	_____

DISCUSSION QUESITONS

Ask group members to name the things that stress them the most. How many of these are related to money, time, work, family, politics, etc? Does a loss of peace seem inevitable to them whenever these stressors show up? What have they been doing to try to overcome the stress in these situations? Have they been mainly trying to eliminate the problem, ignore it, be distracted from thinking about it, or have they been trying to learn how to overcome their negative emotional reactions to it? What works? What doesn't work? Close by praying for all these situations!

MAIN POINTS

- Loss of health comes from loss of peace in the mind or heart.
- Loss of peace comes through entry of negative emotions—these are sins.
- Negative emotions draw power from unresolved issues of the past.
- Unresolved issues reveal a loss of love or trust for God, self, or others.
- Loss of peace indicates that we have a sin issue to deal with (Col 3:15).
- Loss of peace indicates that the other kingdom is manifesting through us.
- We are paying a terrible price for not living in the peace of Christ.

DIGGING DEEPER
The mind-body connection:

Many ordinary illnesses are nothing but the expression of a serious dissatisfaction with life. [10]

Sickness may be the solemn occasion of God's intervention in a person's life. [11]

It is ambition, fear of the future, love of money, jealousy, or social injustice that makes men strive and overwork, invent all sorts of unnecessary tasks, keep late hours, take too little sleep, take insufficient holidays, or use their holidays badly. Their minds are over tense, so that at night they cannot sleep and by day they doubly fatigue themselves at their work. [12]

The fact is that in denying the reality of sin, by giving people to understand that a fault of character is due to the malfunctioning of an endocrine gland, or by calling some impure temptation a "psychological complex," science destroys man's sense of moral responsibility. The present state of the world shows where that leads. [13]

How the body responds to stress:

I have found over the years that with every disease there's usually an emotion linked to that disease. And the emotion that so many Americans have is frustration. We have an epidemic of frustrated Americans here. [14]

The majority of the patients that I see on a daily basis are overstressed, and this contributes greatly to the illness or disease from which they are suffering... Our mind and body seek a state of peace and relaxation, which is called homeostasis... When a person becomes "stressed out"... reactions begin to occur in the body that lead to the general adaptation syndrome... Unfortunately, when most patients finally come to my practice, they are already in [the] final stage of the general adaptation syndrome... I have learned when a person reaches adrenal exhaustion, we shouldn't just treat their body... We must also treat the person mentally, emotionally, and most of all, spiritually. [15]

SWORD AND SHIELD

Texts that speak to health issues abound in scripture, especially in regard to the connection between negative emotions (sins) and physical health—what our science describes as the mind-body connection (see also Pr 3:7-8; 9:11; 16:24).

My son, attend to my words. Turn your ear to my sayings. Let them not depart from your eyes. Keep them in the midst of your heart. For they are life to those who find

---

[10] Paul Tournier, Md., quotation posted at *The Doctor's Page*: www.doctorspage.net/quotes.asp.
[11] Ibid.
[12] Ibid.
[13] Ibid.
[14] Don Colbert, Md., "He's Got the Cure," *Charisma Magazine*; Nov, 2003.
[15] Don Colbert, Md., "The Dangers of Excessive Stress, Part 1 and 2," *Charisma Magazine*; Jan/Feb, 2001.

them, And health to their whole body. Keep your heart with all diligence, For out of it is the wellspring of life.** Proverbs 4:20-23 WEB

A tranquil heart gives life to the flesh, but envy makes the bones rot. Proverbs 14:30

A joyful heart is good medicine, but a crushed spirit dries up the bones.
Proverbs 17:22

The emphasis of scripture regarding our health is on the spiritual food in our daily diet, especially *the fruit* of the Spirit (peace, love and joy), not physical food. Physical food is not seen as a threat to health, if thanksgiving and moderation are maintained (Pr 23:21; Pr 25:16; 1Co 9:25).

Let no man therefore judge you in eating, or in drinking... "Don't handle, nor taste, nor touch" (all of which perish with use), according to the precepts and doctrines of men? Which things indeed appear like wisdom in self-imposed worship, and humility, and severity to the body; but aren't of any value against the indulgence of the flesh. Colossians 2:16, 21-23 WEB

For everything created by God is good, and nothing is to be rejected if it is received with thanksgiving, for it is made holy by the word of God and prayer. 1 Timothy 4:4

Do not be led away by diverse and strange teachings, for it is good for the heart to be strengthened by grace, not by foods, which have not benefited those devoted to them. Hebrews 13:9

PRAYER FOCUS

Are you willing to be H.O.T. for Jesus? Guarding the inward flame of our "first love" will mean that we have to live in an Honest, Open and Transparent way with the Lord and with others. Anything hidden "in the dark" of buried secrets becomes a weapon the enemy can and will use against us. Anything "brought to the light" will become suffused with light and life (Mk 4:22; Jn 3:21; 1Jn 1:7).

Father, in the course of these lessons enable me to be honest, open and transparent before You. Please help me to choose to deal with You and with anything You may want to bring up. Despite the pain I may have to work through, I am determined to break free of my past and truly learn how to live with Your peace established in my heart.

RENUNCIATIONS AND AFFIRMATIONS

Renounce any agreements with untruth; believe Jesus' *truth* as your new *way* of *life*.

Why is it so hard to live a life of grace? A life of grace is a mercy-based, peace-filled life—the very thing we all so deeply and desperately desire which also happens to be the polar opposite of the stressed up or depressed down emotional states we carry around. A life of grace is characterized by living as the Bible says that we are meant to live: by trusting to, reply upon and rejoicing in the grace that is always being given to us (Ro 1:17).

"Behold, his soul is puffed up; it is not upright within him, but the righteous shall live by his faith." Habakkuk 2:4

If such a life has been eluding you, then you need to know what the problem is, but before seeing where the problem really lies, it will be helpful to understand what it is NOT. Be sure to go over this list renouncing any anger, blame or frustration with your life that you have been placing on the wrong culprit for what has been causing "the problem," making it a scapegoat. Then being confessing the truth of Ephesians 2:8: we are saved by grace (which is always being given us by God) *through faith* (that's the only place where the disconnect can happen!).

For by grace you have been saved through faith. And this is not your own doing; it is the gift of God. Ephesians 2:8

The problem is:

Not you
Not God
Not others
Not the world
Not your flesh
Not the devil
Not your sin

Not your past
Not your circumstances
Not your weaknesses
Not your 'personality'
Not your addiction
Not your disease

The problem is what we choose to believe in our heart of hearts about ourselves, our God and our world. Believing the truth—God's truth—with a full heart of faith will always work to set us free (John 8:32). Believing a lie, any lie, will always work to destroy us.

What you choose to believe determines:

- Your immediate and future emotional state (your inner world).
- Your level of contact with REALITY (others, all of creation, God).
- Your consequences. You are not the only player: God, the devil and all of creation are responding to choices you make based upon what you believe deep down and act upon.

PUTTING FEET TO YOUR PRAYERS: STRETCH YOURSELF!

What are some steps you can take to reduce stress in your life? This workbook is intended to help you convert emotional stress back into the peace of Christ through prayer, but there are many practical ways to de-stress as well. Consider these steps that others have found helpful, then add the ones that you will actually do to the second list.

- Laughter.
- Loving—pets, children, anyone and anything you can (in a right way!).
- Getting out in nature—drink in the beauty and grace of our Creator's world.
- Deep, relaxed breathing—letting out stress; taking in peace.
- Stretching, tensing and relaxing your muscle groups from head to toe.
- Imagining a relaxing scene—like walking along a beach or lying in sunshine.
- Meditation—focused awareness, interactive and directed toward the Lord.
- Prayer—casting your cares on Him because He cares for you; sharing the day's burdens.
- Massage and hugging—healthy, legitimate forms of receiving and giving human touch.
- Aerobic exercise—brisk walking, cycling, swimming, or jumping with reasonable intensity.
- Daily quiet time all to yourself with little or nothing to do but relax.
- Playing gentle music, watching wholesome videos, reading good books.
- Sleep—we need between seven to nine hours of sleep a night and more on the weekends.

Things I could stop doing (activities to eliminate, expectations to pare down).

1) _____
2) _____
3) _____

Things I could start doing (to relax stress away, to burn it off, to forget about it).

1) _____
2) _____
3) _____

CHAPTER 2

TRUTH OR CONSEQUENCES

We saw in the previous chapter that there is hope for becoming free of many illnesses, even addictions and mental disorders, since they are rooted in negative emotions and false beliefs that we can learn to overcome. However, this knowledge could become a heavy burden to bear for it means recognizing things we thought were "just emotions" as sins. Since we fall into these sinful emotional states so easily and so often, it begs the question: What is God the Father thinking and feeling about us? Is He angry? Is He losing patience? Is He withdrawing from us? Unless we can discover something about our Father God that will put our hearts to rest, this accurate view of sin could well become cause for even more stress! Thankfully, in God we have the perfect safety our hearts have been searching for all along!

Our homeward journey into His Heart of love begins by taking a necessary "detour" into the thorny question of suffering. Issues of disease raise questions about suffering, such as: Why does a good, *loving* God allow evil and suffering to exist? This series takes the following positions:

1) God is a thoroughly good God—unconditionally loving, abounding in mercy and yet completely just.

2) All suffering exists because evil exists—God is NOT the source or cause of evil.

> *All suffering comes from there being free will, in a real world, with an invisible enemy.*

3) All evil exists because of Satan's sin—his prideful free will decision to go a separate way from God. He led other created beings into rebellion with him, forming an empire of evil.

4) All suffering is due to three things: our free will *abused* (our sinful choices of thought, word or deed), a real world setting (which involves natural consequences for all choices) and the sins of an invisible enemy against us.

There has to be balance and an allowance for mystery when attempting to understand the relationship between God's sovereignty and human free will, as well as the painful issues of why a particular disease and suffering came about. Nevertheless the boundaries are clear: God is not the author of evil, Satan is. In heaven there is a complete absence of sin and suffering, because in heaven everyone is perfectly surrendered to God. We give the enemy countless open doors to bring sin and its consequences into our world through our lack of surrender, our sinful choices. God allows us to say "No!" to Him and to His ways. He does this for the sake of preserving our free wills. He even works through the evils our free will allows to restore us to love and to our lost humanity. Fortunately for us, He has many ways of turning our "No's" back into "Yes's", but in the interval much suffering can happen.

We don't seem to be as committed to our freedom of will as God is. We want *our* will to be free, but not the will of others—especially if they are about to hurt us with it. Or we may want our wills to be free but don't want the real world consequences that go along with it. God, on the other hand, has placed all of us in a real world in which even the demons have freedom of choice. To live with a free will in a real world under assault by an invisible enemy, we will have to learn to love God's ways or face the consequences.

The Inescapable Reality

We have been given freedom of will and are therefore sovereigns over our own hearts. What we choose to believe in our mind and in our heart determines how we will react or respond to people and events (Proverbs 23:7; Matthew 12:34). Every emotion we have is springing up from the core of what we deeply believe. There is no neutral zone in this. We are either coming into agreement with God's truth in our thoughts, attitudes, words and actions, or we are moving into agreement with the enemy's lies (John 8:44). Remember the peace report card from the previous lesson? Tragically, we have to make our decisions on faulty or incomplete understandings of truth and its consequences, all the while a cunning adversary is taking full advantage of our lack of knowledge to enslave us or destroy us (Hosea 4:6; Isaiah 5:13).

Truth or consequences is the unalterable rule of life. Since, our will does not operate in a vacuum, every thought we have—conscious or unconscious—has natural consequences in our bodies in terms of neurological or hormonal responses that affect our organs and even individual cells. That is the universe *within our bodies*. Our inner life also affects the universe *beyond our bodies* through our words, actions and prayers. We live in a very real world. Our choices truly matter. Even when we seem to have no power to make things better, we still hold great power to make them worse. This power is immense: We have actually been given the power to choose life or death.

> **"I call heaven and earth to witness against you today, that I have set before you life and death, blessing and curse. Therefore choose life, that you and your offspring may live."** Deuteronomy 30:19

The Grace That Covers Us

Have you been dressed in stress? From the Bible's perspective, every negative emotion is a sin issue. When negative emotions turn our hearts away from trusting God and loving others, we are not clothed in Christ—which may be very often for some of us. How does the Father see us? Mercifully! Our Father covers us all with great grace. Grace is God's perpetual outpouring of love and mercy that we cannot earn and do not deserve. In revealing His glory to Moses, God could have shown him the starry heavens which declare His glory (Psalm 19:1) or He could have sent down the glory cloud that would one day fill the tabernacle and the temple (Exodus 40:35; 2 Chronicles 5:14). But He didn't. Instead, He chose to reveal all that is magnificent about who He is. It is as if He said to Moses, "I'm glad you asked Me. So many of My children have such terribly wrong ideas about Me. Thank you for letting Me set the record straight and clear My own great Name."

> **Moses said, "Please show me your glory." And he said, "I will make all my goodness pass before you… The Lord passed before him and proclaimed, "The Lord, the Lord, a God merciful and gracious, slow to anger, and abounding in steadfast love and faithfulness, keeping steadfast love for thousands, forgiving iniquity and transgression and sin." Exodus 33:18-19, 34:6-7**

We are also shown the Father's glorious grace in the New Testament. The Father is fully reconciled to us. He has foreseen all that will be needed of suffering and sacrifice, of patience, mercy and grace *on His part* and He is "OK" with whatever is required to save us. In fact the Father was *in Jesus* reconciling the world to Himself. He did this by not holding our sins against us. Instead He held them against Jesus, so that we could receive newness of life (Romans 6:4).

> **But all things are from God, who through *Jesus* Christ reconciled us to Himself [received us into favor, brought us into harmony with Himself]… It was God [personally present] in Christ, reconciling *and* restoring the world to favor with Himself, not counting up *and* holding against [men] their trespasses [but cancelling them], and committing to us the message of reconciliation (of the restoration to favor). 2 Corinthians 5:18-19 AMP**

Apply this passage to negative emotions. God the Father is not "holding it against" us that we have so many negative emotions stressing us or depressing us. He is perfectly able to love us even when we are in the negative emotion "pig pen" feeding the swine! And He is continuously calling to us to come home to His loving embrace (Luke 15:11-32; Hebrews 4:16). This is the truly Good News about His amazing grace.

God's Justice System

Then how does God correct the world? Will not the Judge of all the earth bring justice (Genesis 18:25)? Yet He refuses to accuse or condemn us (Romans 8:34), He refuses to terrify or threaten us (1 John 4:18) and He isn't counting our sins against us (2 Corinthians 5:19). What is left? Love, truth and consequences. By His love, He draws all who are willing, and by His Word, He leads all who are willing (speaking through conscience, nature, scripture and others). If we are not turned into His ways by these "polite" methods, then He allows some of the consequences of our wrong choices to help us realize that we are heading in a wrong direction. Heart-peace, trust and mercy-giving love are the *only* way of life offered to us by God.

Even great grace such as we have been offered does not remove the necessity of our repentance. In the same passage in which He revealed His glorious grace to Moses, God also stated that He "by no means clears the guilty" (Exodus 34:7). Since even grace cannot be forced upon anyone, there is only one way of removing sin and its consequences: repentance. Until we choose to repent and return to Him, He "keeps" mercy for us (Exodus 33:7), but mercy cannot be released to do its full work of restoration until we repent and return to receive it. When the children of Israel were about to enter into their Promised Land, the Lord told them to create a visual picture by having some men stand on Mt. Ebal calling down the curses that would come to those who would not listen and obey Him and others to stand on Mt. Gerizim calling down the blessings on those who would obey (Deuteronomy 27:1-10). The choice is ours!

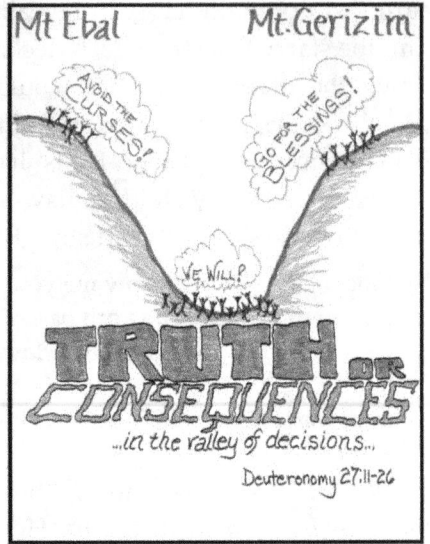

THE VALLEY OF DECISION

The life of faith is not a one-time choice to follow God. We are in "the valley of decision" faced with that choice daily! Will we live by Truth or "choose" to suffer the consequences?

The Curse of the Law

Things that represent the "curse of the law" (the consequence of sin) don't come to us accidentally.

As the bird by wandering... so the curse causeless shall not come. Proverbs 26:2 KJV

The curse of the law may enter our lives through three ways: the sins of others, un-repented sins of our forefathers (generational sins in the family or on the land), or our own sins of thought, word or deed whether known or unknown, including things done or left undone. It is a wonder any of us are sane and healthy! Actually, this too is due to His generosity for He doesn't treat us as our sins deserve (Psalm 103:10). Even so, sin's very real consequences always lead to death. No one gets away with any sin (Exodus 34:7). The law of sowing and reaping applies until repentance comes and even repentance doesn't remove all consequences (Galatians 6:7-8), but it does allow God opportunity to bring restoration and redemption (Romans 8:28). Consider the "little" sin of simple unforgiveness:

1) The first consequence of unforgiveness is that it robs you of joy.

2) Then your peace slips away whenever you think of what happened.

3) You discover the relationship being affected negatively.

4) The longer you hold on to it, the more the remembered pain may intensify.

5) You grow more critical not only of the person, but of other people in general.

6) As your walls go up you feel cut off from God's Presence, His peace and joy.

7) As more walls go up, other relationships are affected.

8) More of your time is fruitlessly robbed from you by dwelling on the past.

9) All this increases the stress-load upon the body and can lead to illnesses.

10) And on and on…

Keys to Health and Freedom

Jesus gives us keys that provide access to His Kingdom's health and freedom. As we saw in Chapter 1, His summary of the law clearly shows us that our primary assignment is to work at building (or rebuilding if need be) relationships of trust and love with God, self and others (Matthew 22:36-40). When these relationships are healthy, God can send many blessings our way—this is His desire. However, we "invite" the curse even in the form of disease when there is a breakdown in one or more of these relationships (Deuteronomy 27-28). This means that there is tremendous hope for all of us that if we are willing to put our primary assignment *first* and do what is needed to get things right *in our hearts*, our bodies may very likely return to full health. Our hearts hold the key!

Keep your heart with all diligence, for out of it is the wellspring of life.
Proverbs 4:23 WEB

Thank God, however, there is one dreaded consequence we never have to fear coming upon us: losing His love. He loves us *unconditionally* (Isaiah 54:9-10; Romans 8:37-39). And that's the truth!

NOTES/JOURNAL

_____
_____
_____
_____
_____
_____
_____
_____

_____

_____

EXERCISE

Can you think of a choice you can make that doesn't have any consequences to it—no matter how slight or how delayed? Can you think of any thought or action that doesn't have some relationship to right or wrong ways, truth or falsehood? This is what it means to be continually feeding upon the Tree of the Knowledge of Good and Evil (Ge 2:17)!

Now consider how many decisions you may have made today. How many of them were you able to make with total knowledge of all consequences, all outcomes, all interrelationships to other persons or events? Gets tricky really fast, doesn't it? No wonder God wanted to spare us this impossible task. What would feeding on the Tree of Life look like compared to this? Jesus is the Tree of Life. Living surrendered to Him—trusting Him and being led by His Spirit—allows us to find a path of life that doesn't require knowing everything about everything! Write down how it would simplify your life—if you gave Jesus more control. What is stopping you? Pray to overcome that obstacle!

Surrendered I wouldn't have to	**Trusting and obeying I would be able to**
_____	_____
_____	_____
_____	_____

DISCUSSION QUESTIONS

Have someone in the group read Deuteronomy 28:1-20 (or more if you can bear to hear all the consequences of not harkening!). Notice especially how consequences (good or bad) come to us based upon our attentiveness (or lack of it) to God's *voice*—not just the words of scripture.

1) Thinking mainly in terms of health issues (for now), ask the group to name all of the ways in which God has been sending His truth to us concerning things to do to maintain good health. Don't just think inside the church box. God "speaks" in all kinds of ways.

2) Then ask them to name consequences that come (eventually) to those who don't heed the words of truth God has been speaking—especially in terms of health issues.

3) Now have them name all of the ways God goes to work to gracefully help us with those same health issues—even though they may have come to us because we didn't listen to Him.

4) Say a prayer of gratitude that we are under a new and better covenant—one that gives great grace. The Lord doesn't remove all of the consequences of our choices from our lives (we live in a real world after all), but at least the covering of mercy and love is perfect!

MAIN POINTS

- Blessings are the consequences of listening to God's Word and walking in His ways.
- Curses are the consequences of *not* listening to God's Word or walking in His ways.
- We have been given free will in a real world with an invisible enemy.
- God is loving us perfectly no matter what choices we make.
- By reconciling Himself to us at the cross, The Father is not holding our sins against us.
- Nevertheless, our choices reap real consequences—for good or evil.
- When we repent God "clears us" of sin and helps with sin's consequences.

DIGGING DEEPER

Trials and troubles can raise the questions: "Am I being punished? Is God upset with me?" Happily the answer is always "No"! We will experience consequences we have to work through at times, but Jesus took the punishment fully and finally. However, we do have an enemy "seeking whom he may devour" (1Pe 5:8), who delights in crushing us with consequences for the very sins he tempted us to do and then makes us feel we are being punished by God instead! Review these basic principles of sifting (going through trials) from chapters 1-3 of the book of Job and from Peter's sifted time (Lk 22:31).

- God in no way afflicts us: Satan does the afflicting.
- Satan has legal rights to enforce the curse of the law on sin.
- Our sins give the enemy open doors by which to enter with the curse.
- God covers (protects) us with lots of grace.
- God sets limits to each sifting.
- Siftings are what we call trials.
- Trials always flush our impurities up to the surface.
- The best way out of any trial is total trust in God.
- God makes it work for our good—He is out to restore more than before.

A word to the wise: Surrendering fully to the Lord takes the fire out of any trial!

Lord, make me willing to be made willing to surrender everything to You.

The consequences of present sins are not the only consequences we have to deal with: Others may come to us from the distant past. Naturally we need to focus on our new inheritance in Christ, but that doesn't mean we don't have another inheritance to make peace with. Every newborn Christian has *an inheritance from the old man*—the person they were before Christ entered in. Depending upon how recklessly, or how extravagantly, we "put on" the old man, there may be a considerable "inheritance" we will have to deal with coming from the ways of the world, the flesh and the enemy that we once embraced.

This is the basis of our "consequence inventory"—things outward and inward that will have to be reckoned with in a faithful way. Fortunately, the Lord is with us to help us work through all of the consequences due to us that grace alone does not remove and which honesty and responsibility call us to face. Jesus will help us grow spiritually as we work through the consequences that make up our inheritance from our pre-Christian self! He will help us:

- **Live with** (in recognition and responsibility leading to acceptance)
- **Live above** (by casting the burden upon Him in our struggles with it)
- **Live beyond** (in finally having them laid to rest—never to appear again)

Now, make a simple list of some of the major consequences that you will need to work through which stem from your pre-Christian or un-Christian ways of the past. Think in terms of relationships lost or broken, finances, career, health, persistent wrong attitudes about yourself or others.

_____
_____
_____
_____
_____

The good news is that our loving Father loves to bring restoration! The only bad news is that He rarely waves a "magic wand" over our lives: He prefers that we become transformed by walking through what it takes to mend our lives. So pray for the grace to follow Jesus on that healing journey!

SWORD AND SHIELD

In the mix of scriptures below, there are passages that speak of the law of sowing and reaping (L), our calling to sow into the lives of others (C), and God's own work of sowing into our lives (G). Circle them "L, C, and/or G" as you study and pray over them. Notice that even the devil sows in hopes of reaping—this principle is so profound and powerful! So, step out into your world and sow good seed as a co-worker with your God—every chance you get!

L C G "Remember: who that was innocent ever perished? Or where were the upright cut off? As I have seen, those who plow iniquity and sow trouble reap the same." Job 4:7-8

L C G The wicked earns deceptive wages, but one who sows righteousness gets a sure reward. Proverbs 11:18

L C G For it is from Israel; a craftsman made it; it is not God. The calf of Samaria shall be broken to pieces. For they sow the wind, and they shall reap the whirlwind. Hosea 8:6-7

L C G Sow for yourselves righteousness; reap steadfast love; break up your fallow ground, for it is the time to seek the Lord, that he may come and rain righteousness upon you. Hosea 10:12

L C G He answered, "The one who sows the good seed is the Son of Man. The field is the world, and the good seed is the children of the kingdom. The weeds are the sons of the evil one, and the enemy who sowed them is the devil. The harvest is the close of the age, and the reapers are angels. Just as the weeds are gathered and burned with fire, so will it be at the close of the age." Matthew 13:37-40

L C G The point is this: whoever sows sparingly will also reap sparingly, and whoever sows bountifully will also reap bountifully. 2 Corinthians 9:6

L C G Do not be deceived: God is not mocked, for whatever one sows, that will he also reap. For the one who sows to his own flesh will from the flesh reap corruption, but the one who sows to the Spirit will from the Spirit reap eternal life. And let us not grow weary of doing good, for in due season we will reap, if we do not give up. Galatians 6:7-9

PRAYER FOCUS

It is important to learn how to pray for grace as we go along when looking into these sobering truths about sin, stress and consequences. Otherwise we could easily become overwhelmed with trying to bail ourselves out of one emotional entanglement after another or deliver ourselves from the sins that we see. No one can do this in their own strength, looking to Self to "conquer" life. Jesus really desires to be our Savior in every way! Let us learn how to cast every care on Him because He wants us to (1Pe 5:7). Here are sample ways of praying for grace:

- *Lord, there is so much I still don't understand. Help me to walk in what I do know and come with further teachings so that I can grow. I cast this care on you.*
- *Lord, I can see that my stress is contributing to my illnesses. Forgive me and please go to work to help me learn to live by trusting you. I cast this care on You.*

- Lord, I suspect that there are so many things about me that need changing that I am overwhelmed. I cast the burden of my whole life on You.

Now, consider the concerns that may be rising up in you and write prayers for grace that will help you cast those concerns on Him.

_____
_____
_____

Finally, end your prayers for grace with this one:

Lord, thank You for taking on these cares and for having a plan already in place for helping me. I am ready to trust and obey You with whatever You show me is my part.

RENUNCIATIONS AND AFFIRMATIONS

Renounce any agreements with untruth; believe Jesus' *truth* as your new *way of life.*

Father, wherever I have believed that I can live without consequences, forgive me. I renounce that false view of Your world and of my life. Whenever I thought that You were punishing me by what You allowed as my consequences, forgive me for shifting the blame for my own choices to You. I take authority and responsibility over my life. Thank You that You have given me sovereignty over my heart and have placed me with freedom of will in a real world. Help me to listen to Your Word and learn from my consequences and turn to Your ways.

PUTTING FEET TO YOUR PRAYERS: STRETCH YOURSELF!

Put a note in your wallet or attach it to your mirror or computer that reminds you:

- My Father is not counting up or holding my sins against me.
- He wants me to talk with Him about everything!

Then start challenging every emotion that comes up during the day that wants to hide from God or keep you from believing in how good the Father's love for you really is. Don't exhaust yourself trying to keep negative emotions and false beliefs from appearing! Just make sure that the wrong thoughts don't capture your focus and attention. You may not be able at first to clear away the thicket of emotions which keep cropping up, but you can learn how to clear a way through them.

CHAPTER 3

THE KEYS TO THE KINGDOM

In the first two chapters we noted the powerful connection between our negative emotions and many diseases and the uncomfortable fact that such emotions of the carnal nature are actually sinful states. How are we to get free? As it happens Jesus has foreseen our need and promised us keys—keys to His Kingdom! In this chapter we will look at what the Kingdom of God means in terms of our daily experience, what the keys are and what it is that the keys unlock.

Jesus has given keys of access to His disciples. The keys are the power to bind and loose. We are to bind the enemy and carry his works captive to Christ and we are to loose people from their sins and release them to God, ourselves included. The keys enable us to access the powers of heaven.

> "I will give you the keys of the kingdom of heaven, and whatever you bind on earth shall be bound in heaven, and whatever you loose on earth shall be loosed in heaven." Matthew 16:19

What Is This Kingdom?

By the above text of scripture we see that these keys are meant to be used "on earth" and they are given to all who receive the same revelation that Peter received—the revelation of Jesus Christ, the Church's great foundation. This Kingdom is a present reality to all believers (Colossians 1:13), but entering into it and accessing its power is evidently not automatic, which is why we need the keys. Consider that every born again Christian receives the "starter kit": forgiveness of sins, the indwelling Spirit, hope of heaven, union with the Body of Christ, knowledge that the Bible is God's Word, and the revelation that Jesus is a very personal Savior and Lord. That's a lot! One would think that would be enough to set us forever free. Yet many experience defeated, miserable lives.

Perhaps, this explains why Jesus wants to give us keys. However, if we are to use the keys we will need to know what they are and what they are for. It will also help us to know some things about the Kingdom of God to which they give us access. A kingdom is the realm where a king reigns—the *king*'s *dom*ain. Paul gives us a clear description of what the Lord's reign is like:

> *For the Kingdom of God is... righteousness, peace, and joy in the Holy Spirit.*
> Romans 14:17

> For the Kingdom of God is not eating and drinking, but righteousness, peace, and joy in the Holy Spirit. Romans 14:17 WEB

Righteousness in the sense of saving grace is "right standing with God"—given to us through the new birth and faith in what Jesus has done for us at the cross. Through justification God has forever separated us from our sins and given us a new righteous status *in Christ*, one we don't deserve because not all of our actual "living" is righteous. Yet this accurate definition of the righteousness that comes by faith may keep us from seeing the vast righteousness of the Kingdom because what is fully meant by righteousness includes everything that is right (good, beautiful and true) which flows from God: Lunch with a friend is righteous; doing a job well is righteous; playing with puppies and babies is righteous; enjoying a sunset or a good book is righteous. It certainly isn't unrighteous! In this wider sense righteousness is anything the Holy Spirit would lead you into doing or appreciating. Such righteousness is the very life of heaven on earth. This kind of righteousness by itself isn't sufficient to get anyone into heaven or the cross of Christ would not have been necessary, but this kind of righteous living is made possible to us through living *in the Spirit*. This is "Kingdom living" in very practical terms.

Like God's righteousness, the peace and joy of God's Kingdom are vast. His peace is different from the peace this world offers, which is so easily lost. The peace of His Kingdom is deep and everlasting—nothing on earth can shake it; nothing on earth can take it from you. Likewise, the world's pleasures are fleeting, but the joy of this Kingdom is available to everyone at any moment for it proceeds from the glad-hearted God who wants to share His joy with us. Unlike mere happiness which depends upon "things going our way," joy can come to us in any moment in which we realize by a living faith who we truly are in Christ and who our God really is. And who can say enough about the Holy Spirit? He is the very Presence and power of Jesus on earth today. This is what the Kingdom is "made" of! Now if we were suddenly told that all the right ways of living, all the peace, all the joy that we have ever wanted *and* the Presence and power of God were on the other side of town just waiting for us, we would be catching the next bus or taking off on foot.

Where Is This Kingdom?

Just where is this Kingdom to be found? Jesus told Nicodemus that unless he was converted (born again) he would neither be able to see this Kingdom nor enter into it.

> **Jesus answered him, "Most assuredly, I tell you, unless one is born anew, he can't see the Kingdom of God..." Jesus answered, "Most assuredly I tell you, unless one is born of water and spirit, he can't enter into the Kingdom of God!"** John 3:3, 5 WEB

Perhaps that has already happened for you. You can now "see" the Kingdom because you have eyes of faith to see the King. And you have been "translated" by the Father out of darkness into the Kingdom of His Beloved Son (Colossians 1:13).

Conversion certainly gets us into a portion of the Kingdom, but are we still searching for entry to that place where all the righteousness, peace and joy can be found? Imagine how it would feel if you were conveyed to the airport of a foreign country, but never left the airport to explore the land or enjoy life with its citizens. So too we may be in the Kingdom of God, but still not be fully sharing in its life. And this life is all around us! Jesus tells us that it is literally as close as the air that we breathe—for it both surrounds and fills us. Amazingly, this Kingdom is always within reach of and always "hiding" inside every believer (Mark 1:15; Luke 17:21). We are in it like fish in the sea: The fish is in the ocean and the ocean is in the fish. As Jesus said, we need to repent—change our way of thinking—and believe this good news!

The Master Key

Consider this: If all of these highly desirable things are already within us and are all around us, what is keeping us locked out? According to Jesus, conversion in the form of the new birth gets us into heaven (John 3:16); becoming as little children gets us into the Kingdom. It is a realm that apparently *requires* childlike trust and cleanness of spirit in order to enter it. In the following scripture note how stringent the warning is: Unless we "repent" (are converted) *and* become as little children we will *never* enter into His Kingdom. The "big key" is becoming like a little child!

> **And He called a little child to Himself and put him in the midst of them, And said, "Truly I say to you, unless you repent (change, turn about) and become like little children** [trusting, lowly, loving, forgiving], **you can never enter the kingdom of heaven** [at all]." Matthew 18:2-3 AMP

Entering heaven is a pure gift of grace given to those who have saving faith in Jesus (John 3:16; Romans 10:9). However, Jesus is not speaking about entry into heaven here. In Matthew's gospel the Kingdom of God on earth is usually referred to as the kingdom of heaven. To this day little children enter the Kingdom on earth and show forth its fruit far better than most believers (Matthew 19:14). And this is true of little children no matter the religion of their parents. In fact most little children haven't even been converted (know and believe in the King) and yet they still live in His Kingdom. What is it about little children?

We can safely assume that Jesus wasn't holding up as an example a little child "in the flesh" but one that was in the right spirit. All such children exemplify the life of the Kingdom (Matthew 19:14; Mark 10:14; Luke 18:16). They are humble, unself-conscious, willingly dependent for all provision upon their parents and freely love the people they meet. They are also teachable, fearless explorers of their world and live with openness and transparency in the present moment. If anything

> *Truly, I say to you, whoever does not receive the kingdom of God like a child shall not enter it.*
> Luke 18:17

troubles or hurts them they run to their parents, are quickly set right and easily let go. In fact when hurts begin to accumulate and they start carrying yesterday and its pains with them, children become self-protective, leave childhood behind and become *like us*—so untrusting that we now need faith in Christ to restore our lost access to God's Kingdom. Jesus says that self-protectiveness—trying to control our life and that of the ones we love—is guaranteed to rob us of life (Matthew 16:24-27; Mark 8:34-37; Luke 9:23-25). His Kingdom doors only open to trusting hearts! We need to take His warning to heart and seriously start learning how to "let go" so that we can reenter the life of grace and freedom we left behind.

Four Essential Keys

We lock ourselves up in a dungeon of pain and bondage without ever realizing what we are doing. Due to an accumulation of life's hurts that we did not release, we left childlikeness behind by binding the pains and injustices of the past to ourselves. Unforgiveness is the number one block to healing and to the Kingdom's peace and power. It leads to unanswered prayer, un-received mercy, hardness of heart, spiritual bondage and painful inner torment. Walls that were erected to keep us safe now imprison us and shut the Kingdom out.

> **"And whenever you stand praying, forgive, if you have anything against anyone, so that your Father also who is in heaven may forgive you your trespasses."** Mark 11:25

> **"And in wrath his master turned him over to the torturers (the jailers), till he should pay all that he owed. So also My heavenly Father will deal with every one of you if you do not freely forgive your brother from your heart** *his offenses***."**
> Matthew 18:34-35 AMP

Hidden and unrecognized unbelief can also bar our entry into the Kingdom because it "hardens" the heart before God as powerfully as un-forgiveness does. Unbelief kept the Israelites out of the land promised to them; it keeps us out of the life that has been promised to us.

> **Take care, brothers, lest there be in any of you an evil, unbelieving heart, leading you to fall away from the living God... So we see that they were unable to enter because of unbelief.** Hebrews 3:12, 19

Without doubt there are many keys to the Kingdom: Some keys are for accessing the supernatural realm to gain power for miracles and healing; other keys are for advancing His governance over the spheres of power and influence that shape nations. Our focus, however, is upon establishing His Kingdom as a superior principle over our inner state, so that both recovery and mastery of the emotional life can be achieved. Towards that goal there are four keys that we will need to learn how to use—frequently!

Key #1) Receive: Confess and repent of recognized sin and receive full forgiveness (consider these as "halleluiah moments"—see below). Receive the grace offered to you.

Key #2) Release: Confess and repent of un-forgiveness and release full forgiveness (towards God, self or others—until no pain is left in the memories). Give grace freely to others.

Key #3) Believe: Confess, repent of unbelief and believe His truth with a full heart of faith (Romans 15:13). No matter what, believe in God and His grace until you are fully liberated by believing truth (John 8:32). This is our real work (John 6:28-29).

Key #4) Discern: Use the key of knowledge: discerning the spirits; discerning truth (Luke 11:52; Hebrews 5:14). This enables you to recognize which of the first three keys needs to be used.

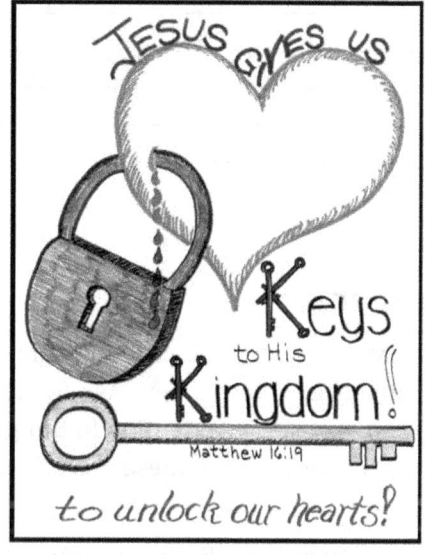

KEYS TO THE KINGDOM

Jesus gives us access keys to His Kingdom of peace and joy, keys that will unlock our true potential and restore childlike vitality. Let's get really good at using them!

Because God gives us sovereignty over our hearts, it is not what happened to us that is the real issue. It is how we have reacted to hurt and injustice that determines our life, our peace and our emotional freedom. Use the keys to forgive others and to fully accept yourself. At first it may seem like this teaching is making the problem worse because you are being shown the connection between physical, mental and emotional health and what the Bible clearly describes as sin issues: bitterness towards others, unbelief, envy, not accepting oneself, living full of stress, etc. However, through repentance, grace and faith there really is a pathway of cleansing and freedom.

Learn to say "Halleluiah!" when the Holy Spirit reveals sin in you that you had not seen before—it means He is getting ready to cleanse you and give you greater entry. So, set your heart "on pilgrimage" (Psalm 84:5) and get really good at using these four keys.

NOTES/JOURNAL

_____
_____
_____

_____
_____
_____
_____
_____
_____
_____

EXERCISE

Make a list of "locks" you may need the four keys to open. Be very honest—don't gloss things over. Ask the Lord to begin helping you in each of these areas. Then, pay special attention to things coming up in the lessons that will prepare you to get victories over these obstacles.

I need to forgive myself for (1st key)   _____

People I need to forgive (2nd key)   _____

Areas of doubt and unbelief (3rd key)   _____

Areas of low discernment (4th key)   _____

DISCUSSION QUESTONS

Ask the group how many of them before this lesson could have said what the keys to the Kingdom are or even what the Kingdom is. Can they tell it now? Have they been taught much about the Kingdom before (is lack of teaching common)? How much did Jesus teach about the Kingdom? Rick Joyner, pastor of MorningStar Fellowship in Charlotte, NC, says that the church has done a good job of preaching the gospel of salvation (getting us into heaven), but has rarely taught the gospel of the Kingdom (bringing heaven down to earth)—and that this gospel of the Kingdom *must* be preached before the Lord returns (Mt 24:14—look it up!).

Discuss the difference between these two gospels. There is much more to the message of the Kingdom than could be covered in this lesson, but of the four keys listed here which are needed the most? Which are used the least? Discuss the relationship between each key and entering into the Kingdom by becoming childlike. (See Digging Deeper for other keys.)

MAIN POINTS

- The Kingdom of God is right ways of living, peace, joy and the Holy Spirit.
- Entering and living in the Kingdom is not automatic, even for believers.
- We enter the Kingdom by conversion and by becoming like little children.
- We lock ourselves out by holding on to un-forgiveness and unbelief.
- Jesus gives us keys to gain access to the Kingdom of God on earth.
- The four keys needed for emotional healing and restoration: Receive forgiveness, release forgiveness, believe truth, and discern truth.

DIGGING DEEPER

This is a diagram of the levels of reality revealed by scripture. Note the fallen counterparts of spiritual darkness to those of light—both centered on the earth. Consider the relationship of the Kingdom of God to other levels of reality—whether of light or darkness. Consider also the relationship of the Kingdom of God to earthly "kingdoms" existing in the natural/physical realm, such as organizations, corporations, municipalities and nations.

Heaven—eternal dwelling of God the Father, Son and Holy Spirit, angels, saints (1Pe 3:21)
  Kingdom of God—invisible, spiritual reign of heaven reaching to earth (Ro 14:17)
    Church—the Body of Christ, partly visible, humanity organized by God (Mt 16:18)
      New nature—New Creation, Christ's life in us, regenerated spirit (2Co 5:17)
        Earth and its heavens—natural realm of five senses and matter (Ps 24:1-2)
      Fallen nature—*sarx*, the flesh, Adam's life in us, spiritual death (Ro 8:6-9)
    World—the *kosmos*, partly visible; humanity organized by Satan (Jn 12:31; 1Jn 2:15)
  Kingdom of darkness—invisible, spiritual realm surrounding earth (Eph 6:12; Col 1:13)
Hell—eternal place of punishment for Satan, fallen angels, demons, the unsaved (Mt 5:30)

There are more Kingdom keys! Add to this list any other "keys" to healthy, happy living that you have discovered along with way.

1) The Key of Authority: Resisting and rebuking the enemy is a key to freedom (see the next lesson for more on spiritual warfare).

2) The Key of Surrender: The grace of yielding to God in any situation frees us in the midst of what we are going through (see "The Disciple's Cross" in the Postscript, page 267).

3) The Key of Praise: The power of aggressive praise frees the heart from heaviness and a host of other burdens (see the "Pick Axe of Praise" page 144).

4) _____

5) _____

Let's combine the key of knowledge with the key of believing and see what the results could be. Since we are "saved by grace through faith" (Eph 2:8) our believing has an enormous part to play in the quality of the life that grace now offers us. Consider this principle: *"The ruling factor is the belief that rules you."*

If in your heart of hearts (not your intellectual or mental beliefs) you believe that you live in a world that rejects you, or that God doesn't really care about you or doesn't love you as He does others, or that your life is worthless or meaningless, or that *only* bad stuff happens to you, or that when you get hurt or suffer loss there is no end to the pain and no good thing really comes out of it...then your heart will naturally feel depressed and heavy. And it should—if that is the kind of world your heart believes you live in. It would be a denial of "reality" to feel good about being yourself and living in such a world. Anybody whose heart believed those things would feel the same way.

But that is not the universe you live in! If you are a believer in Christ, you have been translated out of that awful, seemingly god-forsaken dimension of reality the Bible calls the kingdom of darkness (where many of those things are true for the unredeemed) and has translated you into the Kingdom of His beloved Son.

Let's try to understand the reality that we live in now:

- You are deeply and affectionately loved by the Father—always, at every moment, no matter what shape you are in.
- You are completely forgiven and covered with grace and mercy.
- That same power of forgiveness is available to you for you to be set free from every hurt.
- Everything will actually be made to work for your good, whether you believe it or not.
- Your best Friend is with you and will never leave you or forsake you.
- The greatest Teacher in the world is working with you to help you grow.

Believing these great truths even just a little, will make you begin to feel just a little better. Learning how to believe them a lot will make you feel a lot better! See the connection between the keys? We have to be shown by grace what the truth really is (the key of knowledge); we may need to be helped by grace to fully believe it (the key of active belief).

SWORD AND SHIELD

In light of this teaching about the Kingdom of God, review the following scriptures—just a fraction of what is in the Bible about this invisible realm of God's reign on earth. Note the dynamic tension that evidently exists between earnestly seeking entry and receiving entry as a gift. Seek to understand the presence and *present tense* of the Kingdom. Receive it by faith. Let your eyes be open to "see."

And Jesus said to his disciples, "Truly, I say to you, only with difficulty will a rich person enter the kingdom of heaven. Again I tell you, it is easier for a camel to go through the eye of a needle than for a rich person to enter the kingdom of God." Matthew 19:23-25

Which of the two did the will of his father?" They said, "The first." Jesus said to them, "Truly, I say to you, the tax collectors and the prostitutes go into the kingdom of God before you." Matthew 21:31

"But woe to you, scribes and Pharisees, hypocrites! For you shut the kingdom of heaven in people's faces. For you neither enter yourselves nor allow those who would enter to go in." Matthew 23:13

"For all the nations of the world seek after these things, and your Father knows that you need them. Instead, seek his kingdom, and these things will be added to you. Fear not, little flock, for it is your Father's good pleasure to give you the kingdom." Luke 12:30-32

"The Law and the Prophets were until John; since then the good news of the kingdom of God is preached, and everyone forces his way into it." Luke 16:16

Being asked by the Pharisees when the Kingdom of God would come, he answered them, "The Kingdom of God doesn't come with observation; neither will they say, 'Look, here!' or, 'Look, there!' for behold, the Kingdom of God is within you." Luke 17:20-21 WEB

But Jesus called them to him, saying, "Let the children come to me, and do not hinder them, for to such belongs the kingdom of God. Truly, I say to you, whoever does not receive the kingdom of God like a child shall not enter it." Luke 18:16-17

PRAYER FOCUS

Read through this powerful prayer given to us by Jesus and look for the keys and the ways in which the Kingdom will come as we exercise them. Then pray for His Kingdom to come into your heart, into your life and throughout this course! *Expect* this Kingdom to come.

"Pray like this: 'Our Father in heaven, may your name be kept holy. Let your Kingdom come. Let your will be done, as in heaven, so on earth. Give us today our daily bread. Forgive us our debts, as we also forgive our debtors. Bring us not into temptation, but deliver us from the evil one. For yours is the Kingdom, the power, and the glory forever. Amen.'" Matthew 6:9-13 WEB

RENUNCIATIONS AND AFFIRMATIONS

Renounce any agreements with untruth; believe Jesus' *truth* as your new *way* of *life*.

Father, thank You for translating me out of darkness and into the glorious Kingdom of Your beloved Son! I repent of and renounce all false ideas about where the joy and peace are that I have been searching for—You have placed it all around me and within me! Thank You for showing me these four keys to the Kingdom. Help me to get really good at using them to unlock my heart from un-forgiveness towards myself, You and others and from all the ways in which I have not really been believing in who You are and what You have promised. Help me exercise the gift of discernment that comes with the fourth key. Thank You that it is Your desire to lead me into this Kingdom!

PUTTING FEET TO YOUR PRAYERS: STRETCH YOURSELF!

Get a jump on things: Go back to the exercise lists and begin praying for victory now by forgiving others and by receiving forgiveness for yourself where needed. Give the keys the workout they deserve!

Become a careful observer of little children. Following Jesus' example note well their positive characteristics and then pray for those good traits to be restored into your life (see list below). Take time out during the day to enjoy some moments the way a child would.

Perhaps it would be good to consider the ways of a child in the flesh. Make a list of some that come to mind. Following the example of Paul, have you put off these childish things (1Co13:11)? Childish ways even block little children from being childlike!

Child*like* ways for me to grow into

_____
_____
_____

Child*ish* ways of mine to leave behind

_____
_____
_____

CHAPTER 4

KINGDOMS IN CONFLICT

In Chapter 3 we saw that Jesus has given us keys that give access to the peace and joy of His Kingdom on earth. These are divinely powerful keys they are guaranteed to work—but it is not so easy to get them to work. Someone is resisting us practically every step of the way! Satan's name actually means "Adversary"—the one who "opposes" and "plots against" God and us. In a strange way it is comforting to learn this truth that we didn't mess up our lives or the planet as a whole just by our own foolishness alone. We evidently had lots of help coming from an invisible realm that we may have had no idea even existed. There are plenty of people—including Christians—who don't believe the devil is real or that knowing about him could have any relevance for daily life. C. S. Lewis wryly commented upon this way of the world in his preface to *The Screwtape Letters*.

> *For we do not wrestle against flesh and blood, but against ... spiritual forces of evil in the heavenly places.*
> Ephesians 6:12

> *There are two equal and opposite errors into which our race can fall about the devils. One is to disbelieve in their existence. The other is to believe, and to feel an excessive and unhealthy interest in them. They themselves are equally pleased by both errors.*[16]

We certainly don't want to fall into the ditch of error on either side of this truth. The great thing in the Christian life is our relationship with Christ—not with the enemy. Even so this very deceptive enemy must be exposed in order to be successfully resisted. We would be wise to learn from the elders of the early church who tell us that they took care to beware.

To keep Satan from getting the advantage over us; for we are not ignorant of his wiles *and* intentions. 2 Corinthians 2:11 AMP

An Introduction to the Battlefield

Did you know that you have a personal enemy, even legions of enemies? Did you know that they know your weaknesses and will stop at nothing to bring you down? How can you survive on a battlefield, if you don't know that a war is going on? How can you fight back, if you don't know who your enemy is, or how to recognize him or how to use your weapons? We have been given free will in a real world that is besieged by an invisible enemy (Ephesians 6:12). None of us volunteered to be

---

[16] Preface, THE SCREWTAPE LETTERS by CS Lewis © copyright CS Lewis Pte Ltd 1942, 1943, 1944, 1952.

involved in this war—we were born into it. We can learn to fight in the great battle of our age, or be rendered ineffective, taken captive, or destroyed. We can even have a great love for God and still be defeated by a lack of knowledge (Romans 10:2).

Therefore my people go into captivity for lack of knowledge.
Isaiah 5:13 WEB

My people are destroyed for lack of knowledge. Hosea 4:6

This invisible kingdom of the enemy was in the Garden, but it was kept separate from Adam and, before the Fall, could not interfere with his fellowship with God. Tragically, after Adam and Eve sinned, the nature of Satan—his way of feeling, thinking and believing—began to operate in them and seemed like their own reasoning process (Genesis 3:11).

There are literally hundreds of references to evil spirits, fallen angels and Satan in the scriptures. Instances of demonic oppression abound. In the New Testament there is a linking of sickness and oppression, just as there is a linking of sickness and sin. There is not a shared identity of the two, but a relationship: Not every sickness required deliverance from demons: Not every deliverance from demons involved a physical illness. Nevertheless, disease and death come from the Fall, not the blessing of God. Hence, it is the enemy's kingdom that is at work behind sickness and disease to enforce the curse of the law. Consider these examples.

They brought him all the sick, those afflicted with various diseases and pains, those oppressed by demons, epileptics, and paralytics, and he healed them. Matthew 4:24
(See also Mark 9:23-29, Luke 4:40-41, Luke 8:1-2.)

Behold, there was a woman who had a spirit of infirmity eighteen years, and she was bent over, and could in no way straighten herself up. When Jesus saw her, he called her, and said to her, "Woman, you are freed from your infirmity." Luke 13:11-12 WEB

The spiritual realm of darkness is not inhabited by ethereal forces, but by intelligent beings with malignant natures. Evil spirits have personality, will and desire, but lack bodies through which to carry out their assignments. Jesus says evil spirits prefer to occupy our bodies and think of us as their "house."

"When the unclean spirit has gone out of a person, it passes through waterless places seeking rest, but finds none. Then it says, 'I will return to my house from which I came.' And when it comes, it finds the house empty, swept, and put in order. Then it goes and brings with it seven other spirits more evil than itself, and they enter and dwell there, and the last state of that person is worse than the first." Matthew 12:43-45

The evil spirits that have been cast out and sent into "waterless places" are in torment because they need a means of expressing their nature. They need our agreements with them and the use of our bodies so that they can sin through us. Being in terror of their dark lord, they urgently desire to fulfill their mission by expressing themselves within us and to propel us by inward pressure (fear, anger, lust, shame, etc.) into outward sins as well. All the while they take an unholy pleasure in feeling inside of us the very feelings we don't enjoy; hence, their primary goal is to return to the person they were cast out of. We need to clean our "house" and keep it filled and guarded. Evil spirits gain dominion over us by tempting us to agree with the sin they represent (i.e. a "spirit of fear" promotes fear). Christians cannot be possessed by the enemy, since they are the Lord's possession (1 Corinthians 6:20; Ephesians 1:14). However, they can be and often are oppressed from the inside and/or the outside by this infernal kingdom.

> *We are still in secret agreement with any sin we have not yet fully forsaken.*

Discernment Is Key to Our Freedom

The enemy seeks to veil his work with darkness and deception—that's why discernment is one of the four keys to freedom (see Chapter 3). If we can recognize the working of this kingdom, we can overcome it for light drives out darkness (John 1:5). If we do not discern the spirits, their position and power continues unchallenged. We enter into agreement with the evil spirit whenever we let it express itself through us. When that happens it is no longer sinning by itself—*against us*—its sin has become our sin—*within us*. Sin is an agreement with the enemy—with his ways, his perspective and his desires. Until we fully forsake a sin, we are still in "secret" (unrecognized) agreement with it at some level deep inside our heart. Because the evil spirits so thoroughly believe in the "rightness" of their demented perspective, we have to learn how to break our agreements with the compelling power of *their* entrenched beliefs.[17] We will have to work hard at believing God's truth instead. This is war and war is never easy, but our freedom is well worth the effort it takes.

Consider this in relation to the negative emotions. Every negative emotion has had its source in this kingdom all your life. These evil beings have been sinning against you from birth. We could all easily share David's complaint that an enemy has hated us and laid snares for us "without cause" (Psalm 35:7). The kingdom of darkness is the true source behind all of your pain and suffering as well as your own sinful ways, but you didn't know this in the beginning. You looked around and all you could see was other people and the injustice coming through their sins against you. You were blinded from seeing these three things with enough understanding to stay free, but these truths can liberate you now:

1) The real enemy was the evil spirits who had attacked those people first and were using them against you.

---

[17] "We have to learn to fall out of agreement with the compelling force of the spirit's own belief system and believe instead what God's Word declares to be true in situations that trouble us." From Pastor Ed Kelly, Be In Health® teaching and materials, Dr. Henry W. Wright, Thomaston, Georgia, seminar notes, October 2000.

2) In unintended reaction to your pain it was your own sinful reactions and ungodly beliefs that bound the pain to you.

3) The loving and faithful God was always there with you, preserving your life, just as He is with you now to heal your life.

Now, God is saying to you: *Forgive people for everything*—let Him deal with them—and concentrate on the real enemy. Confess your own sins (including any unforgiveness), resist Satan's kingdom and let God restore your life as you leave justice to Him. All the while, keep your focus on the Lord. Our primary objective is not to crush the enemy, but to love God with our whole being (Matthew 22:37). In terms of spiritual warfare, this translates into trusting and obeying God no matter what the enemy is doing—to surrender and stay surrendered to God. Consider this well: There is no peace without surrender. Yet, even believers often find themselves living without the peace of Christ capturing their hearts. The truth is that whenever we begin to move away from the place of total surrender, we are, *to that degree*, joining the Great Rebellion that began when the enemy used his free will to move away from the will of his Creator and go his own way. Since our ongoing surrender to the Lord is the key to victory, we will surely have to learn how to face the cross of our embattled times and say with Jesus, "Nevertheless, not my will, but Yours, be done" (Luke 22:42).

The Importance of a Fighting Spirit

The language of spiritual warfare can be found throughout the New Testament, but it is in the Hebrew Scriptures especially that we see the importance of maintaining a fighting spirit. They could visibly see their enemy coming to steal, kill and destroy and they responded accordingly! Our battle is not against flesh and blood as theirs was for they were called to be examples to us (in the visible and natural realm) of things that we would experience in the invisible realm of our own spiritual warfare. We have to learn how to "see" by means of faith to win our battle ((Ephesians 6:12).

Now these things happened to them as an example, but they were written down for our instruction, on whom the end of the ages has come. 1 Corinthians 10:11

One of the things which caused the children of Israel to stumble was a great fear about going up against the giants in the land that the Lord had promised to them as their inheritance. They were very reluctant warriors! However, in the battles to come, it was Joshua and Caleb who saw an opportunity for the people of God to grow stronger, just as fresh bread strengthens and revitalizes a hungry person.

"Only do not rebel against the Lord. And do not fear the people of the land, for they are bread for us. Their protection is removed from them, and the Lord is with us; do not fear them." Numbers 14:9

These men had faith that the God *they* believed in was capable of helping them gain the victories they needed against the giants, boldly saying the giants would be "bread for us." Ultimately, it was *only* Joshua and Caleb of that generation who ended up enjoying life in the land promised to all of those who Moses led out of Egypt.

Whether you want it or not, one of the ultimate battles of life lies right before you—to subdue the interior landscape of your own heart by fighting to fully believe and do what God's Word declares to be truth (Proverbs 4:23). What a conundrum it is that we have to be willing at times to fight to live in the Kingdom's peace and joy. Hebrews calls it laboring to enter the promised place of rest.

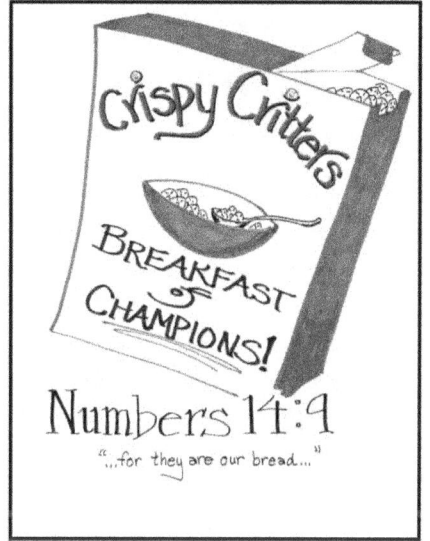

> **Let us labour therefore to enter into that rest, lest any man fall after the same example of unbelief.** Hebrews 4:11 KJV

CRISPY CRITTERS

Evil spirits will burn one day, but in the meantime we are at war! Joshua embraced the battle, declaring that the giants they faced would be "bread for us." By learning to overcome the enemy we grow stronger!

In the fourth and fifth centuries many noble souls "fled" the lukewarm Christianity of the converted Roman Empire to the deserts of Egypt in order to live more totally for Christ. They discovered that like Jesus they were to face some of the stiffest temptations from the enemy in their wilderness. They quickly discovered that it was easy to get the monk (the spiritual athlete, the God chaser) out of Rome, but far harder to get "Rome" out of the monk! Here are a few nuggets of wisdom gleaned by Henri Nouwen from the writings of the desert fathers:[18]

> *The chief task of the athlete is to enter into his heart [and do battle there].*
> Macarius the Great, Desert Father, ca. 300-391.[19]

> *The great work of a man…[is] to expect temptations to his last breath.*
> Saint Anthony of Egypt, Desert Father, ca. 251-356.[20]

> *You should realize that as soon as you intend to live in peace, at once evil comes and weighs down your soul… But if we are vigilant, all these temptations fall away.*
> Mother Theodora, d. 490.[21]

---

[18] Henri Nouwen, *The Way of the Heart* (New York: Seabury Press, 1981), pp. 77, 70, 70.
[19] Macarius the Great, cited in Irenee Hausherr, *The Name of Jesus*, trans. Charles Cummings (Kalamazoo, MI: Cistercian Publications, Inc. 1978, p. 314.
[20] Benedicta Ward, trans., *The Sayings of the Desert Fathers* (London & Oxford: Mowbrays, 1975), p. 71.
[21] Ibid., p. 71.

Even so, the great thing is never the battle, but the "resting in the Lord" and "flowing in the Spirit" times that lie on the other side of each fresh victory.

NOTES/JOURNAL

_____
_____
_____
_____
_____
_____
_____
_____
_____

EXERCISE

Make a list of actual moments when you were quite sure—even at the time—that you had bumped up against real spiritual evil. Pray over those times when the enemy tipped his hand, thanking God for His power and mercy in delivering you from them. Be sure to renounce any fear of the enemy you may have taken on during those times. Ironically, any fear we may have of the demons comes from the demons themselves—so don't buy into it. God is infinitely stronger and you have been granted incredible power and authority over them in the Name of Jesus.

The event	How I felt; what I did; equipping I still need
_____	_____
_____	_____
_____	_____
_____	_____

Now, make another list of all the times you have been tempted to do or to say something wrong. Be sure to include all of the times you have lost peace and joy due to being swallowed up in negative emotions. What's the matter? Don't have enough lines on the paper? Can you see from this that your enemy prefers working under the radar? Forewarned is forearmed!

_____	_____
_____	_____
_____	_____

DISCUSSION QUESTIONS

Ask the group if a few people would care to share their "war stories"—brief (!) descriptions of a time when their life seemed to be heavily assaulted by the powers of darkness. Ask them to make an attempt to give it a clear beginning, middle (the time of struggle) and end. Then ask the group to look for common themes. Keep in mind that the enemy has four main pathways by which he operates: deception, temptation, accusation and destruction. Consider asking:

- Was there an open door that allowed the enemy to come in?
- Was that open door evident at the time, or only in hindsight?
- Did it begin as a flood, or was there a slow, steady descent into the trouble?
- What kinds of feelings were stirred up during that time of assault?
- How easy was it to "tag up" with the Lord while under the assault?
- Did other believers have to be called upon for help?
- In what ways did they help?
- Did final victory come from the Lord alone or did he use the person's cooperation that was under the assault?

Close by praying for the Lord to break the power of any fear or lies that the enemy may have planted during those "close encounters" with spiritual darkness.

MAIN POINTS

- Do you know that you have an enemy? These guys play for keeps!
- Evil spirits have personality, will and desire: Their assignment is to discourage, defeat and destroy you.
- Evil spirits gain power and influence over us by tempting us to agree with the sin they represent.
- In your own strength you are easy pickings; united to the Lord you are powerful!
- We are still in secret agreement with any sin we have not fully forsaken.
- Christians are not possessed, but can be *oppressed* from inside or outside.

DIGGING DEEPER

There are a few things that God didn't tell you when you were born—or even ask your permission to do! Stay with us on this wry look at an imaginary scene in heaven. Suppose the Father had you on His loving knee and asked you if you wanted to help Him out with a little rescue campaign He was operating on planet Earth. You might have said, "Sure!" until He began to explain to you...

Dearest child of Mine,

You will be born without even knowing I exist, much less that I love you as fully as I do. You will be born with a sin nature you won't be able to get rid of and which will cause you all kinds of problems. Your parents will have a sin nature and may sin against you in ways they won't want to, sometimes in ways they won't even be aware of. You will even begin to sin against Me. ("No, heaven forbid!" you cry out!) You will have to wait for other people who didn't know Me either, to come and tell you about Me and what I did for you through Jesus. Otherwise, if they don't come to you, your sins and separation would take you to hell. You will have a very hard time believing them at first. Oh and by the way, there will be legions of the evil one who hate you, will attack you relentlessly and will be invisible to you—and yet you won't really know much about them or believe they are even there until you get to know Me again.

What would you say to being born under these circumstances? So take a deep breath and realize that God knows what you have been up against and what He has to do to help you overcome it!

SWORD AND SHIELD

Not only did the Lord Jesus cast out spirits, so did his disciples both before and after His death and resurrection. Notice who is doing the work in the scriptures below and consider what their level of training may have been. Look up what Jesus called "the children's bread" (Mt 15:26; Mk 7:27). What do you suppose He meant by that? Study the great commission given by Jesus after His resurrection (Mk 16:17-18). Notice any "great omissions" in our actual practice?

> **That evening they brought to him many who were oppressed by demons, and he cast out the spirits with a word and healed all who were sick.** Matt 8:16-17

> **And he appointed twelve (whom he also named apostles) so that they might be with him and he might send them out to preach and have authority to cast out demons.** Mark 3:14-15

> **"And these signs will accompany those who believe: in my name they will cast out demons; they will speak in new tongues."** Mark 16:17-18

> **The people also gathered from the towns around Jerusalem, bringing the sick and those afflicted with unclean spirits, and they were all healed.** Acts 5:16

Some of the evil spirits mentioned specifically in scripture:

The spirit of jealousy (Nu 5:14)	A lying spirit (1Ki 22:22)
The distressing spirit (1Sa 16:23)	The spirit of heaviness (Isa 61:3)

The spirit of harlotry (Hos 4:12)
A spirit of infirmity (Lk 13:10-13)
A spirit of divination (Ac 16:16-18)
The spirit of bondage (Ro 8:14-15)
A spirit of stupor (Ro 11:6-8)

The spirit of the world (1Cor 2:12)
Deceiving spirits (1Ti 4:1)
A spirit of fear (2Ti 1:7)
The spirit of the Antichrist (1Jn 4:3)
Spiritual fornication (Rv 17:2)

PRAYER FOCUS

How can we effectively guard against the enemy? One way is to put on the whole armor of God. Read the following passage and then fill in the blanks below, listing the whole armor and stating how you believe it could help you withstand the enemy better. Pray over each piece as you put on the armor.

> **Finally, be strong in the Lord and in the strength of his might. Put on the whole armor of God, that you may be able to stand against the schemes of the devil. For we do not wrestle against flesh and blood, but against the rulers, against the authorities, against the cosmic powers over this present darkness, against the spiritual forces of evil in the heavenly places.** 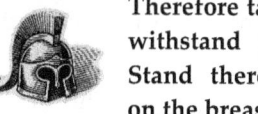 **Therefore take up the whole armor of God, that you may be able to withstand in the evil day, and having done all, to stand firm. Stand therefore, having fastened on the belt of truth, and having put on the breastplate of righteousness, and, as shoes for your feet, having put on the readiness given by the gospel of peace. In all circumstances take up the shield of faith, with which you can extinguish all the flaming darts of the evil one; and take the helmet of salvation, and the sword of the Spirit, which is the word of God, praying at all times in the Spirit, with all prayer and supplication. To that end keep alert with all perseverance, making supplication for all the saints.** Ephesians 6:10-19

Item of armor	Purpose of the armor
1 _____	_____
2 _____	_____
3 _____	_____
4 _____	_____
5 _____	_____
6 _____	_____

Father, thank You for the Blood of Jesus, the Name of Jesus, Your truth, Your Spirit and Your armor—my weapons for offense and defense. You have truly equipped me for fighting the spiritual battles that lie ahead! I place the helmet of salvation over my mind and the righteousness of Christ over my heart. May I always be girded about by Your truth and may my feet remain upon Your path of peace. I take up faith as a shield against the Accuser and wield Your Word as a sword to cut through the darkness as I walk in Your light, praying always for Your Presence and power to guide me!

RENUNCIATIONS AND AFFIRMATIONS

Renounce any agreements with untruth; believe Jesus' *truth* as your new *way* of *life*.

The following is an ancient pattern of renunciation and confession for baptismal candidates taken from the 1979 Episcopal Book of Common Prayer.[22] As you pray over it, confess any previous agreements with the kingdom of darkness (sins of thought, word or deed) and renounce them. Then confess and believe in Jesus and His truth as your new Way of Life (Jn 14:6). If you have never been baptized, seek out a faith community and go for it. Baptism is evidently very important to the Lord (Mk 16:16; Ac 2:38; Ro 6:3; 1 Co 12:13; Gal 3:27).

Question	Do you renounce Satan and all the spiritual forces of wickedness that rebel against God?
Answer	*I renounce them.*
Question	Do you renounce evil powers of this world which corrupt and destroy the creatures of God?
Answer	*I renounce them.*
Question	Do you renounce all sinful desires that draw you from the love of God?
Answer	*I renounce them.*
Question	Do you turn to Jesus Christ and accept him as your Savior?
Answer	*I do.*
Question	Do you put your whole trust in his grace and love?
Answer	*I do.*
Question	Do you promise to follow and obey him as your Lord?
Answer	*I do.*

PUTTING FEET TO YOUR PRAYERS: STRETCH YOURSELF!

Try reading one of Frank Peretti's novels to expand your vision for how these two kingdoms just might be working behind the scenes: *This Present Darkness* or *Piercing the Darkness*; or treat yourself to the all time classic: *The Screwtape Letters* by C. S. Lewis. If you feel ready to move from fiction to fact, look up *He Came to Set the Captives Free* or *Prepare for War* by Dr. Rebecca Brown.

Be advised, however, not try to "go after" this kingdom on your own. If you feel called to spiritual warfare, your first task is to fully engage the battle to see your own heart set free as outlined in a workbook like this one. Then find those who are being used to deliver others and become trained by working in yoked submission with them. Jesus sent His disciples out two by two, all the while making sure that they stayed under His authority and in fellowship with the whole band of disciples.

---

[22] The Episcopal Church, *The Book of Common Prayer* (New York: Church Publishing, Inc. 1982) p. 302-303.

CHAPTER 5

SEPARATION FROM SIN

In the previous lesson we studied the rebel army and saw how its members work to bring us into agreement with their false world view and participate in their sinful rebellion. Since sin is so intimately connected with so much that we may say or do, including our emotional life, it is very easy to fall into the snare of looking at ourselves and others, seeing the sins and going into judgment. How does God keep His own great heart clear of holding sins against us? If we can see from His perspective, we will see the way for our own hearts to live free of holding judgments. We have already seen that the Father's glory is His mercy (Exodus 34:7) and that He doesn't count our sins against us (2 Corinthians 5:18-19). Now let us see the way that He looks upon us.

God Sees Us Differently Than We Do

Our loving God actually sees us as separate from our sins.[23] This is due to the great act of deliverance He accomplished for us when we were born again—He justified us freely in the Beloved giving us an entirely new righteous status based upon Jesus' death for our sins (Romans 3:24). We asked Him to separate us from our sins and He did! He can see sin in us all day long and still see the person we are as separate from those sins—even sins of attitude and emotion, even the desire to sin that dwells so powerfully in us at times. Just consider what Paul is seeking to express:

> *You are not your sins!*

> Now if I do what I do not want, I agree with the law, that it is good. So now it is no longer I who do it, but <u>sin that dwells within me</u>. For I know that nothing good dwells in me, that is, in my flesh. For I have the desire to do what is right, but not the ability to carry it out. For I do not do the good I want, but the evil I do not want is what I keep on doing. Now if I do what I do not want, it is no longer I who do it, but <u>sin that dwells within me</u>. Romans 7:16-20

Whenever scripture, like a parent, repeats something, we need to pay attention. Paul states it twice: "It is no longer I who do it, but sin that dwells in me." This is not Flip Wilson saying, "The devil made me do it." We are not being asked to abandon our responsibility for sin being in us, but we are being shown from heaven's perspective that *we are not our sins*, no *living* human is. The enemy and his kingdom have indeed become their sins, with no possibility of (or desire for) repentance and separation from them. Tragically those who never repent, the

---

[23] For the concept of "separation" in relation to justification: Teaching and insights from Be In Health® teaching and materials, Dr. Henry W. Wright, Thomaston, Georgia, seminar notes, October 2000.

unredeemed who die in their sins, cannot be separated from them and end by being made one with their sins in hell. They actually become beings of sin. But we can be separated from our sins and can repent. The very fact that we repent of sin shows that it is a foreign invader in our lives—it is not who we really are. Never bind anyone to their sins. Right up to the moment of death it is possible for absolutely anyone to seek God for mercy and be set free from indwelling sin.

God has perfect vision. He can see every moment in time at all times. He is able to look upon us and always keep in mind three things about us: 1) the unseen past—who He created us to be, 2) the veiled future—who we will be in heaven and 3) the hidden present—who we really are even now deep down in Christ. He fashioned us in our mother's womb and He knew us before time began (Isaiah 49:15). Since He is not the author of sin in us, His perfect vision still holds the image of who we really are before the fallen nature got attached to us and before generational sins or our own wrong choices began to have their effect. Not only that, but our Redeemer has 20/20 future vision and can always see who we are being redeemed to become as He draws us out of darkness into His light through the sanctifying work of the Spirit and our own belief in the truth (2 Thessalonians 2:13; 1 Peter 2:9). But His vision extends beyond the past and our future; it sees deep within that there is a New Creation in us. He knows (and wants us to know) that this is who we really are now despite any stubborn, temporary agreements we may have with sin. We are not the old nature, we are not our sins and we are not our negative emotions. We are a New Creation!

> **Therefore if any person is** [ingrafted] **in Christ (the Messiah) he is a new creation (a new creature altogether); the old** [previous moral and spiritual condition] **has passed away. Behold, the fresh** *and* **new has come!** 2 Corinthians 5:17 AMP

Why Is This So Hard To Get?

Throughout the creation process, God declared that everything He was making was good. With Adam, however, God went even further. He said that Adam was "very good" (Genesis 1:31). Keep this well in mind: All that God put into you is very good: your mind, your heart, your body, your renewed spirit. You are very good! However, when we allow sin to encroach upon our thoughts, words and deeds we are bringing in a foreign element, something God never put into us when He created us in our mother's womb. Three times in scripture we are shown how the Lord sees us as separate from the sin that dwells in us. The first was God questioning Adam about who he was "listening" to in the Garden (Genesis 3:10). The second time was Jesus rebuking Satan from speaking through Peter (Matthew 16:22-23). The third time came when Jesus rebuked the "sons of thunder" for wanting to call fire down on a village that had rejected Him.

> But the Lord God called to the man and said to him, "Where are you?" And he said, "I heard the sound of you in the garden, and I was afraid, because I was naked, and I hid myself." He said, "Who told you that you were naked?" Genesis 3:9-11

> But he turned and said to Peter, "Get behind me, Satan! You are a hindrance to me. For you are not setting your mind on the things of God, but on the things of man." Matthew 16:23

> But he turned and rebuked them, "You don't know of what kind of spirit you are." Luke 9:55 WEB

Like Adam and Peter, James and John, we may not even be aware that some of our "best" thinking is actually coming from the enemy—disguised as our own ideas and reasoning process. None of them were possessed, but they were giving ear to the enemy and voicing his perspective. Discern the voices: Who am I listening to and letting speak through me? Beware of "stinking thinking."

The real you is somebody both you and God want you to be. He is simply redeeming you to become who He created you to be. He didn't give you a sin nature or any of your patterns that don't match up with Jesus. That was Satan's way of "unmaking" you. God always sees the difference and we can learn to do it too. Grow spiritual eyes to see yourself and others as separate from whatever sins may be present. Because of the reconciliation won for us by Christ (2 Corinthians 5:18-21), God does not separate Himself from us—only from our sins. Our sins break our fellowship with Him—not His with us. Therefore, we can confidently go to God with our sin still clinging to us, knowing by faith that He will love us and help us. In His eyes we who believe in Christ are always "covered" and protected by the Blood of Jesus, even when our need to be "cleansed" by the Blood is at its greatest. This is why He tells us to be bold in coming—He knows that many times we will have to come "slimed" by sin and need to be cleaned up on arrival!

> Let us then with confidence draw near to the throne of grace, that we may receive mercy and find grace to help in time of need. Hebrews 4:16

Deception Is Very Deceiving

The reason we need so much cleansing is due to the way that the "law of sin" wars within us against the new law of Christ (Romans 7:22-25). This law of sin is the often unrecognized teaching of Satan in us which seems like obvious truth (John 8:44-46). For example, it was the devil who "fathered" us into the idea that holding on to bitterness is better than letting go or that being anxious is better than trusting God. The truth is that everyone who sins has been blinded and deceived by an enemy. In compassion God "grants" repentance so that we may know the truth, come to our senses and separate ourselves from our sins and the enemy's snares with God's help. Let this grow mercy in you for others.

> **The Lord's servant must not quarrel, but be gentle towards all, able to teach, patient, in gentleness correcting those who oppose him: perhaps God may give them repentance leading to a full knowledge of the truth, and they may recover themselves out of the devil's snare, having been taken captive by him to his will.**
> 2 Timothy 2:24-26 WEB

One goal of effective spiritual warfare is to expose the real enemy, to reveal the true battleground. The real enemy is not your body, not the disease, not the depression, not the addiction, not the people who may have harmed you, not the people who led you astray. The real enemy is not yourself either! The real enemies are those spiritual powers of darkness whose thoughts masquerade as our own in order to tempt us to think, speak and act to serve their purposes. When we let sinful thoughts, attitudes and feelings dwell in us we are actually fellowshipping with evil beings and establishing Satan's kingdom on earth by doing his will instead of God's. By forgiving everyone (ourselves included) we shift the ultimate blame for evil to the demons who carried people captive into sin in the first place. We can then focus our righteous indignation on the enemy and his kingdom, where God keeps His anger and wrath focused. Certainly Jesus hates the wickedness of the enemy's kingdom.

> **You have loved righteousness and hated wickedness. Therefore God, your God, has anointed you with the oil of gladness beyond your companions.** Psalms 45:7

We, too, need to develop a perfect hatred for sin as the Psalmist did, and yet remember who the real enemy is under the conditions of our New Covenant. Shift the hate and blame from people to the one who enslaves them to do his will (2 Timothy 2:26).

> **Do I not hate those who hate you, O Lord? And do I not loathe those who rise up against you? I hate them with complete hatred; I count them my enemies.**
> Psalms 139:21-22

When we refuse to forgive someone as the law of Christ commands, we are saying to Jesus: "I don't believe your law is right. I believe my law of bitterness is better." God may well ask of us as He did of Adam, "Who told you that?" Through intercession and forgiveness we are to loose people from their sins and bind the real enemy. But when we bind people to their sins, we loose the enemy instead. Remember, we do not wrestle against flesh and blood, but against the invisible powers of evil (Ephesians 6:12). Stay focused. Love God, love people and hate the real enemy!

> **For we do not wrestle against flesh and blood, but against the rulers, against the authorities, against the cosmic powers over this present darkness, against the spiritual forces of evil in the heavenly places.** Ephesians 6:12

Recognize, Discern, Separate!

Cultivating a perspective of separating people from their sins is a process of discernment and recognition—and the best person on which to practice this is yourself. Learn to notice the presence of negative emotions and wrong attitudes—these are not coming from your true self. Any loss of peace should alert you. With practice you can learn to separate yourself from what is not like Christ in you. The good comes from the New Creation that you already are and are becoming (Colossians 1:27). The evil comes from the enemy. Stay in agreement with God and not the devil about who you are. As you learn to practice this with yourself, you will be much better equipped to cover others with the same grace. Once mastering this, you will learn to see everyone as separate from their sins—including yourself. Heaven's perspective is so much better than that of earth, for once you catch on to it you have to admit that it's, well, *heavenly...*

NOTES/JOURNAL

____

EXERCISE

Practicing separation from sin is a process of discernment and recognition. First learn to discern the presence of sinful heart attitudes in you and then school yourself to realize that these are *not you*—not the real you. Make a list of things about you (in your past or your personality) that you have thought of as a part of yourself, but which you will be separated from in heaven.

Patterns I see in me that heaven will remove (not Christ like in me; not really me)

____

Try to see yourself as that New Creation—the one that will fully emerge in heaven. What are those aspects of yourself you can see today that will endure into eternity?

Things about me that will continue in heaven (from Christ in me; the real me)

_____
_____
_____

DISCUSSION QUESTIONS

Once the pathway of repentance is closed by death, unbelievers who die in their sins without Christ to free them actually *become their sins* with no hope of separation from them. Until then we can all learn God's way of repentance from sin and faith in Christ in order to become separated from our sins.

1) Ask the group to try to describe what it would be like to be stuck to one's sins for all of eternity—let alone suffer punishment for it. Imagine that sin growing without God helping you to restrain it. Stir your heart to intercede for the lost. (Consider reading *23 Minutes in Hell* by Bill Wiese.)

2) Then, ask the group to name some notorious kinds of sinful people (no names please). Try to imagine death bed conversions for each one of them in turn. What kind of person might emerge at that point of entry into heaven? What characteristics of the New Creation would spring to life? How would they see their former life? What parts of their former ways could pass in to heaven—separated from their sinful side? Envision them in their future.

3) Now, ask the group to consider infants and how innocent they are—most of the time. What are they like before sins begin to get stuck to them? Do they begin with any sins? Which ones? What do parents do about it—leave it in place or try to separate them from it before it gets established? Do parents still remind themselves of what their children were like as infants? Does it warm their hearts? Wouldn't that do the same for God? Learn to see with His eyes!

MAIN POINTS

- You have been created good in your essence as a person who God loves!
- You are not your sin(s)—you are a New Creation desiring to come forth.
- Whatever is not like Jesus in you is not who you really are—turn from it.
- God sees you as He created you to be, as you will become, as you are deep down united to Him in your spirit.
- God sees everyone separate from their sins so we can learn to do it too.

DIGGING DEEPER

As we have examined in this lesson, one reason that the Father sees us as separate from our sins is because He created us good in the womb and never loses sight of who we really are. He has also redeemed us in a way that forever separates us from our sins: This amazing gift of grace is called justification and it is an immense topic in the New Testament, especially in the letters of Paul.

> "In the Lord all the offspring of Israel shall be justified and shall glory." Isaiah 45:25

> He shall see of the travail of his soul, and shall be satisfied: by the knowledge of himself shall my righteous servant justify many; and he shall bear their iniquities. Isaiah 53:11 WEB

> "Be it known to you therefore, brothers , that through this man is proclaimed to you remission of sins, and by him everyone who believes is justified from all things, from which you could not be justified by the law of Moses." Acts 13:38-39 WEB

> For there is no distinction, for all have sinned, and fall short of the glory of God; being justified freely by his grace through the redemption that is in Christ Jesus; whom God set forth to be an atoning sacrifice, through faith in his blood, for a demonstration of his righteousness through the passing over of prior sins, in God's forbearance. Romans 3:22-25 WEB

> It was to show his righteousness at the present time, so that he might be just and the justifier of the one who has faith in Jesus. Romans 3:26

> Therefore, since we have been justified by faith, we have peace with God through our Lord Jesus Christ. Through him we have also obtained access by faith into this grace in which we stand, and we rejoice in hope of the glory of God. Romans 5:1-2

> Who shall bring any charge against God's elect? It is God who justifies. Who is to condemn? Christ Jesus is the one who died—more than that, who was raised—who is at the right hand of God, who indeed is interceding for us. Romans 8:33-35

> For those whom he foreknew he also predestined to be conformed to the image of his Son, in order that he might be the firstborn among many brothers. And those whom he predestined he also called, and those whom he called he also justified, and those whom he justified he also glorified. Romans 8:29-30

> And such were some of you. But you were washed, you were sanctified, you were justified in the name of the Lord Jesus Christ and by the Spirit of our God.
> 1 Corinthians 6:11

> So then, the law was our guardian until Christ came, in order that we might be justified by faith. But now that faith has come, we are no longer under a guardian. Galatians 3:24-26

Justification is called the "free gift" (Romans 5:15-17). God has chosen to see us as justified before Him. A catchy turn of words has it that this activity of God *justify*-ing us means *"just as if I* had no sin in me at all." Through the Blood of Jesus God is able to separate us from our sins and to give us right standing with Him and restore us to favor, now and forever. He literally sees us just as if we were sinless. He places a new sinless nature inside of us and seals it with the Holy Spirit. This is the basis of our new life. This does not eliminate the reality of our sins or their consequences in this life, but it does establish us in a totally different relationship with God, one that is mercy-based and covered with favor.

SWORD AND SHIELD

Sin defined. Since so much of our freedom and blessing depends upon recognizing sin in order to turn from it and avoid its consequences, the following biblical definitions of sin may be helpful. Keep in mind that God does not see you as your sin. *You are not your sins!* But we still need to recognize sin in us so that we can go to God for forgiveness and freedom from it.

The devising of folly is sin. Proverbs 24:9

For whatever does not proceed from faith is sin. Romans 14:23

So whoever knows the right thing to do and fails to do it, for him it is sin. James 4:17

All unrighteousness is sin. 1 John 5:17 WEB

Sin described. It is also helpful to recognize sin by description: Sin is shown to be a blood-like stain ("scarlet"), a missing of the mark ("falling short"), a breach of the law ("transgression"), a crossing of rightful boundaries ("trespass"), a form of living death ("dead" to God), a torment of death (its "sting"), a bent or crooked way ("iniquity") and a form of self-will over God's will ("idolatry").

"Come now, let us reason together," says the Lord: "Though your sins are like <u>scarlet</u>, they shall be as white as snow; though they are red like crimson, they shall become like wool." Isaiah 1:18

For all have sinned and <u>fall short</u> of the glory of God. Romans 3:23

Yet death reigned from Adam to Moses, even over those whose sinning was not like the <u>transgression</u> of Adam, who was a type of the one who was to come. Romans 5:14

And you were dead in the <u>trespasses</u> and sins. Ephesians 2:1-2

The <u>sting</u> of death is sin, and the power of sin is the law. 1 Corinthians 15:56

"For rebellion is as the sin of divination, and presumption is as <u>iniquity</u> and <u>idolatry</u>. Because you have rejected the word of the Lord, he has also rejected you from being king." 1 Samuel 15:23

PRAYER FOCUS

Separating other people from their sins saves us from the snare of judging. Unrighteous judgment does just the opposite of separation—it binds people to their sins. We are to judge persons as God does (as being worthy of His acceptance, love and mercy) and still judge their sins as needing atonement, intercession and correction. Jesus even says that if we cease judging the person (by removing the plank in our eye), God can then use us to free them from their sins (the speck). Righteous judgment always proceeds from this viewpoint of separation.

> "Judge not, that you be not judged. For with the judgment you pronounce you will be judged, and with the measure you use it will be measured to you. Why do you see the speck that is in your brother's eye, but do not notice the log that is in your own eye? Or how can you say to your brother, 'Let me take the speck out of your eye,' when there is the log in your own eye? You hypocrite, first take the log out of your own eye, and then you will see clearly to take the speck out of your brother's eye."
> Matthew 7:1-5

Ask forgiveness for judging yourself and others. Then cast this concern on the Lord—that He will bring freedom from all unrighteous judgments and raise you to the Mercy Seat with Jesus as an intercessor for sinners, including yourself.

RENUNCIATIONS AND AFFIRMATIONS

Renounce any agreements with untruth; believe Jesus' *truth* as your new *way* of *life*.

Discernment enables us to escape the snare of agreeing with hidden sin (Isa 5:13; Hos 4:6). That wrong thing in you—fearfulness, jealousy, bitterness, shyness, impatience, etc.—*is not you*. Notice what it sounds like (its message) and what it feels like (its pressure) when it goes off inside you. It may have been "a part" of you for so long, it seems like it is just the way you are, but it isn't. Somewhere along the way, it came inside from the outside. Rightly recognizing sin as sin (not you) is half the battle. The Word of God illuminates those dark places and shows us who we are and what we are not. Separate sinners from their sins—self included. Your heart will love the freedom it brings!

> **For the word of God is living and active, sharper than any two-edged sword, piercing to the division of soul and of spirit, of joints and of marrow, and discerning the thoughts and intentions of the heart.** Hebrews 4:12

> **But solid food is for the mature, for those who have their powers of discernment trained by constant practice to distinguish good from evil.** Hebrews 5:14

> **So Jesus said to the Jews who had believed in him, "If you abide in my word, you are truly my disciples, and you will know the truth, and the truth will set you free."**
> John 8:31-32

Father, forgive me for binding people to their sins and holding their sins against them. I repent of and renounce any deeply held belief that this is what You do. I confess that the truth is that You see us all as separate from our sins and can separate anyone from their sins who repents, including myself. Jesus, help me to join You as an intercessor for—not a judge of—myself and my fellow sinners.

PUTTING FEET TO YOUR PRAYERS: STRETCH YOURSELF!

Confession is much more than confessing sins. Most powerfully it is confessing truth. This is because confessing sins (and fully repenting of them) frees you from being dragged downwards by the weight of sin; confessing truth lifts your spirit higher as you lay hold of truths that come from heaven. The sky is not even the limit to how high truth can lift you! The following scriptures are word pictures that describe the life of Jesus that is inside of us. Read and confess them as the truth of who you really are as a New Creation and what you are really like deep down.

Love is patient and is kind; love doesn't envy. Love doesn't brag, is not proud, doesn't behave itself inappropriately, doesn't seek its own way, is not provoked, takes no account of evil; doesn't rejoice in unrighteousness, but rejoices with the truth; bears all things, believes all things, hopes all things, endures all things. Love never fails.
1 Corinthians 13:4-8 WEB

But the fruit of the Spirit is love, joy, peace, patience, kindness, goodness, faithfulness, gentleness, self-control; against such things there is no law. And those who belong to Christ Jesus have crucified the flesh with its passions and desires. If we live by the Spirit, let us also walk by the Spirit. Galatians 5:22-25

Have this mind among yourselves, which is yours in Christ Jesus, who, though he was in the form of God, did not count equality with God a thing to be grasped, but made himself nothing, taking the form of a servant, being born in the likeness of men. And being found in human form, he humbled himself by becoming obedient to the point of death, even death on a cross. Philippians 2:5-8

CHAPTER 6

THE PATHWAY OF TEMPTATION

How is it that we so often fall into sin? Ever since the Fall sinning comes naturally to us. We don't have to *work* at being sinners! We can fall into sin without any effort at all because we already have a fallen nature ready to go in that direction. But there is someone who delights in tripping us up. Satan and his kingdom seek to make us fall by presenting us with deceptive temptations.

> **For this reason, when I could bear it no longer, I sent to learn about your faith, for fear that somehow the tempter had tempted you and our labor would be in vain.**
> 1 Thessalonians 3:5

> **And the great dragon was thrown down, that ancient serpent, who is called the devil and Satan, the deceiver of the whole world—he was thrown down to the earth, and his angels were thrown down with him.** Revelation 12:9

Truth Is the Issue

The heart of the issue of temptation is this: Will we use our wills to agree with the enemy or with God about what is right to believe and to do? Naturally, we want to agree with God, but the enemy is a deceiver and he has had a lot of practice at making the wrong thing seem right and the right thing seem wrong. If he simply came out in the open and said, "My ways are guaranteed to kill you!" we would all turn away and run to God. Instead he twists the truth enough to make his perspective seem plausible and his paths seem desirable—all the while seeking to set his hook into our flesh. Note this about the following seven steps: Before sin ever becomes a struggle in our flesh, it has to gain *the agreement of our will*. To sin or not to sin is essentially a truth encounter, not a will power contest.

The Sin Process According to James

Let's learn to recognize and avoid these seven deadly stages of the sin process that James warns us about:[24]

> **Let no man say when he is tempted, "I am tempted by God," for God can't be tempted by evil, and he himself tempts no one. But each one is (1) tempted, when he is (2) drawn away (3) by his own lust, and (4) enticed. Then the lust, when it (5) has conceived, (6) bears sin; and the sin, when it is full grown, (7) brings forth death. Don't be deceived, my beloved brothers.** James 1:13-16 WEB

---

[24] Teaching and insights about these seven stages of temptation from Be In Health® teaching and materials, Dr. Henry W. Wright, Thomaston, Georgia, seminar notes, October 2000.

Stage 1: Tempted

Temptation begins with the enemy, not you. Images, impulses or ideas that tempt us do not come from God or our flesh, but from Satan's kingdom. Some tempting impression is made upon the mind or heart by an evil spirit. At this point it is not sin, only a temptation to sin. Jesus was tempted in every way we are—so don't take on condemnation for being tempted (Hebrews 4:15). You are being probed by an evil spirit to see if you will agree with it. Usually you will sense something in you shift as your attention is caught by the tempting thought. If the tempting impression is recognized for what it is and rejected out of hand, it ends there. But if the idea is entertained and in some way accepted, then the struggle begins. As Martin Luther once said of temptation, "You can't help it if a bird flies over your head, but you can stop it from building a nest in your hair."[25] Be asking: Whose voice is it? Mine? Or the enemy's!

> But each one is tempted, when he is drawn away... don't be deceived.
> James 1:13-16

There is a very real difference between being tempted and actually sinning—temptation is not the same thing as sinning no matter how strong or wrong it feels. Resist the devil and you may suddenly have a whale of a fight on your hands, but you are still on the right side of the issue. Coming into agreement with the tempting thought and doing what it desires is where the sin lies. Being assailed by tempting thoughts, however strongly they may be tugging at you through your wrong desires, is not sin. In the Garden of Gethsemane Jesus sweated blood in His effort to resist the temptation to avoid the cross, and He remained without sin despite the awful power of the enemy working upon Him. So resist all self-condemnation! Getting us to condemn ourselves for being tempted by him is very much a part of the enemy's game plan and it only makes it harder to fight back. Stay encouraged in the Lord—He sees your efforts to resist the snare. He knows your heart and does not condemn you (1 John 3:20).

Stage 2: Drawn Away

Many think that the enemy's primary objective is to get us to sin, but the great issue of temptation is not what we are drawn *into* (sin), but what we are drawn *away from* (the Lord). Entertaining the evil thought draws us away from the peace and confidence that comes to us as we trust and obey our God. The enemy ever seeks to disconnect us from our source of strength and new life—for it is only in Christ that we are a threat to his kingdom (John 15:1-10). Hence he wants to separate us from heart-peace and trust and then make it seem that such a life of surrender is undesirable or impossible. Even one small step away from being fully surrendered to the Lord is a step in the enemy's direction. The first task of resisting temptation is to reconnect with God and His grace. You know you have been

---

[25] Martin Luther, Letter #1575: to Hieronymous Weller (at Wittenberg), June 19, 1530.

"drawn away" if someone asks you how you are doing and you hear yourself say, "I'm just hanging in there." Hanging in there means, "I am still struggling and trying to be faithful, but it's killing me!" This beats giving up and going back, but it is a far cry from living in the grace that is offered us. On the other hand, if a person is fully surrendered, you usually don't have to ask how they are doing—it shines with a glow all over their face.

Stage 3: By His Own Lust

As temptation increases wrong desires begin to awaken out of the fallen nature. The old you comes back to life, sometimes with a vengeance. When the temptation finds a hook into a wrong desire ("lust" means *any* strong, but wrong desire, not just a sexually immoral one), formerly crucified feelings can sometimes spring back to life in an instant. Don't panic! Before that moment of temptation they had been lying in the grave with the old you, and they will do so again as soon as you get your focus back on Christ. Jesus said the enemy had nothing in Him. We should seek to be the same way by quickly reconnecting with God and His grace, then holding the wrong desire as a captive to His light until we see something in Him that makes it lose its emotional power.

"I will no more speak much with you, for the prince of the world comes, and he has nothing in me." John 14:30 WEB

Stage 4: Enticed

Enticed means to catch by using bait. At this point in the process we have already begun buying into some lie that the temptation represents —that's the bait. *Find the lie and break off the hook!* Otherwise, our will becomes "hooked" by agreeing with that deceptive thought, and negative emotions gain strength to overpower us. The evil spirit can only succeed if it breaks our agreement with God by getting us to agree instead with its own false and distorted belief system (see Chapter 4).

Stage 5: Conceived

Enticement generates a desire to give up the struggle by yielding our will to the enemy. We now want to give in to the temptation more than to resist it. Once such an agreement with sin is made (conceived), the actual sin (of thought, word or deed) is sure to follow. Once we have embraced a tempting thought by giving our heart to it, the temptation has become our sin.

"But I say to you that everyone who looks at a woman with lustful intent has already committed adultery with her <u>in his heart</u>." Matthew 5:28

Stage 6: Bears Sin

Now that the temptation is "treasured" in the heart it has become a sinful thing inside of us (Luke 6:45). By our thoughts, words and deeds it is "birthed" as an expression of sin into the world.

Stage 7: Brings Forth Death

The sin, if it is un-repented, continues to kill and destroy that which the enemy attacks through it—especially our relationships of trust and love with God, self or others. Sin always works to produce death: first within the soul of the one who sins and then into the world around. We have become a servant of the enemy in that area of our life and reap accordingly (2 Timothy 2:24-26).

This whole process can take months, days, or fractions of a second. It can be stopped at any point, but it is easiest to stop in the early stages. The more frequently we give way the more likely it is that we will become enslaved. What began as a seemingly random temptation in a "weak" moment may well become a habit that is very hard to break. Such bondage—not being able to say no—indicates that we have given ourselves as *slaves* to sin (John 8:34).

> **For just as you once presented your members as slaves to impurity and to lawlessness leading to more lawlessness, so now present your members as slaves to righteousness leading to sanctification.** Romans 6:19

Gaining Victory

Temptation is a lie of the enemy knocking on the door of your mind, seeking entrance to your heart. Capture the thought when it first starts knocking and carry it captive to Christ before it carries you captive to what the enemy wants you doing. Be on guard and get to it first. Then, reconnect quickly with God and His grace!

> **For the weapons of our warfare are not of the flesh, but mighty before God to the throwing down of strongholds, throwing down imaginations and every high thing that is exalted against the knowledge of God, and bringing every thought into captivity to the obedience of Christ.** 2 Corinthians 10:4-5 WEB

Even temptation has a redemptive purpose, once we learn to recognize and resist it. God desires to move us from holy innocence to mature holiness by means of choice—maturing us through a growth process of sanctification that preserves and enhances our freedom of will (2 Thessalonians 2:13). God allows evil spirits to tempt us so that we can learn to discern good and evil, believe that His Word is the truth and rely completely on Him (Hebrews 5:14). Whenever we fall, we can still choose to repent, return to God and learn to walk in His ways.

The Pathway of Temptation

For the righteous falls seven times and rises again. Proverbs 24:16

Let us remember that Jesus was tempted in every way just as we are, yet did not sin. There is hope for us in this, because Jesus defeated Satan's temptations as a man, in His full humanity. This is evident because the scripture says that "God cannot be tempted"—so it cannot be that Jesus was tempted in His divine nature (James 1:13). And yet the Word also says that Jesus was tempted just as we are (Hebrews 4:15). By this we see that Jesus, in His humanity, was tempted in *exactly* the same way that we are—by enticements coming from the enemy intended to deceive Him into giving sin a place within Himself.

Jesus, being conceived of the Holy Spirit and sinless, had no place within Him that was attracted to sin. He also was fully connected *by faith* to the Father's love, grace and truth and wasn't about to let anything disconnect Him. As reborn believers we, too, through the Holy Spirit have a new nature (at the core of our being) that is not attracted to sin and now enjoy a new connection to God through faith in Christ that we are meant to fight to maintain. The way that Jesus resisted temptation in His humanity, shows us the way we need to learn in order to effectively resist temptations. Jesus resisted temptations by resolutely holding fast to the truth of God's Word—and by carrying the enemy's lies captive to the Word.

Then Jesus said to him, "Be gone, Satan! For it is written, 'You shall worship the Lord your God and him only shall you serve.'" Then the devil left him, and behold, angels came and were ministering to him. Matthew 4:10-11

As soon as you realize that temptation is seeking to disconnect you, fight the good fight of faith to get firmly reconnected with God's grace and His truth!

NOTES/JOURNAL

_____
_____
_____
_____
_____
_____
_____
_____
_____
_____

EXERCISE

We are often strongly tempted in areas where our flesh is predisposed to desire the sin because of woundedness and deceptive thinking coming out of unhealed events of the past. Temptations expose to the light those wounded, deceived areas of our heart so that ultimately we will pray about them and seek the Lord for cleansing and restoration. Try this exercise to see if it helps you understand better the things you struggle with.

Past unhealed event   Temptations and deceptive thinking coming out of wounds
_____   _____
_____   _____
_____   _____

DISCUSSION QUESTIONS

Ask the group what the enemy's primary purpose is with temptation. What is he trying to get us to do? Let it go the rounds then look up James 1:14. Surprised? Most Christians would answer that it is to get us to sin, but to James this is secondary. The primary purpose is to *draw us away* from the place of complete surrender.

1) Now ask the group to describe what the place of complete surrender to the Lord is like—as a moment in time and as a life-style. Ask what Biblical phrases describe it (ex. abiding in Christ, entering into the rest, walking or living in the Spirit, the glorious liberty, the abundant life). Look up several, examine them in context, and seek to envision this as *a whole new way of living*—which it is.

2) Is this how most Christians seem to be living? Is the enemy accomplishing his primary objective where temptations are concerned? What is he getting out of it? What are we being robbed of by not living fully surrendered? What is the world around us being robbed of by us not living fully surrendered? What steps can we take to reverse this? How can we live more fully surrendered?

MAIN POINTS

- It is not a sin to experience even strong temptation—only to agree with it.
- The enemy tempts us *primarily* to draw us away from our place of trust and complete surrender in the Lord.
- Fully surrendered we are a great threat to his plans because Jesus becomes so "alive" in us that we are advancing His Kingdom as we go.

- Drawn away into survival mode ("hanging in there") we are not much of a threat—the enemy has us on the defensive.
- While we are "hanging in there" he will further tempt us to give up resisting and start giving in to sin.
- The process of temptation can be recognized and stopped at any point.
- Resisting temptation is a struggle to believe truth—not a will power contest.

DIGGING DEEPER

In order to understand this dynamic of the spiritual life and live in the midst of many temptations without taking on condemnation (for being tempted so often) or giving way to sin (by being tempted so often), we need to see that...

1) It is not a sin to have a sinful nature. None of us asked to have a sin nature. God allowed it to be so at our birth. Even in the new birth the Lord does not remove our sin nature. In fact the sin nature will only be removed when we get to heaven. Until then it remains a part of who we are, much as a shadow clings to our bodies on a sunny day, but it is not who we are in Christ.

2) In Christ God crucified the sin nature, so that its power over us has been broken. We can now go a different way than the way of the flesh, because we have a new nature within us that desires the ways of God. Whenever we entrust our life to God through faith in Christ, the sin nature remains crucified within us and we are raised to new life by the power of the Spirit.

3) The new nature within us is the sinless nature of Jesus. When we are tempted *as Christians* we are now much more in the same position Jesus was when He was tempted. Just as with Him, we now have a nature within us that is sinless, given to us through the new birth. We can choose to live in and by this new nature through trusting and obeying the Lord, staying yielded to do God's will—just as Jesus lived His life.

4) Temptations test our commitment to trust and obey God. If we learn to recognize and resist temptation, we can remain in our place of rest, trusting and obeying the Lord as His Spirit keeps the sin nature crucified within us. If we give way to the temptation, the sin nature "springs back to life" within us. Temptations test and grow our allegiance to the Lord.

5) Having a sinful nature is not where the bondage to sin comes from. When the New Testament speaks about the sin nature the language is that of "putting off" the old man as readily as one puts off old clothing and puts on new (Eph 4:22; Col 3:9). However, when the spiritual powers of the enemy are involved, the language is that of a pitched battle in which real resistance and determined

effort are required for victory. These battles usually rise out of stronghold areas that we are called to take down (see Lesson 11).

If you want to get victories over areas of strenuous struggle with sin in your life, you need to know the power you have. You have incredible power! Do you know that the single greatest power in your world lies right there within you—at all times? It is the freedom of will God has given you: the power of choice. If we have power to resist God and His desire to save us, we certainly have power to resist Satan and his desire to enslave us. God says in Deuteronomy that He is calling heaven and earth to "witness against us" (since we keep denying we have this power) that He has given us the power to choose *life* or to choose *death*. He clearly wants us to know that we have already been given the power we need.

> **"I call heaven and earth to witness against you today, that I have set before you life and death, blessing and curse. Therefore choose life, that you and your offspring may live."** Deuteronomy 30:19

Surely this is an awesome power! How does it play out? Simply by saying no—with great resolution and conviction—to that which is death, brings us over to the side of life. We have incredible power to resist temptation. The problem is twofold: a) We don't always have an ability to recognize the temptation as death in disguise and b) We aren't always motivated to combat it. But we can *always* choose life by calling on the Lord for a) discernment and b) His strength.

SWORD AND SHIELD

In the following scriptures about sin, note the language of captivity and dominion.

> "If you do well, will you not be accepted? And if you do not do well, sin is crouching at the door. Its desire is for you, but you must rule over it." Genesis 4:7

> Jesus answered them, "Truly, truly, I say to you, everyone who commits sin is a slave to sin. The slave does not remain in the house forever; the son remains forever. So if the Son sets you free, you will be free indeed." John 8:34-36

> For the weapons of our warfare are not of the flesh, but mighty before God to the throwing down of strongholds, throwing down imaginations and every high thing that is exalted against the knowledge of God, and bringing every thought into captivity to the obedience of Christ; and being in readiness to avenge all disobedience, when your obedience will be made full. 2 Corinthians 10:4-6 WEB

> Let not sin therefore reign in your mortal bodies, to make you obey their passions. Do not present your members to sin as instruments for unrighteousness, but present yourselves to God as those who have been brought from death to life, and your members to God as instruments for righteousness. For sin will have no dominion over you, since you are not under law but under grace. Romans 6:12-14

PRAYER FOCUS

Since the primary purpose of the enemy is to draw us away from the place of full surrender to the Lord, our greatest weapon against temptation is to focus in prayer, praise and thanksgiving upon our God, so that living fully surrendered to Him comes more easily and naturally. Spending time in His Presence by intentionally seeking to give worship to the Lord throughout the day makes running to Him so much easier when we come "under fire" in the times of temptation. To worship means to "ascribe worth" to something or someone. Do not seek the *feeling* of His Presence, seek the rightness of your heart in the act of showing or telling Him how much He means to you. Consider adding into your day times of:

- Giving thanks for His blessings as you experience them.
- Praising Him frequently for His love, mercy, wisdom, and saving power.
- Singing along with worship CDs or songs you know by heart.
- Stopping to "smell the flowers" — simply enjoying His creation.
- Offering yourself to Him body, soul and spirit.
- Send, allow, withhold: "Only let me trust and obey You through it all."
- Asking for Him to help you surrender fully.

Father, the foremost temptation I will need to overcome is that of living by trusting and obeying myself, rather than You. Help me turn my life around! Make me willing to be made willing to surrender everything to You. According to Your love and wisdom, send whatever You desire to send of Your grace and blessings, allow whatever You have to allow of free will and its consequences, ask of me whatever You desire or require of inward and outward obedience, withhold me from and withhold from me whatever is necessary to fulfill Your plans. Help me to fully trust that You are working in and through all things for my good and Your glory. Then strengthen me to say in the midst of all temptations, "Not my will, but Yours be done."

RENUNCIATIONS AND AFFIRMATIONS

Renounce any agreements with untruth; believe Jesus' *truth* as your new *way of life*.

Hate the bait! The bait that the enemy is hoping you will reach for is the lie hidden away inside the temptation (Step 4, above). Find the lie and break the hook. That temptation is the effort of an enemy to steal, kill or destroy — why do you keep reaching for it thinking it is a way of life?

Temptation I keep falling into	The lie of the temptation that I keep believing
_____	_____
_____	_____

_____   _____
_____   _____

Now, renounce the lie and confess some truth from God's Word that counters it!

PUTTING FEET TO YOUR PRAYERS: STRETCH YOURSELF!

Don't give up! Repeated failings, though discouraging, can actually help us 1) grow a perfect hatred for the sin (and so learn to better resist it); 2) gather a deeper humility and compassion for others in their sins (by realizing daily our own weakness and need of grace); and 3) gain a firmer confidence in God's mercy (as we discover again and again His patience with us).

Since repentance is something fallen angels and demons will never do, don't expect temptation to cease, though specific ones may diminish in power and intensity, once deliverance is gained. Rate your progress at growing in the grace that is coming to you even in your area of struggle: 1 = some progress; 5 = lots of growth. Be encouraged!

Area of struggle	Hatred of sin	Humility/compassion	Confidence in mercy
_____	1 2 3 4 5	1 2 3 4 5	1 2 3 4 5
_____	1 2 3 4 5	1 2 3 4 5	1 2 3 4 5
_____	1 2 3 4 5	1 2 3 4 5	1 2 3 4 5
_____	1 2 3 4 5	1 2 3 4 5	1 2 3 4 5
_____	1 2 3 4 5	1 2 3 4 5	1 2 3 4 5

CHAPTER 7

RECOGNIZE AND REPLACE!

In the previous chapter we explored the seven stages of temptation, noting that the enemy's primary objective is to draw us away from our rightful place of surrender and union with Christ. Since our salvation—in all of its forms—comes to us by grace *through faith* the center point of the enemy's attack quite naturally is to disconnect us from trusting in and relying upon our God and His grace. As soon as a potential disconnect begins, we start losing the peace of Christ which is meant to rule in our hearts *at all times* (Colossians 3:15). This loss of peace is the Holy Spirit "throwing a flag on the play," alerting us that we are being drawn in the wrong direction. Noticing that loss of peace—and understanding what it means—gives us a choice: We can choose life by seeking to reconnect with our source of new life (Jesus) or we can choose death by continuing to let the temptation gain ground within us.

> *But when he came to himself, he said..."I will arise and go to my father, and I will say to him, 'Father, I have sinned'"*
> Luke 15:17-19

Every fresh challenge or temptation, therefore, presents us with daily opportunities to grow spiritually *into Christ* or to fall back in reliance *upon Self*—our old nemesis and former god. Remembering this, recognizing the opportunity and taking advantage of it means that we need some principle of simplicity by which to ingrain the new ways. We call ours: *recognize and replace!* You have an enemy actively "seeking whom he may devour"—always wanting to separate you from your God and His ways by breaking the trust connection or detouring your path of obedience. If you don't want to be robbed of your sweet surrender and the sense of peace and confidence it gives you, what can you do? *Recognize and replace!* Recognize that the emotions stealing over you are not coming from Christ in you and replace them with the emotional life Jesus desires you to have. For this you will often need to act fast to reconnect. Although difficult at first, eventually, the way of replacing our junk (past issues and present negative emotions) with His grace will become as practiced as riding a bicycle with no hands.

A.C.T.! Fast to Reconnect

Here is an example of a typical episode involving the sudden appearance of negative emotions: The peace of Christ is given to you as you surrender, trust and follow Jesus. So now you feel confident in God and are *flowing in the river of peace, flowing in the river of peace, flowing in the river of peace.* But wait: A challenge just came to the flow! Interruption of peace! Alert! Battle stations! Something has come up *in* you or come down *on* you so that your peace is gone. You either have to deal with it or you will run from it; fight your way through it or surrender to it. Don't be passive! The enemy will use that to drag you down further. You are under attack, so *A.C.T.!* fast to reconnect.

A) Admit: Admit right up front that you need help handling the situation or your emotions. That's why you feel weak and want to run, or hurt and want to lash out. Alone you are powerless to get the victories you need. The devil knows it. God knows it. So admit that you really do need God to be helping you *right now* with this situation, with your feelings, with your attitudes and desires—so that His peace can be restored.

C) Call: Call on Him! All who call on the Name of the Lord *will* be saved (Romans 10:13), so start praying like your life depends upon it! Call for help, confess your need, come clean about any sin and cast that care on Him. You need His help right now, so ask, seek and knock. He is eager to help you, but you have to ask Him in—it's a free will issue. Has your sense of failure or moral weakness got you feeling condemned, unworthy? *Don't hold back.* Go boldly to His throne of grace anyway (Hebrews 4:16). That's exactly what He wants you to do—to receive the mercy and help you need.

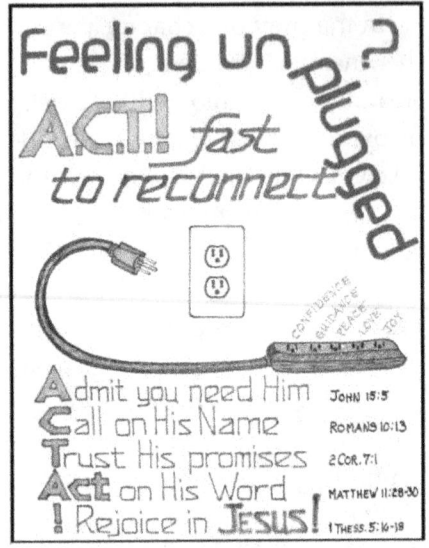

FEELING UNPLUGGED?
We have to be ready to "plug back into the Lord" whenever we start losing the peace and confidence He gives us. A.C.T.! fast to reconnect! Restored peace is always His sign to you of a "good" faith connection on your part.

T) Trust: Trust yourself to God by laying hold of some lifesaving promise that offers you help and hope for this situation. Hold on tight to the truth of the promise. All kinds of good things are promised to you but you have to learn how to hold on to the truth of the promises when your emotions are under attack. You are separated from His peace and from seeing the way through, which is why you have to learn to live in the meantime by relying on His promises. Grab one or both of these: "I will never leave you or forsake you;" "No weapon formed against you will prosper." Put it in first person: "All things are being made to work for my good," "Not even this can separate me from my Father's love." Bet your life on it! *Our new life is lived out in this Land of Promises!*

A.C.T.) Act: Put steps A, C, T together *and act*. Don't be passive—this is war! Obey whatever it is that you honestly believe the Lord wants you to do. Sometimes it is just "be still and wait." At other times it may be "deny yourself and take up this cross" (do the very thing you don't want to do). Or it may be something totally easy or unexpected that the Spirit will show you. Stay open but *be ready to act as soon as that idea takes shape*. Learning to obey Jesus is the new way of life that leads to fullness of joy. Step out in His direction!

!) Thank Him: Begin thanking Him even before you see *His action* coming your way. Thank Him that His promises are true. Thank Him that He is teaching you to trust His promises. Thank Him that you can come so quickly to His throne of grace, that He reminded you to call on His Name and helped you to do it. Thank Him and praise Him that what the enemy meant for evil (in seeking to disconnect you from God and His peace), He is now using (through *your ACT-ions*) to reconnect you.

Ah, now peace is restored! The peace of Christ is given to you as you surrender, trust and follow Jesus. Once again you are *flowing in the river of peace, flowing in the river of peace, flowing in the river of peace*. But wait: A challenge just came up! Here we go again...

Dislodging a Stronghold: The 6 R's

There may be a further problem, however, if the disconnect is happening in an un-mended area of your life where you have never experienced much of a "reconnect." If you have never yet known the peace or the victory of Christ in that area of your life, then you may need a deeper work in order to get a breakthrough over the power of that stronghold. A.C.T.!-ing fast to reconnect is intended to give you quicker victories over negative emotions in the midst of normal life. This is a powerful way to achieve mastery over your inner state so that you can stay connected to Christ and *keep the river flowing*. But what if that particular river has never flowed properly for you? What if you need recovery and restoration of your emotional state from unresolved past issues before you can practice mastery?

The following six steps to freedom will help you return to walking in the light.[26] If you are stuck in a pattern and want to get free of it, you may need to break up what is now a hard work of repentance into these easier to understand steps. You may need to practice these six steps very deliberately *at first* in order to get effective victories in the stronghold areas that we will be exploring in later chapters. As toddlers we all had to learn to walk in the natural; these are spiritual "baby steps" which will help you walk in the Spirit in areas where you still need restoration and recovery.

1) Recognize: Unless you can see that *your way* is amiss then there is no way to get back on track. Let the Holy Spirit turn on the lights, showing you by a loss of peace that there has been a loss of trust or obedience on your part. Learn to discern where sinful attitudes have taken over. Separate yourself from what is

---

[26] For the "R" repetitions in these steps of repentance: Dr. Henry W. Wright, Be In Health®, Thomaston, GA, seminar notes, October 2000.

not you. The good is Christ *in you*—that's your core. The rest comes from the enemy. If it is not of God, it is not the real you (see Chapter 9). *That wrong thing in you* (fearfulness, jealousy, shyness, etc.) *is not you*. Notice what it sounds like (its message) and what it feels like (its pressure) when it goes off inside you. It may have been "a part" of you for so long that it seems like it is just the way you are, but it isn't. Somewhere along the way *it came inside from the outside*. Break all agreements with the enemy and repent of any sinful reactions to originating events you may have had. *Rightly recognizing sin as sin* (that it is not good, not you and that it has to go) is half the battle (2 Timothy 2:25-26).

2) Responsibility: Own it. Take responsibility for your part in it. Others may have sinned against you, but how you reacted to what they did is *fully* your responsibility. Allow yourself no excuses, no avoidance and no denial—repent of every attitude and action that missed the mark. True maturity is accepting and taking responsibility for what you recognize in you *that is not of God*. If it got in, you let it in or kept it in—stop blaming others. Don't look for a way out: Face it. Taking responsibility enables you to confess and repent honestly to God and to acknowledge that He is right, rather than seeking to vindicate your ways (Psalm 51:3-4).

Taking responsibility restores you to being the true sovereign over your own heart and will. Your emotional reactions are the result of your own deeply held beliefs about right and wrong ways of responding to what is going on around you. If you try to make other people responsible for what you feel and do, you will always be ruled by their words and actions. But you are the head and not the tail when it comes to your emotional life: You can carry any thought or emotion captive to Christ and you can repent of your ways and choose to believe in God's ways. Eventually this change in believing (when it goes deep enough) will bring about a shift in your emotional reactions in the future (Proverbs 23:7; Matthew 15:19; Mark 7:21). By submitting your emotional life to Christ He enables you to rule over it (see Negative Emotions in the Postscripts).

3) Return: Make a quick return to the Father. *Reconnect with His love and mercy* (James 4:7). Some wrong turns were made inside your thought-life that carried you away from being fully trusting of His love or fully submitted to His ways, allowing the stronghold to form in you. Turn back to God and His ways now.

Don't delay like the prodigal son did, fearing that he wouldn't be received in love. There is "a refreshing" promised to those who repent, for it leads to freedom once we turn and reconnect with God's grace (Luke 15; Acts 3:19; Hebrews 4:16). Cast all your cares on Him!

4) Renounce: Fall totally out of agreement with the enemy: Declare sin to be sin; declare its half-truths to be total lies; declare God's truth to be truth; and declare yourself to be committed to God no matter what. Then keep confessing God's truth that counteracts the lies behind the sin you have been walking in. Cultivate a perfect hatred for that sin (Psalm 97:10). Make sin the enemy—not any person. Fall out of agreement with anything that excuses or condones the sin. Discover and renounce the hidden lie the sin used to entice you, and confess the truth that God's Word declares. Carry every thought about it captive to Christ (2 Corinthians 10:4-5).

5) Remove: If need be, have someone pray with you to cast out any spirit that is not removed through repentance (Luke 11:20-26). Get rid of the things in your life that are causing you to sin (Acts 19:19). Be aware of this dynamic: If you want God, the Holy Spirit alerts you to dangers; if you want the sin, the enemy puts people and temptations in your path. Separate from "friends" who pull you down and away from Christ.

6) Resist: The spirit will try to come back and the stronghold will seek to reassert itself, so be prepared to keep resisting. Give the burden of the struggle to God. Don't try to strong arm it in your own strength. Run to Jesus instead. Draw near to Him first, then through His power and support, resist the temptations (James 4:7-8). It takes time to break old mental habits and start new ones. Don't give up: perseverance always prevails (Ephesians 6:13; Hebrews 12:1-2)!

Pray, Persevere and Press in!

Restoration takes time and many individual moments of repentance. Give yourself grace and work through these steps little by little. Let God reveal to you what you need to deal with and let Him set the pace. Be gentle on yourself. Be a friend to yourself. But be very courageous about facing the truth (John 8:32). Being saved by God requires a love of the truth—over and above the love of Self. Without total honesty, openness and transparency about your sins and stronghold areas, repentance is shallow at best.

"Pressing in" to the Kingdom is when you exercise faith to believe for freedom even under attack and keep pressing forward to trust and obey as fully as you can. No matter how bad things are, no matter how badly you may seem to be doing, no matter how bad you feel you *always* have a God who loves you, has covered you with mercy, is working all things for your good and who deeply desires you to reconnect with Him. Return to Him first, refresh your heart with His love and mercy, and then receive the grace and strength to keep going.

NOTES/JOURNAL

_____
_____
_____
_____

_____
_____
_____
_____
_____
_____

EXERCISE

If we are the ones who fall into sin, then we will indeed need to become well versed in how to take steps that lead us back out into the way of life. To help familiarize you with the six steps, write the name of the step that matches the word or phrase which is involved in it (some may be a part of more than one step). The six "R" steps are: 1) recognize, 2) responsibility, 3) return, 4) renounce, 5) remove, and 6) resist.

Descriptor	Step (# and name)	Descriptor	Step (# and name)
Contrition	_____	Revelation	_____
Confession	_____	Repentance	_____
Deliverance	_____	Passed it on	_____
Cleaned house	_____	Embraced the grace	_____
The lights came on	_____	Stood fast	_____
Owned up	_____	Turned around	_____
Stopped denying	_____		

DISCUSSION QUESTIONS

Have the group read Jesus' story about the prodigal son (Lk 15:11-32)—a classic case of repentance and return. How many of the six "R" steps can they find in the story? What steps are left out? Which steps do they think are always necessary? Is it possible to take some of the steps in a different order? What might that look like? Are the steps necessary for God or for us? (Answer: God is not a legalist—but we sometimes need all the help we can get in turning around!)

Ask for someone in the group to tell of a practically instantaneous turnaround that they may have experienced sometime—to give everyone a sense of how quickly the steps of revelation/repentance/return can go. Ask if someone else has a (fairly brief) story of "getting it" that took them through at least the first four steps.

MAIN POINTS

- In any area where you have had a breakthrough, ACT! fast to reconnect if you sense your peace and freedom in that area slipping away.
- Receiving restoration in areas where you need initial breakthroughs is a process of recovery that can include many steps of repentance.
- The first step is discerning sin—recognize whatever is not Christ in you.
- Taking responsibility (Step 2) by not blaming anything or anyone for it.
- Run to the Father (Step 3)—even under attack, making a quick return.
- Resubmit your heart to trust and believe in His love and grace.
- Renounce all agreements (Step 4) with the sin and confess God's truth in its place, especially truths that directly confront the problem you face.
- The other steps may be necessary for complete victory to be established: removing and resisting.

DIGGING DEEPER

There are two realities we all have to deal with regarding our emotional state and they are directly connected to being dis-connected from our God:

1) Left unattended, the heart of the old nature fills up with the garbage of negative emotions quicker than a dumpster and can be just as hard to clean out.

2) Left unattended, the heart of your new nature empties out quicker than a colander, so you have to keep it positioned under the water of revelation and Spirit-life that is always flowing your way. Otherwise, you will leak away the fruit of the Spirit that He is pouring in.

There is that place inside all of us where we sense our peace, joy and confidence level rising or falling throughout the day. We are usually being either uplifted or dis-spirited as the day progresses, ever shifting from an empowered to an unempowered emotional state. We can be up one moment, get a troubling phone call and be down the rest of the day. On the other hand we can be absolutely pinned down by terrible fears or depressing thoughts, stumble into a moment graced by God and be gloriously set free! We have probably all been conditioned to believe that external causes are the problem, but that is just not true. We are completely in charge of our inner state and can learn how to manage it so that we can be free of both past and present negative emotions that stress us up. Note what the Lord is saying in this scripture:

Keep your heart with all diligence, for out of it is the wellspring of life.
Proverbs 4:23 WEB

According to scripture, who has God placed in charge of your heart? Who is the one who can determine every moment of the day whether your inner state is "springing up" into life or sinking into death? Is this God's job? No, it is yours. We are the ones called by the Lord to guard or keep our hearts. *We are the ones in charge of our own inner state.* Notice that He says "with diligence." That always means it's going to take active, intentional effort on our part to reap the blessing. The truly remarkable thing is that although outward events can dramatically shift our inner state, we are actually the ones in charge of how we feel on the inside. We can access any inner state we want to! We do not have to be the playthings (emotionally speaking) of whoever out there wants to sink our inner state, we can actually learn how to align with heaven, get quick recoveries (when stuff happens) and stay "powered up," ready for anything.

There are at least two levels of attainment available to us:

1) Restoration: Preparing our inward state to hold up under the pressures of daily life requires recovery of the natural grace that got lost along the way. For countless reasons—not least of which is getting free of the pain—we need to recover from any emotional brokenness emanating from our past.

2) Mastery: As we learn to manage our emotional life, we not only receive freedom from the past, but we gain the graced ability to reign with wisdom over our own emotions, making it possible to live even the most active or embattled days with deep peace and Spirit-led resourcefulness!

What a blessing! To be able to not only manage our inner state, but actually master it. Every point of disconnect can become a staging ground for charging up to heaven to exchange any emotion you don't want for something the Lord actually desires you to be feeling. He wants you living in that empowered state with His joy, peace and confidence carrying you along like a river. It may take a good deal of "diligence" in learning His ways: It may be hard, but it's doable!

SWORD AND SHIELD

These lovely images of returning to God show a restoration of rest, of refreshing and of relationship. These blessings are promised to those who return to God, seeking to reconnect with Him and His ways.

> **Return, O my soul, to your rest; for the Lord has dealt bountifully with you. For you have delivered my soul from death, my eyes from tears, my feet from stumbling; I will walk before the Lord in the land of the living.** Psalm 116:7-9

> Return, return, O Shulammite, return, return, that we may look upon you.
> Song of Solomon 6:13

> "I have blotted out your transgressions like a cloud and your sins like mist; return to me, for I have redeemed you." Isaiah 44:22

And the ransomed of the Lord shall return and come to Zion with singing; everlasting joy shall be upon their heads; they shall obtain gladness and joy, and sorrow and sighing shall flee away. Isaiah 51:11

Now after John was arrested, Jesus came into Galilee, proclaiming the gospel of God, and saying, "The time is fulfilled, and the kingdom of God is at hand; repent and believe in the gospel." Mark 1:14

"Repent therefore, and turn again, that your sins may be blotted out, that times of refreshing may come from the presence of the Lord." Acts 3:19-20

PRAYER FOCUS

The really critical issue is recognition. Without God "turning on the lights" by giving us the grace of repentance, we are still in the dark, caught in patterns that aren't working, but unable to figure out what's going wrong or what to do about it. The Holy Spirit is the only one who can reveal truth in such a way that we can discern our error or our need to change. However, He often desires to speak to us through other people; hence, we would be wise to cultivate a "teachable" spirit.

And the servant of the Lord must not strive; but be gentle unto all men, apt to teach, patient, In meekness instructing those that oppose themselves; if God peradventure will give them repentance to the acknowledging of the truth; And that they may recover themselves out of the snare of the devil, who are taken captive by him at his will. 2 Timothy 2:24-26 KJV

If we are wise there are tried and proven things that we can do to put ourselves in the path of revelation. Pray for grace to take these steps into the light:

- **Stay in scripture:** Seek to be teachable; pray regularly to receive correction.
- **Live in fellowship:** Be open, honest, transparent; let others speak into your life. Try not to be controlling of the flow of "feedback" your way.
- **Enter into worship:** Isaiah recognized a lot about himself during worship (Isa 6:5). The closer we approach the Lord, the more clearly His light shines upon things that are still dark in us.

RENUNCIATIONS AND AFFIRMATIONS

Renounce any agreements with untruth; believe Jesus' *truth* as your new *way* of *life*.

A model prayer of self deliverance:

Father forgive me for these sins of _____ . I repent of them and renounce my previous agreements with all they represent. Thank you for your steadfast love and mercy—and your goodness that has led me to repentance.

I come against you spirit(s) of _____. I bind and break your power over me in Jesus' Name and I command you to go where Jesus wants you to go. I renounce all ties to you. My hope is in the Lord and in Him I will trust and not be afraid.

A model prayer for a quick reconnect:

Father, somehow I have lost the peace in this area of my life and can't seem to get it back. I need Your help! Forgive me and work with me to restore me to trust and obedience. I embrace what You have promised me in Your Word, especially _____. Show me any steps I will need to take. Thank You for helping me learn to "guard my heart" and walk more closely with You.

PUTTING FEET TO YOUR PRAYERS: STRETCH YOURSELF!

Nothing works like doing the work. Persevere. Work through the issues. Consider these tips on doing the six "R's" from the second part of this lesson.

1) Do the steps with a friend. A friend to talk your struggles and issues over with is invaluable for seeing aspects of a step or steps you may not be taking and for encouraging and helping you to take steps that you may be stumbling over (Ecc 4:10).

2) Do the steps in any order. You don't have to do the steps in a lock step manner, but if you are really being stumped it may help to go thoroughly through each one in proper order. Otherwise, skip directly to the step that you seem to need to take at the moment.

3) Just do the steps! Sometimes the steps can be taken in an instant; sometimes they need going over again and again to get the victory and release you desire. Don't give up: Freedom is worth it (Ro 5:3).

4) Keep your eyes on the Lord—not your footwork. Don't focus on your sin—focus on the Lord who loves you and wants to deliver you. Keep casting these cares on Him (1Pe 5:7).

SECTION TWO

Image Bearing

*But we all, with unveiled face beholding as in a mirror
the glory of the Lord, are transformed
into the same image from glory to glory,
even as from the Lord, the Spirit.*
2 Corinthians 3:18 WEB

CHAPTER 8

BEHOLDING THE TRUE IMAGE

In Chapter 7 we saw that the first step out of a stronghold depends upon recognition of sin and the second involves our willingness to take full responsibility for the sin we recognize. Both of these steps are directly impacted by the images that we carry in our heart of hearts. If we "see" that our true self looks like Jesus (His nature now in us as our new nature), then we will be able to discern that anything in us that doesn't look like Jesus must be coming from sin—*not our true self*. But we won't be able to see what God may want to show us or be willing to take much responsibility for sin that is in us if we are carrying a distorted image of the Father, making us want to run and hide from God in shame as Adam did (Genesis 3:10). In this chapter we will look into the all-important place that image-bearing holds for us. Then in the following two chapters we will study first our own image and then the Image of God the Father, as they are both now being restored to us through the revelation of Jesus Christ, the God-Man.

The Power of Beholding

Since our hearts have "eyes," we need to learn how to keep our inward focus on the Lord (Matthew 6:22-23; 2 Corinthians 4:3-6; 2 Corinthians 5:7; Ephesians 1:18). We have been warned, therefore, to be careful what we behold, because we inevitably become like what we behold. Consider the transformation that takes place on the countenance of women when they see a baby or on the faces of children when they watch a fireworks display. Now, recall how most folks look when they are worried about a problem: quite a difference! What gets our attention gets us. As it gets us, it *transforms* us, thus the power of beholding. Israel was forbidden to create images to depict God—the second commandment (Deuteronomy 4:15-18). Since, no created image can do justice to the true Image of the Creator, God didn't want His children beholding and thereby becoming like any false image of Him. They were specifically warned against bowing down to (worshipping) and serving false images.

> **"You shall not make for yourself a carved image, or any likeness of anything that is in heaven above, or that is in the earth beneath, or that is in the water under the earth. You shall not bow down to them or serve them."** Exodus 20:4-5

We become like what we behold.

Worship and service are intimately connected for we will serve throughout the day what our hearts are focused upon (Matthew 6:24). By "bearing" (or carrying deep within) what we behold, we then begin "birthing" that image into life—by our thoughts, words and deeds. We actually become like what we are worshipping—what we are focusing upon. We are made over into the image we bear in our heart of hearts; this applies both to the Image of God and to the image of man.

Any distortion of either image will hinder our walk and deplete our joy, because emotions always tend to match up with what has our focus. Fortunately, we can get our emotions released by putting our focus back where it belongs—on the Lord. Just imagine how quickly all your emotions would change if Jesus *visibly* entered your room right now. Now, realize that *by faith* you can "see" Him at any time your believing matches your level of need—and get an emotional shift. Psychologists call the speed by which emotions shift when focus shifts, the "cascade effect."[27] Let it work for you! You get to choose to believe and see—if you want to.

Beholding Is Key to Transformation

This awesome power of beholding is what the Father is using to save and transform the world. Consider the following fourfold series of revelations designed to completely transform us. What changes us all along the way is not our work—our righteousness—but the grace of looking to Jesus and seeing in Him the answer to everything that is dark or needy in us. Let these truths propel you into a lifetime adventure of "getting the look that gives the shift" (see illustration, p. 89).

Power 1) Beholding Initiates Life

The revelation of Jesus Christ brings us into the Christian life. By the Fall we lost the capacity to behold our God. We became spiritually blind as our hearts were veiled.

> **And even if our gospel is veiled, it is veiled only to those who are perishing. In their case the god of this world has blinded the minds of the unbelievers, to keep them from seeing the light of the gospel of the glory of Christ, who is the image of God.**
> 2 Corinthians 4:3-5

...I received it through the revelation of Jesus Christ.
Galatians 1:12

With salvation we now behold Him with eyes of faith—as Jesus our Savior is revealed to us. This revelation ushers in the new birth.

> **He said to them, "But who do you say that I am?" Simon Peter replied, "You are the Christ, the Son of the living God." And Jesus answered him, "Blessed are you, Simon Bar-Jonah! For flesh and blood has not revealed this to you, but my Father who is in heaven."** Matthew 16:15-17

---

[27] "Cascade effect" concept is from a Lance Wallnau teaching, www.LanceLearning.com, message on CD.

But when he… was pleased to reveal his Son to me. Galatians 1:15-16

But I received it [his conversion] **through a revelation of Jesus Christ.** Galatians 1:12

Power 2) Beholding Saves and Sustains

The revelation of Jesus Christ saves us and sustains us. We cannot live the Christian life in our own strength—looking to ourselves for the righteousness, wisdom, abilities or saving power we need. Calling upon the Lord in prayer is God's way of training us to behold Jesus, rather than some lesser source of help or hope, such as Self or others. We learn to look to Jesus every step of the way, seeking to see in Him something that we need to see in each moment of our need. Do you need forgiveness? Look to Jesus. Do you need wisdom? Look to Jesus. Do you need someone to carry your burdens? Look to Jesus. And keep looking until the concern is lifted. Faith looks through the veil and sees Him as He really is. Then believing becomes restored trust, and once restored, trust can become renewed obedience (Isaiah 51:1; Micah 7:7).

> **"Look to me, and be you saved, all the ends of the earth; for I am God, and there is none else."** Isaiah 45:22 WEB
>
> **Let us run with endurance the race that is set before us, looking to Jesus, the founder and perfecter of our faith.** Hebrews 12:1-2

Power 3) Beholding Transforms and Sanctifies

The revelation of Jesus Christ transforms us in this life.[2] When we behold Him (even dimly) by faith, we bear His Image and begin to become like Him. The new nature which is Christ in us, or the life of the Spirit in us, comes to life whenever we look to Jesus and see something in Him that lets us surrender everything to Him. Until this happens and our trust and obedience are flowing freely again, we are still caught up in trying to live our lives *our* way. "Let go and let God" have His way and watch new life begin to flow. Whenever this happens, we are no longer "hanging in there" trying in our own strength to live the Christian life, we have surrendered, become transformed and the Holy Spirit is lifting us and carrying us. We have passed from "crucifixion" with Christ into resurrection (Galatians 2:20). Jesus begins living through us! This is the Spirit's work of raising us into the new life of grace whenever we get our focus and our faith restored.

Jesus' life comes into us when we are born again (as inward sight is given); His life flows out through us at any moment when we surrender everything to Him (as inward sight is restored). When we look to Him, we walk in the light whenever we see in Him something that enables us to trust and surrender. The old nature is laid to rest like a shadow behind us and we are released to walk by His Spirit (Romans 8:1-4). That newer, better, more loving version of you comes forth and breathes the sweet air of freedom. This is the graceful transformation of our lives from the inside out which no work of the flesh can accomplish (John 6:63). Religious practices and moral striving don't accomplish this—or we would have something to boast about (Ephesians 2:9). The Spirit does it all—*as we behold Jesus*.

> **But we all, with unveiled face beholding as in a mirror the glory of the Lord, are transformed into the same image from glory to glory, even as from the Lord, the Spirit.** 2 Corinthians 3:18 WEB

> **And have put on the new self, which is being renewed in knowledge after the image of its creator.** Colossians 3:10

Power 4) Beholding Glorifies

The revelation of Jesus Christ will complete our transformation in heaven. God will not have to change what he has already been doing to bring forth our new life there. In heaven sight will replace faith as the veil of time and space is forever lifted. We will clearly behold Jesus and instantly become just like Him! We will see Jesus in all His matchless glory and that will bring the new life in us fully into being. Our ultimate glorification flows out of the power released by fully beholding our glorious Lord.

> **As for me, I shall behold your face in righteousness; when I awake, I shall be satisfied with your likeness.** Psalm 17:15

> **Beloved, we are God's children now, and what we will be has not yet appeared; but we know that when he appears we shall be like him, because we shall see him as he is.** 1 John 3:2

Let us praise God for the power of beholding Jesus. Looking to Him we are saved "to the uttermost" (Hebrews 7:25). We call this pattern of losing spiritual sight and regaining it: "Eyes off? EYES ON!" Learn to "get the look that gives the shift"—and keep getting it!

Let Beholding Grow You

Even the five vital requirements for growth listed below do not automatically transform us. Every Christian needs to be actively cultivating all five of these God-given means of staying connected with Jesus, our Living Vine. Even so, we would be wise to understand that they are not foolproof or automatic ways of becoming like Christ. These necessary, very wholesome, elements of our discipleship can actually be used by the enemy to draw us away from our place of surrender into pride, complacency and self-righteousness. We can do these as ritual or routine—but beholding Jesus *through* them is what transforms us.

1) Bible study: The Pharisees knew the scriptures, but many couldn't recognize Him.

2) Prayer: The publican prayed even longer than the sinner, but left unchanged.

3) Worship: Lucifer led worship, but got his eyes on himself instead of Jesus.

4) Fellowship: Can be superficial or supernatural. Are you being honest, open, transparent?

5) Service: Can easily become a work of the flesh. We serve in Him, by Him and unto Him, not to meet our own needs.

Repent of and renounce any of the ways that these five disciplines may be building self-righteousness in you. Instead, seek to use each discipline as a way of making sure your inner focus is upon the Lord. Your peace and joy levels should be going up as you practice them, indicating that you are connecting with His grace and truth. Then pray for God to help you learn to guard the Image of God inside your heart that is being renewed within you.

Keep your heart with all diligence, for out of it is the wellspring of life. Proverbs 4:23

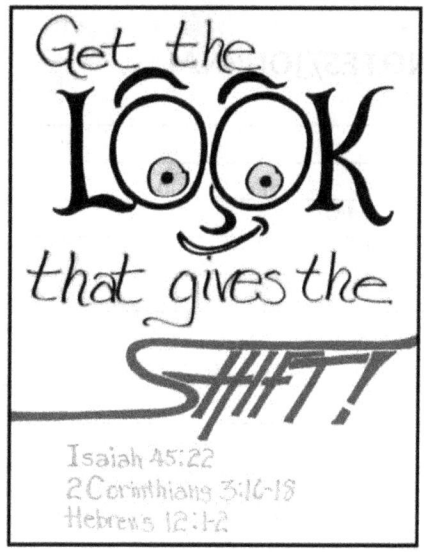

GET THE LOOK!
The secret to a positive emotional state is seeing in Jesus *the very thing you need to see in Him* in order for your trust to be restored. Master the art of getting your focus back on Jesus. The rule is "Eyes off? Eyes ON!"

The Way of Restoration

Being restored to the life God intends for us to live depends upon recognizing when our inward focus has shifted away from beholding by faith the One whose image we were created to bear.

1) The first step of restoration is receiving a living faith in Jesus Christ—all else depends upon that!

2) The next is taking full responsibility for having built one's life around trusting and obeying Self, instead of Jesus: Repent and renounce all desire to live in rebellion, un-surrendered and un-submitted to His leadership. Let His peace fill your heart!

3) Turn to the Father and release gratitude for the grace-filled way He has of transforming us through beholding His Son!

NOTES/JOURNAL

_____
_____
_____
_____
_____
_____
_____
_____

EXERCISE

This exercise may be difficult, but it will be worthwhile. It is called "Finding Grace in His Face." Like Adam (and having his nature in us) when we are aware of our guilt and shame we tend to run and hide from God—the very opposite direction we need to be going! Shame also makes us want to cover our face and not look the other person in the eyes. Moses could not bear to look upon God (Ex 3:6). Neither could Peter (Lk 5:8). Yet our God says "Seek My Face" (Ps 27:8) and invites us to come boldly into His presence to receive mercy (He 4:16). So let's learn to do it! Let's learn to look beyond our shame to see our Savior's Face!

Make a list of the things that you think, say or do (present or past) that make you feel most ashamed before God. Then write down what you would need to see in God to no longer feel any shame (as long as this is something you have already repented about). Finally, find a scripture that will help you get the victory. He says He is not ashamed to be called our God (He 11:16) or to call us brethren (He 2:11). Start with that but keep going... (Note: You may want to just use abbreviations in case someone other than God sees your notebook.)

What I saw in me (sin)	**What I need to see in God** (to let it go)	**Scripture**
_____	_____	_____
_____	_____	_____
_____	_____	_____

DISCUSSION QUESTIONS

Have the class consider and discuss what the Image of God and of man were like:

- **Before the Fall**: What might their "knowing" of God" have been like for Adam and Eve—before they lost sight of His true Image?

- **After the Fall**: What image of "human nature" began to appear in Adam's children? Whose image does it really belong to?
- **After the Flood**: What were the images of false gods that began to be worshipped? What did they look like? What did they personify?
- **After the Law**: Why were images of God not allowed in the synagogue or temple? What carved images were allowed?
- **After the Incarnation**: Why are images of God allowed in churches now?

Why couldn't we look upon God in the past? Why can we look upon God now?

> "But," he said, "you cannot see my face, for man shall not see me and live."
> Exodus 33:20

What have their own journeys been like in terms of any distorted images of God that they have had to deal with? Have their images of self been affected by these distorted images of God? Or vice versa? How did the Lord work to clear their spiritual sight?

MAIN POINTS

- The images we hold in our heart of hearts are powerful—for good or ill.
- Jesus came to restore two images lost in the Fall: that of God and that of us.
- Whenever we behold His Image rightly we are transformed—as the Holy Spirit works through our faith to open our eyes and release our spirit.
- Beholding simply means seeing something about Him we need to see in Him—that matches the need we have, so that trust can be restored.
- The new nature (who we really are) comes to life as we behold Him—even if it is just a glimpse!
- It will take continually catching such glimpses to be continually raised into new life. This is definitely a daily process.
- The power of beholding *alone* is what transforms us. All else is self-effort!

DIGGING DEEPER

Contrasting the head and heart: Enlightenment culture and the pride of man have over-emphasized the place of the mind. Following the lead of European post Renaissance culture Western Christianity became overly rational and has tended to boil the Christian life down into maxims, rules, pious platitudes and dry doctrines. As important as rational truth is (we are depending upon it in this teaching), we were never meant to seek it alone and neglect the heart's imaginative capacity of beholding and bearing images.

The mind is a gateway—all thoughts have to pass through it—but the heart is the seat of power and controls the deep issues of life as well as our deepest, most cherished beliefs about God, ourselves and the world we live in. Our mind may hold very correct theology, but our heart can still think and act like a two year old! Who reigns in your heart—Satan, Self, or Jesus?

> **"For from within, out of the heart of man, come evil thoughts."** Mark 7:21
>
> **Keep your heart with all diligence, for out of it is the wellspring of life.**
> Proverbs 4:23 WEB

Consider these traits about the head (intellect/brain) and heart. What the head can do is good, but look how much further the heart can take us into life! Then pray for grace to walk a "path of the heart" that mirrors His:

Lord, don't let my walk with You become a head trip. Lead me into paths with a heart!

HEAD	HEART
Knowledge, facts	Wisdom, understanding
Physical sight	Spiritual insight
Likes	Loves
Thinks by logic	Reasons by feelings (deeply held beliefs)
Analyzes, chooses	Meditates, wills
Holds consciousness	Held by conscience
Ego resides	Jesus resides
Center of the mind	Center of the spirit
Makes identifications	*Holds identity*
Holds ideas of God	*Beholds the Image of God*
Stores memories	Treasures remembrances
Believes	Trusts
Hears the words of others	Listens to the hearts of others
Sees, plans, decides	Dreams, envisions, determines
Chooses	Wills

SWORD AND SHIELD

Notice the emphasis upon spiritual sight in scripture. Look for it. Grow eyes to see.

> "Your eye is the lamp of your body. When your eye is healthy, your whole body is full of light, but when it is bad, your body is full of darkness. Therefore be careful lest the light in you be darkness. If then your whole body is full of light, having no part dark, it will be wholly bright, as when a lamp with its rays gives you light."
> Luke 11:34-36
>
> **But whenever one turns to the Lord, the veil is taken away. Now the Lord is the Spirit and where the Spirit of the Lord is, there is liberty. But we all, with unveiled face beholding as in a mirror the glory of the Lord, are transformed into the same image from glory to glory, even as from the Lord, the Spirit.** 2 Corinthians 3:16-18 WEB

Beloved, we are God's children now, and what we will be has not yet appeared; but we know that when he appears we shall be like him, because we shall see him as he is. And everyone who thus hopes in him purifies himself as he is pure. 1 John 3:2-3

Do not lie to one another, seeing that you have put off the old self with its practices and have put on the new self, which is being renewed in knowledge after the image of its creator. Colossians 3:9-10

PRAYER FOCUS

Let your prayer time be a time when you seek to behold Jesus better—not only a time for going through a wish list or a to do list or a confessional. Seek to behold Him with an unveiled face (2Co 3:16-18). Exact vision is not required! Just a "glimpse" or vague impression is all one usually needs or gets.[28]

Don't be discouraged if you get off to a slow start. In devotional exercises we usually begin without inspiration as someone once remarked, "I begin in the flesh and end in the Spirit." In other words we begin with effort to approach God, even in dryness or heaviness. Consistency and perseverance in simple expectancy allow the Spirit to bring a greater grace. But don't try to force any special moments to come! You are the peaceful garden basking in "Son-shine" (see Ps 131). Let the Lord be free to come and go like a butterfly that just might drop in! In seeking to behold Him it is very helpful to "unveil" your face. An unveiled face signifies:[29]

- **A tender heart**: We are not closed or hardened by bitterness, fear or shame.
- **An honest heart**: We remain open and transparent about our pain, weaknesses, failings and sins. We live in the light (1Jn 1:7). We don't hide how we really feel or who we are.
- **A confident heart**: We are willing and able to take the veil off because we believe in grace!

We can exercise consistency in the routine without any loss of confidence before God since even un-anointed, yet transparent praying works wonders for our transformation. Be honest with God about everything, even about the lack of apparent anointing or seeming "deadness." Just don't let it become a stumbling block to you and eventually you will get past it.

---

[28] Mike Bickle, "Beholding God's Glory by Encountering His Emotions," *Intimacy with God Series*, (Kansas City, MO: International House of Prayer, August 1, 2009).
[29] Ibid.

RENUNCIATIONS AND AFFIRMATIONS

Renounce any agreements with untruth; believe Jesus' *truth* as your new *way* of *life*.

Repent of and renounce any of the ways that these five necessary disciplines (Bible study, prayer, worship, fellowship and service) may be building self-righteousness in you. Then pray for God to help you learn to guard the Image of God inside your heart (Pr 4:23).

Father, I renounce trying to change myself by my own efforts. Only by beholding Jesus am I actually transformed. Make me aware of those times when my heart turns away from beholding Him. Help me cast down all false images of myself, of others and of You. By Your grace make me willing to be made willing to surrender everything to You.

PUTTING FEET TO YOUR PRAYERS: STRETCH YOURSELF!

Here are seven ways of beholding the Lord. Try to do at least one a day and all of them at least once a week for the first week. Then see which ways are most fruitful for you and pursue them, but don't entirely abandon the others!

1) Personal prayer and quiet times: Seek to "see" Him as He really is, full of grace and truth.

2) Corporate worship: Direct your words to Him personally: With songs of the cross, imagine Him at the cross; with songs of heaven, imagine Him in heaven, etc.

3) Meditation on the scriptures: Dialog with Him; follow Jesus' movements in the gospels; look to see how God is described in dreams and visions of the prophets.

4) Pray in the Spirit with a focus on Him: Pour your heart out; open your mind; let Him fill you.

5) Silence: Gaze in adoration towards Him believing that He is present (which He is).

6) Christian art and symbols: Let them direct your thoughts toward Him.

7) Intercession: Let your heart hold an image of how willing and capable He is as you lift people and situations up to Him in prayer.

Whenever we behold the Lord even a little bit by faith, the Holy Spirit goes to work shifting our emotional state back under grace and freeing us from focusing on whatever it was of the world, flesh or the devil that was robbing us of our trust and vital life in Christ. *So let's all learn to get the look that gives the shift!*

CHAPTER 9

OUR NEW IDENTITY

The all-important issue of identity determines so much about how we will live and what we will do with our time here on earth. No one who has a poor self-image can truly enjoy living, yet the gospel has not come to tell you how great you are. Jesus says: "Without me you can do nothing" (John 15:5), and Paul writes, "For I know that in me (that is, in my flesh) nothing good dwells" (Romans 7:18). Hardly a formula for pride based self-esteem! So what is the answer to our identity questions? Discovering who we really are—now that Jesus has come to live inside of us. And our sense of self-worth? It is based upon the solid rock of His love for us. Period. You are *His beloved*—just try to wrap your heart around the enormity of that blazing truth. He lived and died and lives again to bring you fully to life. Everything else you could hope to get out of life—compared to this—is chump change (Philippians 3:7-8).

Identity and the Lost Image

What could be of more practical value to us than discovering who we really are? There are two great questions that challenge every human being: Is there a God and who am I? Socrates, after his encounter with the oracle of Delphi, believed he was commissioned by God to teach wisdom to men. The foundation of his teaching? *Know thyself.* Our fundamental problem is that we do not know who our God is; therefore, we do not know who we really are. We are suffering from a massive loss of identity made even worse by our failure to realize it and face up to it.

The fall from grace created our identity crisis. We tend to think mainly of the Fall as a fall into sin and into the sin nature, which it certainly was. We say rightly that fallen man, once created in the Image of God, no longer reflects that image. But one essential effect of the Fall was that, in dying spiritually, Adam could no longer behold his God. Both the Image of God and the image of man *fell* from his sight. Adam could neither see who God is nor could he see who he himself truly was, since who we are is entirely defined in relation to God who created us. Jesus has come to restore both our lost vision (see Chapter 8) and our true identity.

New Creations

Now that faith in Christ has come to us, we are New Creations. This is the miracle of new birth (John 3:3-7; 1 Peter 1:23) which raises us from our sin and separation from God into eternal life in union with our God (John 3:16; John 17:3; 1 John 5:11-13).

Therefore if anyone is in Christ, he is a new creation. The old things have passed away. Behold, all things have become new. 2 Corinthians 5:17 WEB

What does it mean to be New Creations? We still see a lot of the old nature and the former ways of living, thinking and feeling, but new things have been added that radically change *all* things. However, before we look at the things that have become new, let's review what has not changed or passed away. Paul is not telling us that we no longer have a sin nature to contend with or sins to resist. Above all the apostles, he lays out the ongoing struggle between the New Creation (spirit) and the old nature (flesh) in texts too numerous to fully mention (see Romans 7:17-20; Romans 8:1-8; 1 Corinthians 5:5; 2 Colossians 7:1; Galatians 5:13-17; Galatians 5:24-26). So what does pass away?

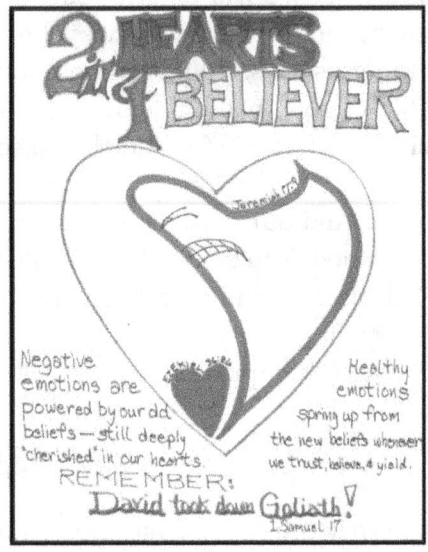

2 HEARTS IN 1 BELIEVER

When we accepted Jesus as our Savior, God placed a new heart within us: we are already just like Jesus at the core of our being! But the New Creation often has to fight it's way past the "Goliath" of the old heart.

1) The person who did not know that Jesus is both Savior and Lord no longer exists. That person (your former self) has indeed passed away now that the revelation of Jesus Christ has come. If a blind person regains sight and sees the sun, even if the blindness returns, they will never be the same.

2) Before conversion, we were one with our sins. With our repentance and faith in Christ, the Father separated us from our sins by forgiving them and justifying us (Romans 3:24). There is still an ongoing battle with sin, but continuing in sin is a spoiled thing for New Creations for two main reasons: one, the conviction of the Spirit; two, the sense of separation from Christ. Both overshadow the former pleasures of unrighteousness, enabling us to learn to hate sin. Many of our old ways, therefore, change with conversion, but not all. We are engaged in an all new process of ongoing conversion, which includes cleansing and growth in Christ (2 Thessalonians 2:13).

3) We are no longer "on the outside." We were formerly not a people, but now we are a part of God's family. We were strangers to the covenant, but now have been brought near (Ephesians 2:19).

This way of seeing the new birth (by what passed away) is like looking in the rear view mirror while driving. The really stunning, forward-looking view is how we now appear as New Creations!

- We have been spiritually reborn through the revelation of Jesus Christ.
- We can no longer measure anything without reference to Christ (2 Corinthians 5:16; also see Chapter 8).
- We have been given a new heart and a new spirit—a new nature! (Ezekiel 36:26).
- We live under a new covenant of immense mercy (Jeremiah 31:31-34; 2 Corinthians 5:18-19).
- We received the Holy Spirit, the righteousness of Christ, the Name of Jesus.
- We are not our past, not our sin, not our negative emotions—we are New Creations!

We are also a mystery even to ourselves. God is bestowing a new identity upon us only He knows. Who we now are is only revealed whenever we trust and obey Jesus—we are "hidden" in Him. He is the key! As we die to Self (the false god), we live through Christ (Romans 6:5-11).

For you have died, and your life is hidden with Christ in God. Colossians 3:3

Then Jesus told his disciples, "If anyone would come after me, let him deny himself and take up his cross and follow me." Matthew 16:24

Our acceptance by God as New Creations is absolute, complete and unwavering. Try to fathom the massive liberation that God has accomplished.

It was God...in Christ, reconciling *and* **restoring the world to favor with Himself, not counting up** *and* **holding against** [men] **their trespasses** [but cancelling them].
2 Corinthians 5:19 AMP

This incredible Reconciliation covers all that we have been in Adam and will be in Christ. Faith is what God gives us so that we can receive this grace and be translated from the kingdom of darkness (in Adam) to the Kingdom of His Son (in Christ), but faith did not in any way change God's Heart towards us, which is love, or His reconciliation to our sins, which Jesus accomplished fully at the cross. In conversion the former self (that had no life in Christ) passed away and the true self (that lives through trusting Christ) has been reborn/regenerated. The New Creation is a redeeming of the old, not an elimination of all that was former. We have a new start and a new center from which to live at any moment.

We Are New, But the Old Is in Us

The New Creation "comes to life" in us whenever we trust in the One who is our new life. As we "walk in the light" trusting God through Jesus Christ (1 John 1:7), our old nature is laid to rest like a shadow lying down behind us (Romans 6:6; Galatians 2:20). However, the one Paul calls "the old man" wants back in. Our old nature "comes back to life" in us whenever we cease to rely upon our God. Are we going to live by a resuscitation of the old self, or by a resurrection of the new life? The choice is ever before us.

> **I have been crucified with Christ** [in Him I have shared His crucifixion] **it is no longer I who live, but Christ (the Messiah) lives in me; and the life I now live in the body I live by faith in (by adherence to and reliance on and complete trust in) the Son of God, Who loved me and gave Himself up for me.** Galatians 2:20 AMP

The old nature draws power from false ideas of self shaped by the world. Some of us carry elements in our personality that we think of as ourselves. They are in us—but not us!

Nervous energy/anxious feelings	Deep wellsprings of grief
Perfectionism (people pleasing)	Feelings of persistent loneliness
Addictions/compulsions	Depression, heaviness of heart
Drive to achieve (self-salvation)	Nuclear reactivity/panic mode
Flashes of anger (hot temper)	Impatience (prickly, irritable)
Excessive sensitivity (easily hurt)	Stubbornness (pride, rebellion)
Timidity/shyness (fear of man)	Impulse to control/be in control

These ideas of self are not who we really are! Any or all of these may describe our personality as we have known it up until now, but they are not who we really are—not our God-given personhood in Christ. They reveal where the fallen nature still has power to block the life of the New Creation from coming forth, but they tell us nothing of what the Father created us to be before the enemy began "unmaking" us. Consider these two things:

1) In the womb these negative traits weren't in us. Even as young children we trusted and loved freely—no baggage!

2) When we die and go to heaven, these traits will have to be removed from us. They are not God's desire for us.

Restoration of our true life begins by breaking agreement with false beliefs about ourselves and choosing instead to embrace what God is speaking to us about our true identity. Two images fell when Adam fell—that of God and that of us. Get your image rightly set by seeing His. Whatever does not look like Jesus in you, isn't the real you. Refuse to be deceived by your enemy about who you really are. Apply the six steps to freedom in Chapter 7! Never settle for anything less than "Christ in you, the hope of glory" (Colossians 1:27). Proper self-love is accepting

God's view of us—it is not pride, false humility, or self-absorption. Let's get purified from all false ideas of ourselves (1 John 3:2-3).

The Great Exchange

Apart from Christ we will be weak, foolish, sinful and ignorant in many ways, but in Christ we are complete, secure and sustained by His life. As Archbishop François Fénelon wrote, "Expect nothing of yourself, but all things of God. Knowledge of one's own hopeless, incorrigible weakness combined with absolute confidence in God's power are the two foundations of the spiritual life."[30] God is not asking us to perfect ourselves or change ourselves, but to turn to Him and learn to see and believe all of life from His perspective. Heaven's perspective on our life is always liberating. Take a moment to "look through" to heaven with your eyes of faith and seek to catch a glimpse of who you are in your eternal being. This is the real you—the eternal you. Then let the power of that glorious vision be released with "prophetic decree" into your own heart *now*. If you are in Christ, then read and confess with full faith:

- I am eternally the beloved bride of my Savior Jesus, who has promised never to forsake me.
- I am eternally a receiver of God's love, mercy, wisdom, saving help and never-ending life.
- I am only a sinner in need of forgiveness for a short while—during my brief time on earth.
- I am in Christ and He is in me. Who I am in Christ looks a lot like Him.
- I am an eternal being with a spirit as free as the wind and a soul of dazzling beauty and grace.
- I am indestructible in my being, because of His unending gift of life to me.
- I am worse in my fallen-ness and better in my new created-ness than I ever imagined.

The Way of Restoration

Joy is produced in us whenever we realize by an active faith who we really are in Him. Even so, the truly great joy is not who we are in Christ, but who He is to us!

1) Learn to recognize all false images of self that don't match up with Jesus and which block your new life from coming forth.

2) Take full responsibility for your attachment to these false ideas of self: Repent, renounce and break all agreement with the enemy about who you are, confessing the truth instead.

---

[30] François Fénelon, *Spiritual Letters to Women* (New Canaan, CT: Keats Publishing, Inc., 1980). p. 55.

3) Turn to the Father and release gratitude that who you are in Christ already looks a lot like Him—you are a New Creation!

NOTES/JOURNAL

_____
_____
_____
_____
_____
_____
_____
_____

EXERCISE

List the things you usually say when asked about yourself by someone you just met for the first time.

Hi, I'm _____, I...
_____
_____

Now try describing yourself in ways that have nothing to do with relationships or work roles you are fulfilling that will pass away when you get to heaven: Think in terms of who you are, not what you do.
_____
_____

Better yet, describe yourself by the calling upon your life and by your dreams.
_____
_____

DISCUSSION QUESTIONS

Identity theft has become a huge financial problem in our day, but there has always been a thief at work who seeks to steal from all of us our true identity.

1) Name the movies and books you have enjoyed that deal with

identity issues. For starters: *The Bourne Identity, Catcher in the Rye, The Matrix, Les Mis*, etc. Why was identity so important to the story and how was it resolved/not resolved by the end? Why is your true identity important to you? Has it been resolved yet in your life story—to your entire satisfaction?

2) Now consider movie stars and pop singers. How does the search for identity play out in the media? Do the "stars" seem to have their own true personalities or are they crafting images to cultivate a fan base? Where do they seem to go to get the image they may be promoting?

3) Where have you been going to get yours? Discuss/admit ways in which we, even we, may be taking on the "protective coloration" of views, styles, appearances that are popular.

MAIN POINTS

- The New Creation is something the world is yearning to see (Ro 8:19).
- The New Creation looks just like Jesus in us, living through us (Col 1:27).
- The New Creation comes to life when we surrender, trust, obey (Gal 2:20).
- We are new (deep down) but the old is still in us (wanting to take over!).
- The life of the New Creation is hindered by false images of self.
- Fall out of agreement with all wrong images. Believe who you really are.

DIGGING DEEPER

As New Creations we cannot define ourselves by anything less than who we now are in Christ without damaging our self-image, security, sense of worth and purpose. Therefore we need to make a quality decision not to accept *any* lesser definitions of who we are. Do not regard even yourself "according to the flesh."

> **From now on, therefore, we regard no one according to the flesh. Even though we once regarded Christ according to the flesh, we regard him thus no longer.**
> 2 Corinthians 5:16-17

The following is a great C. S. Lewis quote from *Mere Christianity*—the last two sentences. Then back up and read the rest of the book!

> *Look for yourself, and you will find in the long run only hatred, loneliness, despair, rage, ruin, and decay. But look for Christ and you will find Him, and with Him everything else thrown in.*[31]

We can rest secure that our "position" in Christ is unassailable—no matter what the enemy brings against us, no matter what happens…

---

[31] MERE CHRISTIANITY by CS Lewis © copyright CS Lewis Pte Ltd 1942, 1943, 1944, 1952.

No Matter What Happens

Since you can't keep the bad stuff from happening no matter how hard you try,
isn't it good to know that...

No matter what happens
> I will always have You with me—and You are my greatest joy.

No matter what happens
> You will always be loving me, forgiving me, accepting me—just as I am.

No matter what happens
> I can always be growing in knowing You, loving You and trusting You.

No matter what happens
> You will never leave me or forsake me.

No matter what happens
> I can always cling to You, call on You, seek You and find You.

No matter what happens
> You will always share wisdom, guidance and encouragement.

No matter what happens
> I can always find something to do to worship You and serve You.

No matter what happens
> You will always be redeeming the bad and making good plans for the future.

No matter what happens
> I can always be learning to believe in You and fighting to live for You.

No matter what happens
> You will always be carrying me to heaven.

No matter what happens
> I can learn to let go and let You be the God who saves me.

SWORD AND SHIELD

Are you willing to live the life that is hidden with Christ in God? Let's go for this!

> **For you have died, and your life is hidden with Christ in God. When Christ who is your life appears, then you also will appear with him in glory.** Colossians 3:3-4

> **To them God chose to make known how great among the Gentiles are the riches of the glory of this mystery, which is Christ in you, the hope of glory.** Colossians 1:27-28

Our Acceptance as New Creations

> **But to all who did receive him, who believed in his name, he gave the right to become children of God.** John 1:12

> **"No longer do I call you servants, for the servant does not know what his master is doing; but I have called you friends."** John 15:15

> **But he who is joined to the Lord becomes one spirit with him.** 1 Corinthians 6:17-18
>
> **For He foreordained us (destined us, planned in love for us) to be adopted (revealed) as His own children through Jesus Christ.** Ephesians 1:5 AMP
>
> **And ye are complete in him, which is the head of all principality and power.** Colossians 2:10 KJV

Our Security as New Creations

> **There is therefore now no condemnation for those who are in Christ Jesus.** Romans 8:1
>
> **What then shall we say to these things? If God is for us, who can be against us?** Romans 8:31-32
>
> **No, in all these things we are more than conquerors through him who loved us. For I am sure that... [nothing] ...will be able to separate us from the love of God in Christ Jesus our Lord.** Romans 8:37-39

Our Worth as New Creations

> **"As the Father has loved me, so have I loved you. Abide in my love."** John 15:9
>
> **"You did not choose me, but I chose you and appointed you that you should go and bear fruit and that your fruit should abide."** John 15:16
>
> **Do you not know that you are God's temple and that God's Spirit dwells in you?** 1 Corinthians 3:16-17
>
> **I can do all things through Christ, who strengthens me.** Philippians 4:13 WEB

PRAYER FOCUS

Pray for the Lord to open your eyes to see more and more who you really are in Him as a New Creation. But do not get stuck by trying to see what He sees in you! The wrong is coming from the enemy's work in you, the old nature. Resist it. The good is Jesus in you united to you, the New Creation. Rest in that. Pray for faith to believe that He and Father and the Spirit really do love to look upon you in love.

Then pray for the grace to see others the same way He sees you. Since we reap what we sow, if we sow seeds of judging others, we will reap a harvest of inner condemnation (Gal 6:7). Counter this, by asking Him to give you eyes to see the New Creation potential of others—even in unbelievers.

> *Father, as a New Creation I cannot define myself by anything less than who I now am in Christ without damaging my sense of self. I will therefore accept no lesser definitions of who I am. Help me break all agreement with my former ways of seeing myself and others and trust completely in Your heavenly perspective!*

RENUNCIATIONS AND AFFIRMATIONS

Renounce any agreements with untruth; believe Jesus' *truth* as your new *way* of *life*.

Renounce and break all agreements with false ideas of self. Repent of any ways in which you have thought of yourself as if these patterns of the flesh were a part of who you really are. Ask the Father to go to work to break these patterns off of you. Commit to cooperating with Him as His Spirit leads. Then rest in His ability, casting these cares on Him (1Pe 5:7).

Father, I renounce thinking of myself as if _____ (Nervous energy...) were a part of me. Forgive me for believing that false image of myself and break the power of it off of me. Forgive me for binding others to these same judgments.

Nervous energy (anxious feelings)
Unresolved grief (carried too long)
Timidity or shyness (fear of rejection)
Excessive sensitivity (too easily hurt)
Nuclear reactivity (panic mode)
Stubbornness (pride and rebellion)

Addictive personality (compulsions)
Feelings of persistent loneliness
Flashes of anger (hot temper)
Depression, heaviness of heart
Impatience (prickly, irritable edges)
Impulse to control or be in control

PUTTING FEET TO YOUR PRAYERS: STRETCH YOURSELF!

Breaking patterns begins with prayer, but requires conscious effort over time. The 3 P's that move mountains are definitely needed here: prayer, patience and perseverance. If you want to be free of shyness, for instance, the 6 R's of Chapter 7 are a good beginning, but the time will come when you have agreed to do something (like attend a party or teach a class) and the old shyness pattern will try to get in the way. That is where perseverance really puts feet to your prayers. Do it shy. Do it afraid. Do it anyway. Or the enemy will be able to stop you every time.

Be sure to get the outward victory (doing the thing shyness wants to avoid) and the inward victory will eventually show up (being free of shy feelings). Now, look over the above renunciations and then write the active thing you can do to persevere past the pattern!

Pattern I renounced   **Pattern breaking activity I can do**

_____   _____
_____   _____
_____   _____
_____   _____
_____   _____

CHAPTER 10

THE FATHER'S HEART OF LOVE

In the previous lesson we looked at how Jesus is restoring to us the lost vision of our true humanity. We saw that the image of ourselves we carry in our hearts must match up with who we are as New Creations remade in His Image, or we will unwittingly block our own growth with false understandings of who we are. Here is another marvel: Jesus, because He is fully human *and* fully divine, also restores to us a true Image of what our Father is really like. All false images of ourselves and of our God are alike demolished and replaced by looking to Jesus! It is an incredible thing that God can restore these two glorious images, once lost and broken through the Fall, by means of revealing the God-Man, our Lord Jesus Christ.

The Danger of a Distorted Image

We have been created in God's Image to be *bearers* of His Image—not just to reflect His Image. Image is everything in the spiritual life. Not the image we can recite, but the image we "bear" or carry deep within our heart. The image we hold of God the Father hidden away in our heart of hearts will determine: How we will seek the Father; how we will respond to what He allows in our lives; how we will act towards others. Jesus kept His spiritual eyes constantly focused upon a true vision of the Father. All that He did flowed out of that ongoing faith connection (John 14:9-11). This is the all-essential matter of keeping the heart rightly set (Proverbs 4:23). Unfortunately, the idea we have of Father God is often misshaped by Adam's nature, earthly fathers and church tradition. It can be a fallen image buried in our heart distorting the true Image. Consider the powerful influence of these three image shapers:

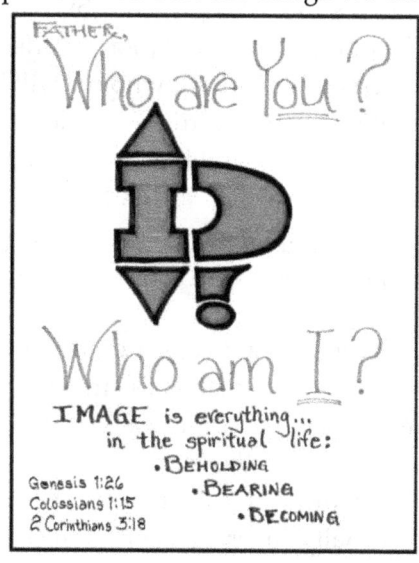

IMAGE BEARING

Looking to Jesus with eyes of faith, we "bear" God's image afresh: we become like the One we are beholding! This awesome power of beholding is what the Father is using to save and transform the world.

1) Adam's nature is in all of us: It still seeks to hide from God in guilt and fear of punishment and shame of having our sinful "nakedness" exposed.

2) Our birth fathers (and mothers) may have been uncaring, distant, overbearing, unaffectionate, abusive, threatening, harsh in discipline, angry in punishment, and sinful—creating powerful, but false impressions of what God the Father is like.

3) Our spiritual fathers (and mothers), even beloved pastors and teachers may have planted wrong images of the Father as being different from Jesus in His ways with us—less loving, more judgmental, easily offended, stern and strict.

None of these distorted images reveal Father God. They actually resemble the enemy instead. These false images must be cast down! We cast them down first by forgiving the ones who sowed distorted images in us, and then by renouncing the lies that were planted and confessing the truth in their place.

The Image Formed by Our Birth Family

Our fathers (and mothers) can contribute to a distorted image of Father God because they are as a god to us when we are little—teaching us right from wrong and exercising power over us. As children we are looking to see God in our fathers—all the more so since our hearts are blocked from knowing the heavenly Father's love and presence by the sin nature. No earthly father entirely measures up, but a solid foundation of affection, love and proper discipline makes a huge difference in forming who we will become. The lack of this solid foundation leaves a void, often a hurting wound, which the enemy has many ways of poisoning. There are crucial things we all needed our fathers to say to us, but which many of us never heard:

I love you.	I'm proud of you.
I'm glad you were born.	You're a good child.

Every home needs a godly father. Godly order in scripture shows us that the head of the woman is the man; the head of the man is Christ; the head of Christ is the Father (1 Corinthians 11:13). The father sets the emotional tone of a household and provides the moral framework of laws or rules for living in the family. The first word babies often say is "dada." Fathers and/or husbands who are not spiritually covering their families leave children as spiritual orphans and wives as spiritual widows.

Statistics give us a sense for the emotional and societal damage caused by failed fathering. In the USA over 90 percent of prisoners are males; 95 percent of those on death row hated their fathers. Many prisoners don't even know who their fathers were. The "father wound" is pervasive and deadly.[32] We all carry the "first father

---

[32] "Father Wound" concept and statistics from Gordon Dalbey, *Father and Son* (Nashville, TN: Thomas Nelson, 1992), 4-7.

wound" stemming from Adam's sin. Many of us also bear the "birth father wound" from our parents, a "father in God wound" from our religious upbringing and a "father impostor wound" from the enemy's direct working. The "father wound" carries a societal curse—a heavy consequence "in the land." Small wonder that so much restoration is needed in our own day.

> **"Behold, I will send you Elijah the prophet before the great and terrible day of Yahweh comes. He will turn the hearts of the fathers to the children, and the hearts of the children to their fathers, lest I come and strike the earth with a curse."**
> Malachi 4:5-6 WEB

Clarifying Our Image of the Father

In truth people often think they begin with knowing God the Father. Actually we only know *about* Him by name as Father God, but relate to Him more as "the great high God"—distant and unknowable until a living faith through Christ is birthed in us. Jesus came to reveal the Father personally and much more intimately as *Abba*, just as He also came to baptize us with the Holy Spirit. The order of the three great pilgrimage festivals that Israel was commanded to observe reveals spiritual realities about our new life in Christ which are very interesting. Passover came first in early spring, prefiguring Jesus the true Passover Lamb. Next came Pentecost in late spring, a celebration of the "early harvest," which exactly coincided with the outpouring of the Holy Spirit upon the Early Church. Finally, Tabernacles, the great Feast of Harvest, arrived at the end of summer after a long growth period. Drawing a Trinitarian analogy to the Festivals, Tabernacles, therefore, relates to the Father. An intimate relationship with the Father is not automatic—it often comes only after a long period of growth (if at all), but it is absolutely necessary for establishing our hearts in sufficient grace that we may dwell (tabernacle) with our God.

The revelation of the Father's glorious grace began in the Old Testament. God the Father revealed His glory—the glorious nature of His grace-filled Being—to Moses.

> **The Lord passed before him and proclaimed, "The Lord, the Lord, a God merciful and gracious, slow to anger, and abounding in steadfast love and faithfulness."**
> Exodus 34:6

This is what Paul refers to when he tells us that our sins consist in falling short of God's glory (Romans 3:23). Our selfish and unloving choices in no way reflect our Father's glorious ability to shower love and mercy, grace and goodness, upon the whole of His creation. So great is His glorious grace that our Father in heaven does not even hold our sins against us. He hates our sins and in His goodness will patiently work to bring us to repentance so that we can be separated from them, all the while maintaining a Spirit of reconciliation towards us in His great Heart.

It was God [personally present] in Christ, reconciling *and* restoring the world to favor with Himself, not counting up *and* holding against [men] their trespasses [but cancelling them], and committing to us the message of reconciliation (of the restoration to favor). 2 Corinthians 5:19 AMP

Our grace-filled Father affirmed His only begotten Son by expressing His love for Jesus in public displays of affection. There are three audible words of God which Jesus heard that are recorded for us in scripture. In all of them the true Father affirmed His Son: at His baptism (Matthew 3:17); on the mount of transfiguration (Luke 9:35); and before the cross (John 12:28). Astoundingly, the Father has the same love for all who are in Christ by faith. If you are a believer, Father God desires to affirm and express His love to you. There is no one He loves more than you. There is no one He loves less than you—He doesn't play favorites. He loves us all as much as He loves Jesus! If these scriptures fail to move your heart, pray for fresh grace to be amazed by the stunning implications of what Jesus is saying about the Father's love *for you*.

> *For the Father Himself loves you.*
> John 16:27

"For the Father himself loves you, because you have loved me and have believed that I came from God." John 16:27

"I in them and you in me, that they may become perfectly one, so that the world may know that you sent me and loved them even as you loved me." John 17:23

This is what our gracious Father is really like:

- The Father delights to give us the Kingdom (Luke 12:32).
- The Father has no darkness about Him—there is no shadow or possibility of evil coming from Him (1 John 1:5).
- He is the giver of every good gift (James 1:17).
- The Father disciplines only in love—it is the goodness of God that draws us to repent (Proverbs 3:12; Romans 2:4).
- The Father is unconditional love—blessing all alike (Matthew 5:44-45).
- The Father has completely accepted us in Christ—He is totally reconciled to us the way we are (Ephesians 1:5-6; 2 Corinthians 5:19).
- He has chosen to favor us with right standing in His sight (Romans 3:24).
- He has never been angry with you and never will be (Isaiah 54:7-11).

Let Jesus Reveal the Father to You

Jesus came on a mission to reveal the Father and restore His true image to us. Both by His life and by His death His stated intention was to reveal the Father.

Philip said to him, "Lord, show us the Father, and it is enough for us." Jesus said to him, "Have I been with you so long, and you still do not know me, Philip? Whoever has seen me has seen the Father. How can you say, 'Show us the Father'? Do you not believe that I am in the Father and the Father is in me?" John 14:8-10

Here is the idea made simple: The Father is just like Jesus! The New Testament not only gives us permission, it makes it a requirement of faith that we cast down every image of the Father we may have been given that does not match up with Jesus.

"I and the Father are one." John 10:30

[But] **in the last of these days He has spoken to us in** [the person of a] **Son... He is the sole expression of the glory of God** [the Light-being, the out-raying or radiance of the divine], **and He is the perfect imprint** *and* **very image of** [God's] **nature, upholding** *and* **maintaining** *and* **guiding** *and* **propelling the universe by His mighty word of power.** Hebrews 1:2-3 AMP

If this is who God really is to you and for you (and it is), then actually knowing and believing it will produce joy and peace in you and love through you in any moment of your life in which you touch this living reality by faith (Romans 15:13). Active, believing faith always has that kind of power. Faith is what puts us in touch with *reality*. Not to live in a faith like this is to live a bad dream from which One Day we will all be awakened in His Presence. Why not awaken now?

As we behold the true image of the Father our hearts become established. So let us learn to run to "Home Base." Begin each day intentionally checking to see if your heart really believes these five great liberating truths about God the Father. Your Father is always:

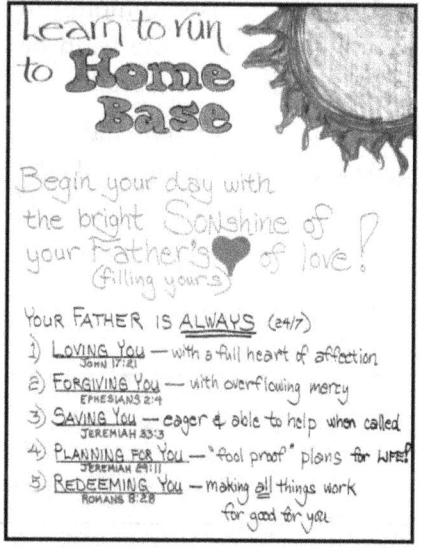

RUN TO HOME BASE

Jesus came to reveal our gladhearted Father who is the Source of life and love. School your heart in these five glorious truths and begin each day by basking in the bright Sonshine of your Father's heart of love!

1) **Loving you**—with a heart full of affection (John 17:23).

2) **Forgiving you**—with overflowing mercy (Hebrews 4:16).

3) **Saving you**—eager to help when called (Jeremiah 33:3).

4) **Planning for you**—for a hope-filled future (Jeremiah 29:11).

5) **Redeeming you**—all things working for good (Romans 8:28).

If your heart doesn't believe these truths, then it's time to roll up your spiritual sleeves and go to work, attaching your faith to His scriptures. Jesus said that believing the truth about God is our most important *work* (John 6:29). Repentance is turning back to the love that never turns away from you. So, don't make Father do all the running—learn to run to Him!

The Way of Restoration

Having our hearts restored to a condition of deeply trusting our Father to never fail us or forsake us will require recognizing the moments when we begin "bowing down to" and "serving" a lesser image of God: Feeling unworthy, anxious or driven to perform are clues we need to heed.

1) Pray for the Holy Spirit to open your eyes to see any distorted images of the Father that you may be carrying: Forgive the ones who planted them; repent, renounce those fallen images.

2) Pray for Jesus to more fully reveal the Father to you: Repent, renounce all unbelief; confess the truth of His perfect love, abundant mercy, saving help, great plans and total redemption.

3) Turn to the Father and release gratitude for His never-ending love and grace-based way of saving You!

NOTES/JOURNAL

_____
_____
_____
_____
_____
_____
_____
_____

EXERCISE

Write a list of what your earthly father seemed to be like when you were very young. If he was absent by death or duty or had abandoned the family, be sure to put that on the list—even if you didn't actually know him. Perception is often more important than reality in the shaping of our emotional life. "No dad" **can be** just as difficult overcome as "bad dad." Remember the world, flesh and devil were at work to mis-shape your personality when you were very young. Having been wounded is *not* your fault; having "acted out" is.

Write another list of what *deep down* you thought or feared your heavenly Father was like when you were in painful or scary trials. Trials have a way of bringing the secret thoughts of our hearts up to the surface (see Job 23:13-17). Don't gloss over your feelings with a religious veneer. Remember them just as they were.

_____
_____

Do you see any connections? Make careful note of them and pray over them.

_____
_____

DISCUSSION QUESTIONS

Have you had times in your life when you questioned the Father's love for you? It is no secret to Him, nor does it weaken His love for you, so be honest! What were those times like outwardly? How did it feel inwardly? How did it influence you to act whenever you were in real doubt about the Father's perfect love for you personally? Was your behavior worse than it might have been? Now consider the plight of the prodigal(s):

1) Why did the prodigal son take so long before he finally went home to the father (Lk 17:15-19)? What kind of image of his father did he seem to carry in his heart? Why do you suppose he left his father in the first place? Think in terms of his possible mis-perceptions of his father's ways, not just the beckoning of the world to his carnal nature.

2) Why does it sometimes take you so long to return to the Father, when you have wandered away? When you find you have strayed, how hard is it for you to take the express elevator (Heb 4:16) to Your Father's wide open door? What could help you shorten the time of return?

MAIN POINTS

- We are commanded not to bow down to or serve false images of God.
- We become like (serve) the Image of God that we carry deep in our hearts.
- The deep images even Christians carry are often distorted ones.
- Distorted images can come through Adam's nature, our birth parents (or those who raised us) and church traditions.
- Jesus came to reveal the Father: He says that the Father is just like Himself.

- We need to recognize and cast down all distorted images and hold fast to the true Image that Jesus has fully revealed.
- As we keep our faith focus on the Father's perfect love our hearts can become established.

DIGGING DEEPER

Jesus says that He reveals the Father in all that He says and does.

> **Philip said to him, "Lord, show us the Father, and it is enough for us." Jesus said to him, "Have I been with you so long, and you still do not know me, Philip? Whoever has seen me has seen the Father. How can you say, 'Show us the Father'? Do you not believe that I am in the Father and the Father is in me? The words that I say to you I do not speak on my own authority, but the Father who dwells in me does his works."**
> John 14:8-10

Study the way of Jesus in two "books." Both of these books reveal the Father.

1) First, in the pages of *the gospel*, look to see how Jesus handles situations and people—this will show you exactly what the Father is like. The letters paint word portraits too (see 2Co 13:4-8, Php 4:4-8, and Gal 5:22 to see Him better).

2) Then review the pages of *your inner diary*. Take careful remembrance of the times you have been touched by Jesus, encountered Jesus, been loved or rescued by Jesus—those also are revealing the Father to you. He would never have been that way with you, if He hadn't seen the Father wanting it to be so.

SWORD AND SHIELD

Study these scriptures. Look them up. Take them to heart. Commit those to memory that you most need to believe in your times of fear and doubt.[33]

I am loved by the Father...

He has loved me with an everlasting love. I have never not been loved (Jer 31:3).

God loves me so much He gave His only Son to die for me so I might have life (Jn 3:16).

The Father loves me so much He wants to express His love to me (Jn 16:27).

The Father loves me just as much as He loves His Son Jesus (Jn 17:23, 26).

Even when I have sinned, the Father loves and seats me with Him in Christ (Eph 2:4-6).

The Father wants to fill me to overflowing with His love (Eph 3:19).

God has extended His love to me and called me His child (1 Jn 3:1).

---

[33] Compiled by Shiloh Place Ministries, Conway, SC: distributed as a flyer that is no longer in publication.

Even when I was ungodly, a sinner, an enemy, the Father sent Jesus for me (Ro 5:6-10).

I am accepted by the Father...

I am called a child of God (Jn 1:12).

I am called Christ's friend (Jn 15:15).

In Christ it is just as if I had never sinned (Ro 5:1).

I belong to the Father (1Co 6:19).

I am a member of Christ's body (1Co 12:27).

The Father is not holding, counting or imputing my sins against me (2Co 5:19).

I have been adopted by Father God (Eph 1:5).

I am complete in Christ (Col 2:10).

God is not ashamed to be my God (He 11:16).

I am secure in the Father...

I am free forever from condemnation (Ro 8:1-2).

The Father will always be for me (Ro 8:31).

Nothing can separate me from the Father's love (Ro 8:35).

God has redeemed me and forgiven all my sins (Col 1:14).

I am hidden with Christ in the Father (Col 3:3).

I am a citizen of heaven (Php 3:20).

I have not been given a spirit of fear but of power, love and a sound mind (2Ti 1:7).

I can go boldly to the Father and find grace and mercy in my time of need (Heb 4:16).

Father God's perfect, unconditional love casts out all of my fears (1 Jn 4:18).

I belong to God, and the evil one has no right to touch me (1 Jn 5:18).

The Father does not accuse me or condemn me (Ro 8:31-33).

The Father does not judge me (Jn 5:22).

The Father forgives me and cleanses me from all my sin as I confess it to Him (1Jn 1:9).

I have purpose in the Father...

I am the salt and light of the earth (Mt 5:13-14).

I have been chosen to bear fruit (Jn 15:16).

I am a witness of God to the world (Ac 1:8).

I am a minister of reconciliation for God (2Co 5:18).

I am God's ambassador to the world (2Co 5:20).

God is at work in me to will and to do His good pleasure upon the earth (Php 2:13).

I can do all things through Christ who strengthens me (Php 4:13).

PRAYER FOCUS

Forgive your parents and claim your God-given heritage through them. Forgive spiritual leaders and church traditions and release them to God.

Dear Heavenly Father, in the Name of Jesus, I choose by an act of my will to forgive my father/mother for all the ways that he/she failed me or hurt me. I repent for agreeing with the enemy in bitterness about my father/mother. I renounce those things in my life. I gratefully accept Your forgiveness of me and I choose to forgive myself and to fully accept myself as the child of the father/mother You gave me. Holy Spirit please come. Heal my broken heart: Show me and tell me your truth.

RENUNCIATIONS AND AFFIRMATIONS

Renounce any agreements with untruth; believe Jesus' *truth* as your new *way* of *life*.

Confess and renounce any unbelief in the Father's perfect love for you. Confess and choose to believe the truth by an act of your will. Stand on the Word!

Father, I confess that I have let the enemy and my own life experiences build up false images about You that have kept me from running to You. But those days are ending now! From now on I will fight to believe in the truth about You that Jesus is revealing to me. I will fight to run to You when I am tempted or in need. I will seek Your grace even in my places of deepest disgrace. Let Your perfect love cast out all of my fears!

PUTTING FEET TO YOUR PRAYERS: STRETCH YOURSELF!

Learn to run to Home Base! This one exercise can change the way your whole day will go. Begin each day intentionally checking to see if your heart really believes these five great liberating truths about God the Father and watch the Son rise in your heart. Your Father is always:

1) **Loving you**—with a full heart of affection (Jn 17:23).
2) **Forgiving you**—with overflowing mercy and grace (He 4:16).
3) **Saving you**—eager and able to help when called (Jer 33:3).
4) **Planning for you**—to give you a hope-filled future (Jer 29:11).
5) **Redeeming you**—making all things work for good (Ro 8:28).

If your heart doesn't believe these truths, go to work! Jesus said that believing the truth about God is our work (Jn 6:29). Repentance is turning back to the love that never turns from you. So, don't make Father do all the running—**learn to run to Him!**

SECTION THREE

Strongholds

*For the weapons of our warfare are not of the flesh,
but mighty before God to the throwing down of strongholds,
throwing down imaginations and every high thing
that is exalted against the knowledge of God,
and bringing every thought into captivity
to the obedience of Christ.*
2 Corinthians 10:4-5 WEB

CHAPTER 11

STRONGHOLDS

Up to now we have been laying a foundation for understanding our emotional and spiritual life. We have seen the connection between stress and disease and between our negative emotions and what the Bible calls sins. Then we looked at the pathway of temptation into sin coming from spiritual darkness and the way out that separates us from sin and reconnects us for greater entry into God's Kingdom. Finally, we focused upon the all-important role of image bearing and how the power of beholding can uplift us or cast us down according to the Image of God and of our self that we carry deep within our hearts. Now, we are entering into the real "battlefield" of the course.

This is the section where we will explore the major emotional strongholds that disconnect us from the peace of Christ and all too often hold us captive to stress (as anxiety) or distress (as depression). The strongholds we will explore are generational sin, unbelief, accusation, bitterness, trauma, rejection, self-rejection, envy and jealousy, the occult, fear and addictions. That's quite a list! First, however, we will have to study what strongholds are, how they are formed and how they can be brought down.[34]

Jesus is our true stronghold—the Rock that we run to when threatened by sin or danger, our new shield of protection against the enemy's encroachments. David couldn't say enough about trusting the Lord as His Protector, Provider and Pardoner.

The Lord is my rock and my fortress and my deliverer, my God, my rock, in whom I take refuge, my shield, and the horn of my salvation, my stronghold. Psalm 18:2

Strongholds of the Flesh

The enemy creates *counterfeit* strongholds in our flesh. These are un-surrendered, un-healed or un-crucified areas of the old nature or self-life. They rise up and resist the Spirit-given life. Self-protectiveness built them and maintains them, aided by the lies and temptations of the enemy. We are to resist them by pulling them down. Like David we don't need self-protection any longer—we have the Lord to protect us! His grace is all-sufficient!

For the weapons of our warfare are not of the flesh, but mighty before God to the throwing down of strongholds, throwing down imaginations and every high thing

---

[34]:Teaching and insights concerning "strongholds" as emotional and spiritual blocks from Be In Health® teaching and materials, Dr. Henry W. Wright, Thomaston, Georgia, seminar notes, October 2000.

that is exalted against the knowledge of God, and bringing every thought into captivity to the obedience of Christ. 2 Corinthians 10:4-5 WEB

Strongholds are habit structures of thought.[35] When we ask Jesus into our life, God gives us a new heart (Ezekiel 36:26), but we have to change our former mental and emotional habits. We do this by working with the truth and grace He supplies. Habits are thoughts or actions repeated so often over time that no conscious thought is required for them to take place. Thoughts begin as seeds but, if unchecked, can become as firmly rooted as trees (Hebrews 12:15). Strongholds are built upon seemingly apparent and self-evident truths which are actually distortions of eternal truth. Our continuing agreement with them keeps them built up and strengthened. Stronghold thinking is "stinking thinking"!

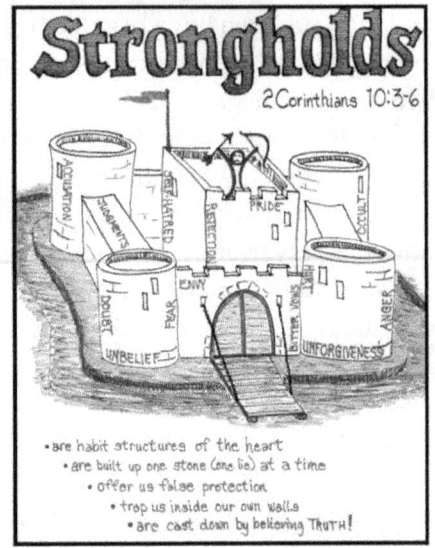

Such thinking springs up from the murky depths of the heart of our fallen nature which is "deceitful above all things and desperately wicked" according to the Lord, who alone can search it out (Jeremiah 17:9). Yes, as if the new life weren't complicated enough, we now have to deal with the reality of having two hearts in one believer. It is very comforting to know that the new heart we have received is entirely good. Indeed, it is Christlike for it comes from Him and stays ever ready to power up the New Creation life, whenever we break free of the strongholds that entrap it.

STRONGHOLD PROTECTION

Jesus is our true stronghold. The counterfeits are un-healed or un-crucified areas of the old nature. We are to resist them by pulling them down. Our walls may make us feel secure, but they trap us inside loveless strongholds.

The old heart, however, is the "stronghold maker." It draws its power from all of the deeply cherished (false) beliefs and (unchristian) coping strategies we developed along the way with the enemy's help. These become the wellspring for our negative emotions, for any emotion is merely the passionate expression of a deeply held belief. This helps explain why living the new life is so easy whenever we are free of negative emotions (it flows gracefully from our new heart) and yet so difficult whenever negative emotions hold us in their power (their power comes from our old heart's most deeply held beliefs). We are literally wrestling within ourselves at times over which belief system to believe—the one that comes with Jesus or the one that we lived by before He made His entrance. If you are

---

[35] For strongholds as "habit structures of thought": Jack Frost, Shiloh Place Ministry, Myrtle Beach, SC, cassette teaching. The phrase, "stinking thinking" is widely credited to Zig Ziglar.

wondering which is which, then know that believing from the new heart always produces life and peace *in any moment*; believing out of the old heart's strongholds doesn't. Let's go for freedom!

The Power of Strongholds

The stronghold is fortified by false beliefs which we are to pull down by carrying those thoughts captive to Christ, once the hidden lie has been exposed by the truth of God's Word. This requires some diligence, especially in the beginning (Proverbs 4:23). In the stronghold we encounter the self-life's negative power coming against us as feelings and as unbelieving thoughts. Be on guard if you find yourself thinking: "I feel it so strongly, it *feels* like it must be true." To counter this we need to wake up and realize that our feelings are lying to us. Never rely upon your feelings to declare the truth! In fact the more powerful the negative feeling is, the greater the lie that the emotion is pressing upon us. However, not all positive feelings can be trusted either (see Negative Emotions).

A second problem arises whenever we "hear" ourselves thinking: "I just don't see how God's truth can be right about this situation." We need to realize in advance that in certain situations our understanding is going to be worthless to us. His ways and His thoughts really are higher than ours (Isaiah 55:8-9). We are told in Proverbs to get understanding, but not to *lean* upon it. Cast down what you think you know if it is keeping you from trusting. You can at least understand this: He loves you, He is not lying to you and He will never fail you. Tell *that* to your doubts and fears!

Strongholds are fortresses of thought built up within our flesh which can be used by the enemy to harass and oppress us. Generational sin patterns that left gaping holes in our covering, pain and problems encountered during childhood and the unhealed wounds of traumatic events often cause strongholds to form. Usually they have been built "stone by stone" (thought by thought) over a long period of time, so long in fact that we have forgotten that we ever believed or felt anything different or that life was ever different from how the stronghold now makes it seem. In that area of experience we have come to see life from the perspective of the stronghold. Like the keep of a medieval castle it is well-fortified. We feel protected by believing it, but it "keeps" us a prisoner on the inside. We are held captive by our own walls, and these walls also keep others from leading us out. Choose to take your walls down and let others (and the truth they bring) in.

Discerning a stronghold area in your life is a necessary first step towards bringing it down. If you can't just say no to the flesh, you are dealing with a stronghold built upon that area of your fallen nature. Another way of picturing these strongholds of the flesh is like having your arm gripped by someone dragging you along with them against your will. The enemy gains a strong *hold* upon our flesh in areas where we have repeatedly given our beliefs and actions over to his twisted ways.

Strongholds are habit structures of thought, not evil spirits. A stronghold may be occupied or unoccupied—this is by no means easy to discern. Try to attack someone else's stronghold head on and it may seem well-occupied and well-defended against all the reasons you bring. This *may* be an indication of the enemy's direct involvement. Likewise, if a spirit is oppressing you *through* a stronghold of your own, you may sense the power of the negative feelings it stirs up and the tenacious hold those thoughts and feelings have over you. Evil spirits are very stubborn, not easily giving way to truth and to the exercise of our wills to resist them. Fortunately, it is not necessary to know if a spirit is oppressing you. Let the Holy Spirit show you what sins to confess and what false beliefs to renounce, then choose to submit to God and His truth. Genuine submission to God undercuts the evil spirit's right to remain, and determined rebuking makes them flee (James 4:7-8).

> *For the weapons of our warfare are not of the flesh, but mighty before God to the throwing down of strongholds...*
> 2 Corinthians 10:4

Strongholds take advantage of the enemy's great lie that you can never really feel good about yourself or be at peace within yourself unless everything is going your way and the people you care about are all affirming you. What a formula for disaster that is, since it so often happens that something or someone fails to fall into place the way we'd like. Stemming from this kind of thinking we may find ourselves living under an inner demand to a) never goof up, b) never get rejected and c) always be capable of solving problems (a) and (b) if they do occur. Protestant Reformers called this "works righteousness"—tying to advance our cause by our own works. We call it perfectionism and performance orientation. Either way it's a snare of the enemy. The truth is that you can feel incredibly good about yourself whenever you choose by a living faith to get your eyes off yourself and back on to the One who remains steadfast at loving you and patiently leads you step by step whenever you trust Him enough to do it. Chapters 17 and 18 will provide more help with this. The "4 A's" (Affection, Achievement, Approval, Acceptance) describe performance orientation coming out of these lies:

> *Because of a lack of Affection I sought Achievements in order to gain Approval so that I could feel Accepted. The answer in Christ: Now I can rest secure at last in the Father's unending acceptance and affection for me—and give up striving and stressing over seeking achievements and approval.*

Pulling Down Strongholds

How are strongholds brought down? The things that bring strongholds down are the very things that would have kept them from forming in the first place—having sufficient understanding of how to apply the truth of God's Word to the hurtful situation or wrong desire. So now in the present moment when new situations trigger the stronghold, we can do what we didn't do then and begin taking the stronghold down one victory at a time, under the Spirit's power. We do this by carrying their "high" thoughts captive to Christ. This is primarily a truth encounter on our part. We choose by an act of our will to cast down our understanding and break agreement with our feelings. As we agree with the truth (that the enemy's stronghold is a lie and the Word is the truth), then the Holy Spirit strengthens and raises us. Confessing truth and renouncing the lies need to be done by the one seeking freedom—thought by thought, "stone by stone."

Either we will carry wrong thoughts captive to Christ, or those wrong thoughts will carry us captive to do their will (see 2 Timothy 2:24-26). Therefore, there is a great need to pray for revelation because if we lack knowledge (discernment) the un-recognized thoughts have greater power (Isaiah 5:13; Hosea 4:6). Recognizing stronghold thinking and being willing to challenge it with the truths of God's Word gives us the weapons needed for victory. Truth is always liberating—if you truly believe it.

So Jesus said to the Jews who had believed in him, "If you abide in my word, you are truly my disciples, and you will know the truth, and the truth will set you free."
John 8:31-32

Basic discipleship and inner healing dismantle strongholds. Basic discipleship is the part we play by doing our best with the faith and self-discipline that we have available to us. Disciplines act as a restraint upon the power of temptation and of our fallen nature and its strongholds. If you think that restraining your flesh isn't working, just imagine abandoning the discipline or the faith you still have left to you and "see" how disastrous that would likely become. In the grip of a very trying time, we usually can't see how to make things better, but we certainly can make them worse! What are the disciplines? Regular prayer, Bible study, worship, fellowship and service to others combined with seeking to trust and obey the Lord form the backbone of basic discipleship.

FRUIT AND ROOTS

The disciplines (prayer, Bible study, worship, fellowship, service) act as a restraint upon the power of temptation. Inner healing gets at the root issues that caused strongholds of the fallen nature to form in the first place.

Basic discipleship enables us to prune unwanted fruit off our spiritual tree; inner healing gets at the root issues that caused strongholds to form bad fruit in the first place. Where there is bad fruit, there is almost always a root issue to deal with

(Hebrews 12:15). Inner healing removes or breaks the power of temptations and of our fallen nature by bringing release from the pain and/or ungodly beliefs trapped inside due to past traumatic events (see Chapter 16). Now that we understand the need for "pruning shears" and "garden spades" we are ready to explore specific stronghold areas in each of the chapters that follow.

The Way to Freedom

There is an underlying pattern to finding freedom from the negative emotion strongholds. It is the way of "returning and rest," of repentance and restoration by entrusting the whole of our life to God, especially in the area of our present trouble.[i]

1) The first step to freedom from any stronghold is realizing that you have lost the peace of Christ, are being held captive instead by a negative emotion, and that this is a spiritual problem.

2) The next step is to take full responsibility for agreeing with the enemy in that area which the stronghold represents: Repent, renounce and carry it captive to Christ until you see something in Him that restores your trust in God and willingness to obey.

3) Turn to the Father and release gratitude to Him for the mercy, love, power and promises He showers upon you by His grace!

NOTES/JOURNAL

___

EXERCISE

This is a test to reveal the power that hidden strongholds may have over your feelings. Can you whole-heartedly and joyfully affirm the following three statements? Remember how you think and feel *when you are down*—being "down" has a way of pulling up what we actually believe deep down.

1) There have been no "unforgivable" sins done by me—I *never* cringe or feel shame or regret at the remembrance of anything I have ever said or done.

2) There have been no unredeemable past or present losses or failings—I am *entirely* OK with all that has happened to me and trust great good to come from everything I have ever experienced.

3) God the Father is *always* loving me with pure, unbounded affection. Even in my worst moments He is not holding any of my sins against me and is eagerly helping me—with His love and wisdom guiding all He sends or allows.

If you cannot agree from the depth of your emotions with these truths (especially on your "bad" days), then strongholds may be present which are binding negative feelings to you. List what you discovered and try to understand the stronghold thinking your feelings represent. Then pray for God to go to work on it with you, for you and through you.

Negative feeling   **Stronghold thinking**

_____   _____
_____   _____
_____   _____

DISCUSSION QUESTIONS

Ask the group to consider examples of stronghold thinking in our culture. For example: people from cults who come to your door, atheistic evolutionary advocates, extreme positions in favor of abortion.

1) Have they ever been able to change anyone's mind on these subjects? What do we end up doing—after first getting frustrated and angry of course!—and what works?

2) Now ask them to consider the kinds of strongholds that individuals they have met have had—no examples of anyone present or known to the group, please. This is not for gossip, but for understanding the dynamic. What was it like trying to talk past the stronghold? What worked? Did anything work?

3) Then ask them to offer up (if they are willing) an example of a stronghold (not shameful, painful, or embarrassing) in their own emotional life. Not for therapy or counsel, but for prayer. Then pray for all that have been mentioned for the Lord to go to work to pull those strongholds down. Then let each one on their own give special attention to the relevant stronghold teachings that are scheduled to come up in the series—no back seat drivers!

MAIN POINTS

- Strongholds are areas of our fallen nature that still have power over us.
- Unhealed trauma and generational sin patterns in the family system are breeding grounds for strongholds.
- Strongholds are rooted in lies that seem self-evidently true.
- Strongholds are habit patterns of thought that require no effort to believe.
- Strongholds are negative emotions that have a "strong hold" on us.
- If we don't carry the thoughts of strongholds captive to Christ, they will hold us captive to the enemy.
- Pulling down strongholds is a truth encounter, not a will power contest.

DIGGING DEEPER

Discerning between the flesh, strongholds and evil spirits. Study the following principles for weighing what you may be wrestling with.

1) Your flesh cannot be cast out, nor does it need to be. It is always there with its tendency and disposition to sin. One day, when we enter into His glory, God will separate us from our fallen nature (1Co 15:53-54), but until then it is dangerous for us to try to eradicate the flesh ourselves. In fact to try to eliminate our flesh is an act of unwitting disobedience to God's Word, because Jesus has already defeated it for us (Ro 6:5-14). Whenever we can truly trust in and rely upon the Lord our flesh (the old man) is laid to rest by His Spirit and the new nature carries us forward in peace and freedom (Ro 8:1-2). Any failing of trust or obedience on our part and the flesh is only too ready to spring quickly back to life. The New Testament scriptures are clear that if what we are struggling with is an issue of the flesh, then we are to put off the flesh like soiled clothing—to just say no and turn from it (Eph 4:22-24).

2) The flesh is essentially a dead thing, crucified by Christ and, like a shadow now seen by the Light of Christ within us, the flesh has no power of its own to overthrow those who walk by the Spirit. But if we get our eyes locked onto our shadow we may easily trip and fall! The way to keep this from happening is to keep our eyes on Christ and by so doing abide in continual trust and obedience. In this way the knowledge of the reality of our flesh and of its total depravity (no redeeming thing about it) helps to humble us and remind us to keep our focus on our Savior (Col 3:9-10).

3) Strongholds are a different matter. To the degree that "putting off the flesh" is difficult, to that degree a stronghold has likely been built into our flesh by the prior activity of the enemy in our lives. Such areas of the flesh, when they are touched by present situations (words, events, desires) are very difficult to simply set aside and a struggle ensues within us if the sinful desire of the flesh is to be overcome. *We are to carry the thoughts of these strongholds captive to Christ*—a much more intense image than "putting off" the old nature.

4) "Heavily defended" strongholds may be occupied by alien intruders—the evil spirits of the kingdom of darkness whose temptations and deceptions built the strongholds in the first place. Here we are told to resist the devil and he will flee from us and even to cast out the evil spirits in the name of the Lord who conquered them at the cross. Such "occupied" strongholds cannot be defeated by simply shifting our focus back to Christ. They require the harder work of the 6 R's (Lesson 7). Even so, victory is assured us (Ro 8:37).

SWORD AND SHIELD

Scriptures that connect victory over strongholds to the battle for truth.

> "Therefore my people go into exile for lack of knowledge." Isaiah 5:13

> So Jesus said to the Jews who had believed in him, "If you abide in my word, you are truly my disciples, and you will know the truth, and the truth will set you free." John 8:31-32

> Do not be conformed to this world, but be transformed by the renewal of your mind, that by testing you may discern what is the will of God, what is good and acceptable and perfect. Romans 12:2

> The Lord's servant must not quarrel, but be gentle towards all, able to teach, patient, in gentleness correcting those who oppose him: perhaps God may give them repentance leading to a full knowledge of the truth, and they may recover themselves out of the devil's snare, having been taken captive by him to his will. 2 Timothy 2:24-26 WEB

> For the word of God is living, and active, and sharper than any two-edged sword, and piercing even to the dividing of soul and spirit, of both joints and marrow, and is able to discern the thoughts and intentions of the heart. Hebrews 4:12 WEB

> But solid food is for those who are full grown, who by reason of use have their senses exercised to discern good and evil. Hebrews 5:14 WEB

PRAYER FOCUS

Even very long journeys begin with a single first step in the right direction. Perhaps by now you have caught a glimpse of the Kingdom with its glorious possibilities of life and it seems a far distant thing from the way your life has been. Perhaps you have also noticed a stronghold or two that are holding you captive to stress and negative emotions of one kind or another. Perhaps it is time to take that first good step to launch a journey into the heart of God. Since every advance is first birthed in prayer, here's one for the road:

Father, I have lived inside the walls of my strongholds for so long they have become a part of me, but I do want to find out what life in Your Kingdom is like on the other side of these walls. Lead me in the way of childlike trust and simplicity of heart! I ask you to help me take all of my strongholds down, untruth by untruth, and rebuild with Your truths the godly walls of love and mercy, faith and grace around the renewed heart You are giving me through Jesus. What I can't tear down, will You? Come charge my walls! Send, allow, withhold—do whatever it takes so that our two hearts can meet and beat as one in this life.

RENUNCIATIONS AND AFFIRMATIONS

Renounce any agreements with untruth; believe Jesus' *truth* as your new *way* of *life.*

In the grip of the stronghold we exert our will to choose to believe truth. Consider the ways you have often felt when a powerful negative emotion has taken you captive. Then pray:

I renounce the lies my feelings and inner thoughts press upon me.
I cast down my understanding, and choose to trust God's wisdom and His ways.
I choose by an act of my will to believe God's Word and to obey Jesus by _____.

PUTTING FEET TO YOUR PRAYERS: STRETCH YOURSELF!

Some fruitful questions to ask within the stronghold. As you ask them, wait upon the Lord to see or hear what He may show you. Then pray to believe the truth that sets them to flight. (For more on finding freedom from strongholds see Negative Emotions in the Postscripts, page 263.)

Lord, what am I really angry about?
Why do I feel so guilty and ashamed?
    Help me fully forgive others and fully receive Your forgiveness.
What am I really afraid of?
    Help me match Your truth to my deepest fear until the fear is released.

CHAPTER 12

REVERSING THE CURSE

The Stronghold of Generational Sin

While still in the womb, without any initiation or cooperation on our part, the devastating consequence of Adam's sin was imparted to us: We were all born with a sin nature separating us from God. This is the deep wellspring of all the generational sins against us which followed and it will not be removed in our lifetime, unless the Lord returns first. Fortunately, we can become free of the impact of ancestral sins in our generational line by reducing or eliminating their "strong hold" upon us.

As it happens, the first unavoidable strongholds any of us encounter are not our own, though they may very well become our own. They are the strongholds of generational patterns of sin in families. Before we were conceived these strongholds were already in place. Since no one is perfect, every family line has sin patterns somewhere along the way. God tells us in His Word that He visits the iniquity of the fathers upon succeeding generations. We can see the evidence of this: Children of alcoholics often become alcoholics, many diseases run in families and some children are born with dreadful genetic defects. Life is tough enough, so it hardly seems fair that the sins of previous generations could be allowed by God to have any impact, let alone a devastating impact at times, on the lives of innocent newborns. The question has to be asked: How can it be right for children to be "punished" for the sins of their ancestors? Why do we suffer from sins in the past?

Why the Problem Exists

The important thing to keep in mind about issues of generational sin is that because God lives outside of time, un-repented sin is always a fresh stain before the eyes of the Lord. He sees the sins of our ancestors and their wrong as a *present* sin. This is why generational sin continues to "live on" even after the person who sinned has died—that sin was their choice and God sustains the reality of the world formed by our choosing. This is the dignity and the terrible responsibility of being given free will in a real world. Upholding the "moral order" we choose to create is part of God's self-revelation to Moses: The sin ledger isn't canceled at death.

> *Un-repented sin doesn't just evaporate.*

> **The Lord passed before him and proclaimed, "The Lord, the Lord, a God merciful and gracious... but who will by no means clear the guilty, visiting the iniquity of the fathers on the children and the children's children, to the third and the fourth generation."** Exodus 34:6-7

Un-repented sin doesn't just evaporate. Un-repented sin continues to wreak havoc in the generations. The blood still cries out from the ground (Genesis 4:10). Lest we get the wrong idea, God is not the one doing the punishing—He punished Jesus for our sins fully and completely. God does not willingly desire to see us afflicted (Lamentations 3:31-33). It is the reality of choice that He gives to "the fathers" that releases the consequences of their iniquities on the earth. As surely as we choose sin, we "choose" the consequences of sin to come, even to the following. God has "no choice" but to allow the consequences of abused free will to continue to visit the earth with the "punishing" effects of sin until someone recognizes it as sin, takes responsibility for the sin and carries it captive to Him. We may rightly cherish our heritage (generational blessing is very real), but we need to also be honest about the sinful side and bring it to God. This kind of responsible repentance is what God desires—not the consequences of sin having to fall upon successive generations (Daniel 9:1-19).

> *No one has to walk in the sins of previous generations.*

"**But if they confess their iniquity and the iniquity of their fathers… and they make amends for their iniquity, then I will remember my covenant with Jacob.**"
Leviticus 26:40-42

The Pattern Is Not Compulsory

No one has to walk in the sins of their fathers (or mothers). The reality of sin's effects on the generations does not mean that children have no free will, but that un-repented sin creates a negative legacy within the family and the nation. For good or ill, whether intended or not, "like begets like" by an invariable mandate of the original creative process (Genesis 1:24). In Ezekiel the Lord speaks of each individual's responsibility for their sin and the ultimate penalty (death). The son will not die as a direct result of the father's sins; each person stands (or falls) as an individual.

"**The soul who sins shall die… Now suppose this man fathers a son who sees all the sins that his father has done; he sees, and does not do likewise… he shall not die for his father's iniquity; he shall surely live.**" Ezekiel 18:4, 14, 17

The command is clear that the sins of the father are not to be entered into or the curse (sin's consequence) will come. Although, the righteous avoidance of the father's sins is a shield against the curse, only repentance can remove sin and its effects (past or present). Remember that God as a responsible Creator has to maintain true justice and therefore He "by no means clears the guilty" (Exodus 34:7). He can only put sin and its consequences under the Blood of Christ if one of us repents and asks for mercy. Until then we, who still hold dominion over the earth, are choosing (often unknowingly) to let the curse of past misdeeds remain in effect. Let us also keep in mind that God's stated desire is to pass on blessings.

Surely He chooses our parents to pass on the blessings of their generations—not the curses.

> **"Visiting the iniquity of the fathers on the children... but showing steadfast love to thousands of those who love me and keep my commandments."** Exodus 20:5-6

How the Patterns Get Passed Down

We were "programmed" by the enemy from birth—set up by sin in the generations going all the way back to the Garden. God makes us "very good" in the womb (Genesis 1:312), but even as He is working to create us in His Image, the sin of Adam and the sins of our fathers were also at work, "unmaking" us into something less than God intended. The enemy is working against us before we are born, hating us "without cause" (Lamentations 3:52). If we fail to understand this reality, we will unwittingly blame God by "crediting" Him for fallen ways that we and others may have: "I hate being shy (or hot tempered or nervous, etc.), but that's just the way God made me!" No it isn't, that's the way the enemy bent and bruised you by sinning against you through your generations in ways that you couldn't notice or can't recall. Our personality structure according to psychologists is shaped in early childhood.[36] How much of that shaping process do you remember? Consider these two powerful personality shapers that are not of God:

1) Adam's sin passed down through the generations has blocked all of his children from being born as God intended—with a direct connection to The Father's love and a conscious awareness of His abiding presence.

2) The sins of preceding generations as they reached us through our bloodline, through the womb, and through our home environment began to set root issues and carnal patterns in us.

There are three ways that the curse (sin's consequences) may be passed down the generations:[37]

1) Nature: Our genetic inheritance can be physiological and psychological. Any damage in the genetic code at birth does not come from God's design or intervention, but results from the effects of the Fall upon humanity. All of God's creative work is "good"—without defect.

2) Nurture: The emotional environment and training in the home shapes each child.[38] The good that is in us often passes into our children (we like that!), but so does the bad (Genesis 1:24).

---

[36] Robert B. Ewen, *An Introduction to Theories of Personality*, Third Ed. (Hillsdale, NJ: Lawrence Erlbaum Assoc., Publishers, 1988) p. 523.

[37] Teaching and insights about these three ways that generational curses are transmitted from Be In Health® teaching and materials, Dr. Henry W. Wright, Thomaston, Georgia, seminar notes, October 2000.

[38] Thomas Verny, MD, *The Secret Life of the Unborn Child* (New York, NY: Dell Publishing, 1981) p. 49.

3) Spiritual: Spirits drawn to families (due to habitual sins) may carry patterns of the curse down the family line (see Leviticus 19:31 for "familiar spirits").

Evidence for Generational Patterns

It doesn't require faith in God or the Bible to see evidence of generational patterns. For instance, doctors routinely take family histories because many diseases are known to run in families. As with prayer or anything else God does, we cannot exactly describe how He works or prove spiritual realities against all doubt. Nevertheless, consider the following story as further uncanny evidence for the truth of both generational sin and blessing.[39]

A study was done in the eighteenth century of the lives of two men.[1] One of them, Max Jukes, lived in New York in the late 1700s. He did not seem to believe in Christ or pursue a Christian manner of life. He had 709 known descendants though 1200 were estimated to exist. These included 280 pauperized adults and 140 criminals. There were 7 murderers, 128 prostitutes, 280 described as harlots and 60 who became thieves. Of the 20 who learned a trade, 10 learned it in a state prison. His family members cost the state $1,308,000 (a staggering sum in those days)—and they made few positive contributions to society.

> *The truth is that living for oneself alone is not sufficient motivation for anyone. It was never meant to be.*

Jonathan Edwards lived in the same state at the same time. He loved the Lord and saw that his children were in church every Sunday. He served the Lord to the best of his ability. Of his 1394 descendants there were "practically no lawbreakers": by actual count, more than 100 lawyers, 30 judges, 13 college presidents, over 100 professors, 60 authors or editors with 135 books of merit, 60 doctors, over 100 ministers and missionaries, 75 military officers, 80 elected to public office, including several congressmen, 3 senators and one vice president of the United States (Aaron Burr). His family never seems to have cost the state one cent but contributed immeasurably to the common good. Take this as further proof that although you cannot change your ancestors, you can significantly impact the generations that follow you.

The Motivational Power of This Truth

This lesson on the consequences of generational sin is not meant to put anyone on a fear trip (about what sins may lie with their ancestors) or a guilt trip (about what they may be passing on to their children). Let it be a *reality* trip. The fact is

---

[39] Compiled. The survey on the Jukes family was done by Richard Dugdale in 1877; the one on Edward's family was done by A. E. Winship in 1900. There are exaggerated versions on the web, but these figures go back to the original reports.

that our lives powerfully impact other people—especially our natural or spiritual children—whether we want them to or not. It is important to know this because one of the enemy's favorite tactics is discouragement when we are down: "No one cares about you...your life doesn't matter to anyone." That's a lie! All of heaven cares about you and stands ready to pass on your every effort to be faithful as a benefit to someone else down the line. There is at least an echo of this reality in the psalmist's choice to make his stand for Truth be something that would powerfully affect *all* later generations. And do you know something? It has! God preserved that psalmist's witness and it continues to uplift us even to this day.

I will sing of the steadfast love of the Lord, forever; with my mouth I will make known your faithfulness to all generations. Psalm 89:1

The knowledge of this truth can be a powerful weapon in our arsenal against the enemy. Let it spur you on to heroic efforts of hanging in there when the going gets tough, because your life really matters! Desperate or discouraging moments may come when we are going to need motivations larger than ourselves to keep our feet moving in the right direction. The truth is that living for oneself alone is not sufficient motivation for anyone. It was never meant to be. If we are only seeking our own comfort, or success, or satisfaction, then those self-centered motivations will often fail us in the times of trial. We will need to learn to reach for better, stronger and higher motives if we want to find the inner strength to keep from quitting when the chips are down.

God supplies that strength whenever we realize that the lives of people we love hang in the balance. It matters to your children that you are trying to be faithful—even if they don't know it, even if it is killing you, even if it doesn't seem to be making any difference in your eyes. It even matters to the generations that haven't been born yet. And in addition to natural children, God also supplies those in our lives who are a spiritual heritage. Like Paul we are all raising the next generation (1 Thessalonians 2:11; 1 Timothy 5:1). Will it be for good or for ill? You decide!

"But as for me and my house, we will serve the Lord." Joshua 24:15

The Way to Freedom

Many generational patterns of sin are hard to recognize because it seems like that's just the way things are: "Doesn't everyone act that way?" Other patterns are hard to escape because from an early age we resented family members for sinning against us and those bitter judgments bound us to their behaviors.

1) Once you discern that a family pattern is not of God, be sure that you fully forgive the family members who are caught in it.

2) Then take full responsibility for agreeing with it and walking in it yourself: Repent, renounce and carry it captive to Christ until you can release it to Him for His help in removing it.

3) Turn to the Father and release gratitude to Him that He is working to overturn every curse with a greater good!

NOTES/JOURNAL

_____
_____
_____
_____
_____
_____
_____
_____
_____

EXERCISE

Fill out the family tree provided and see what spiritual problems there may be in your generations that you may need to deal with through prayer. Consider things like disease, committed or attempted suicide, murder or tragic death, untimely deaths, severe trauma, commission of an abortion, repeated miscarriages, divorce, abuse, mental illness, involvement in the occult, sexual sins, other habitual sins, addictions.

This is not to slam your ancestors! This is to understand what negative influences you may be dealing with so that you can pray representative repentance for your family line and break the power of the curse. It may also help you to see what you have been influenced by without your knowledge. Some sinful patterns are hard to recognize because we grew up with them all around us and they just seemed normal.

	Problem in the generation	Similar pattern in my life
Mother	_____	_____
	_____	_____
	_____	_____
M's father	_____	_____
M's mother	_____	_____
M's grandparents	_____	_____
	_____	_____

Father   _____   _____
                   _____   _____

F's father   _____   _____
F's mother   _____   _____
F's grandparents   _____   _____
                   _____   _____

DISCUSSION QUESTIONS

Have the group name examples of generational sin that have affected whole people groups and nations. Consider wars and their aftermath. Consider exploitation of land. Consider injustices between ethnic or religious groups and blood feuds. Are they aware that intercessors from around the world are being drawn to these "hot spots" to pray to break generational patterns and curses? Do they have any stories to share?

Now consider national or ethnic characteristics that get passed on. Not all of these are negative of course. Are any or all of these cultural stereotypes accurate in terms of the individuals that they have met? Do individuals they have met tend to "play into" their cultural stereotype or repent of it when it is negative?

Do some in the group have tales of stunning examples of generational patterns coming out of their own life and family experience? Were these patterns that needed to be broken? Did they get broken? How? If not, pray for the Lord to break those generational patterns.

MAIN POINTS

- Generational sin includes the sin of Adam (that separated us from God), the sins of our ancestors and the sins of our parents.
- Un-repented sin remains a fresh stain before the eyes of the Lord.
- It can be passed on by natural, environmental or spiritual means.
- The reality of choice is what causes the consequences of sin to be passed on to succeeding generations.
- God is not the one doing the punishing—it is the choices of the previous generations that are reaping sin's consequences down the line.
- Only repentance can remove sin and its consequences from the earth.
- Our lives powerfully impact others—for better or for worse. Knowing this can strengthen us in hard times.

DIGGING DEEPER

Sometimes we need to find freedom from inner vows and bitter judgments. Inner vows are misguided attempts to avoid repeating behaviors we reject or dislike in others or to avoid situations that we hate or fear (Such as: "I'll never speak in public again!" or "I'll never become a drunk like my father!"). They can be a naïve way of trying to break generational patterns or correct our behavior in our own strength.

Unfortunately, the bitter judgment binds us to the pattern and the vow inadvertently puts all the burden of transformation on Self instead of upon the Lord and therefore blocks the one who vowed from being able to receive the grace (God's help) needed to overcome the behavior. Inner vows, like spoken vows, are very binding as the scriptures reveal (Dt 23:21-23; Ps 56:12; Ecc 5:4-5). Fortunately, the Lord, as Father and Husband, has preserved a way to annul our rash vows prompted by the enemy's deceptions, if we go to Him seeking to be released (see Nu 30:1-8).

The only difficult part to breaking inner vows is recognizing where we may have made them. Ask the Lord for discernment and recollection. We need discernment because there are vows that we may have made as freewill offerings to Him—these we would be wise to keep. Recollection is needed because there may be other vows—vows made out of our hurt and anger—that the enemy used to bring us into agreement with his plans for our life. Such vows have often been hidden by him in our forgetfulness. These the Father readily disallows once we repent and renounce them.

Father, I repent of making bitter judgments against _____ and I renounce the inner vow(s) I made to _____. Forgive me and break their power off of me.

SWORD AND SHIELD

Scriptures that reveal the reality of generational sin and the Father's compassion.

> "But if they confess their iniquity and the iniquity of their fathers in their treachery that they committed against me, and also in walking contrary to me... if then their uncircumcised heart is humbled and they make amends for their iniquity, then I will remember my covenant." Leviticus 26:40-42

> For he does not afflict willingly, nor grieve the children of men.
> Lamentations 3:33 WEB

> "The soul who sins, he shall die: the son shall not bear the iniquity of the father, neither shall the father bear the iniquity of the son; the righteousness of the righteous shall be on him, and the wickedness of the wicked shall be on him."
> Ezekiel 18:20 WEB

PRAYER FOCUS

If we want to be free to receive the blessing that God intends to come our way through our generations then we will have to forgive and fully accept the parents (and ancestors) that He has given us. Remember that God did not choose them for the sake of what was wrong in their ways, but for the sake of what was right.

Not to forgive and accept our parents or family heritage is actually to reject *ourselves* for we truly are their offspring; it is also a definite—though often unrecognized—*rejection of God* who chose them for us in His love and wisdom. Just take it in faith that the Father always has good things up His sleeve (Jas 1:17), believe for the blessing He wants you to receive, and do the forgiving—no matter how much you have may have been wronged.

Your faithfulness endures to all generations. Psalms 119:90

Dear Heavenly Father, I choose by an act of my will to forgive my parents or family members for all the ways that they failed me or hurt me. I renounce all the sins in my generational line and I repent for having walked in them myself. Forgive me and break their power over me. I put the Blood of Jesus between me and any generational sin and I cancel all assignments of the enemy in Jesus' Name. I choose to fully accept myself as the child of the family line You have given me and look forward to how you have positioned me through them to serve Your purposes in my generation.

RENUNCIATIONS AND AFFIRMATIONS

Renounce any agreements with untruth; believe Jesus' *truth* as your new *way of life*.

Remember the family tree exercise? Now would be a good time to pray through the issues you may have discerned. Here is a prayer pattern you could follow—let the Holy Spirit tailor it to fit your situation. Be specific: Naming is important.

Father, I renounce ____ in the generations of my fathers and I repent of having walked in it myself. I repent of my own sin of _____. Forgive me and break its power over me and off my generations. Please put the Blood and the cross of Jesus between me and my generations going back to Adam and Eve. I cancel all curses and assignments of the enemy against me and my generations in the Name of Jesus.

PUTTING FEET TO YOUR PRAYERS: STRETCH YOURSELF!

Name the people in your life whose lives are impacted by you through the choices you are making and the way you are living. Let their direct connection to you motivate you!

Family
_____   _____   _____

Friends
_____   _____   _____

Coworkers
_____   _____   _____

Church members
_____   _____   _____

Others
_____   _____   _____

Now make an imaginative list of people you haven't even met whose lives might be impacted by you—for better or worse! (Examples: the hurting, lonely, needy or lost.)

_____   _____   _____
_____   _____   _____

Seek to find motivation in this for toughing it out when the going gets tough. Make a very short list of the very best motivations and keep it with you or beside your bed—so that when the alarm goes off, you will know why it is important for you to get up and be faithful. Be sure to include living for the Lord in some way that holds real meaning for you—He is our greatest motivation. For instance knowing Jesus better was at the top of St. Paul's list of motivations (Php 3:8).

My very best motivations (beyond myself) for sticking with the Lord and His ways:

1) _____
2) _____
3) _____
4) _____

CHAPTER 13

THE POWER OF BELIEVING

The Stronghold of Unbelief

Due to Adam's sin, we were all born into a condition of not knowing our God. Unbelief, therefore, is the primary obstacle that every person on earth needs to overcome, since the faith connection to God has to be restored in order for us to be saved by His grace (Ephesians 2:8). Surprisingly, unbelief continues to be the primary obstacle that believers need to overcome. But wait! Wouldn't it make more sense to say this of un-believers? Certainly, unbelief is a huge obstacle for them—they're still spiritually blind from birth—but that doesn't diminish its power and effectiveness against those of us whose eyes have been opened by faith. In fact it is often (if not always) the thing that we don't see which trips us up. All Christians will tell you that they believe in Jesus. But have we been "blinded" by the light? The all-important issue of believing doesn't end there. The demons also believe that the Father and Jesus exist, but *they take no joy or peace in believing it,* nor do they live yielded to Him in trust and obedience.

You believe that God is one; you do well. Even the demons believe—and shudder! James 2:19

Since we are saved by grace *through faith,* it is entirely by means of faith that we are meant to access all that grace so freely supplies. For instance, God's Word says that we who *believe* can be filled with all joy and peace "in believing" (Romans 15:13). If this is not what you are experiencing *all day long,* then perhaps there are a few things you still need to learn about recognizing and overcoming the stronghold of unbelief which may be quenching your faith.

The Active Power of New Life

Believing is the active power of the new life—the power that activates the life that God desires to give us by His grace. The critical issue is believing God's written Word with a *full* heart of faith. John says that he wrote his gospel in order for us to believe and to find life *by believing* (review Chapter 8).

But these are written so that you may believe that Jesus is the Christ, the Son of God, and that by believing you may have life in his name. John 20:31

What John means by life is more than mere existence and it is not limited to heaven only. John is writing about a quality of life that is filled with joy, peace and love—what the Bible calls eternal life, New Creation life, or abundant life. Peter says that *through believing* we can find joy in the midst of trials and even receive the "end" or goal of our faith, the "salvation" of our souls—that is, experience peace and confidence of heart and mind *in this life*.

In this you rejoice, though now for a little while, if necessary, you have been grieved by various trials... Though you do not now see him, you believe in him and rejoice with joy that is inexpressible and filled with glory, obtaining the outcome of your faith, the salvation of your souls. 1 Peter 1:6, 8-9

There is evidently a way to hold our faith, even in the midst of hard trials, so that we have inexpressible and glorious joy—deep, inward encouragement. This is not will power. You cannot fake this kind of joy or work it up by your own efforts. This joy is something anyone can experience by learning to fully believe God's truth in the midst of a trial. But not just any truth will do! The feeling of being tried in our faith comes directly from a lack of trust in God about the situation. Therefore, being united by faith to the *right* truth about God will automatically begin producing joy in you as your trust is restored (Romans 15:13. That is the power of the Holy Spirit. Such joy is the fruit of dealing with unbelief and learning to activate faith with the truth of God's Word (Hebrews 4:1-2). But know this: Very often your feelings, your understanding and your circumstances will seem to be shouting out that God's Word can't be true for you.

Unbelief is a stronghold that the enemy has built into every believer. We all have limits to what we are presently able to believe *about* God ("Does He love me *in this*?") and to what we are able to believe God *for* ("Will He help me *with this*?"). If this were not so we would already be filled with the joy that Peter says can be ours in the midst of our trials—just as Paul and Silas experienced in prison (Acts 16:25). If we are not there yet, it is vital that we begin to learn to recognize the ways in which our own unbelief is limiting our growth in the Lord and keeping us bound to patterns of the past. Unbelief is also a block to healing. Jesus could not do many healings in Nazareth because of the town's spiritual climate of unbelief (Mark 6:5-6). The lack of miraculous healings and supernatural events in the Western church may be a warning sign that a climate of unbelief surrounds us also.

THE SILENT KILLER

Unbelief is a silent killer stalking the Christian's land of promise. Whenever we lose bright hope for our future, confidence in God's love, deep peace or joy, we have been robbed by unbelief crushing life out of our faith.

Believing God at His Word

Biblical faith in God is fully believing God at His Word, even in the face of great adversity. Such faith believes that God is honest—true to His Word as a Person of great integrity (Psalms 56:4 and 119:81). Unbelief is the opposite of faith in God and His Word. Unbelief is the sin of hardness of heart that doesn't trust God's Person, purposes or promises. Unbelief is the stronghold that kept God's people out of the land promised to them as their inheritance.

> **Therefore, as the Holy Spirit says, "Today, if you hear his voice, do not harden your hearts as in the rebellion… As I swore in my wrath, 'They shall not enter my rest.'" Take care, brothers, lest there be in any of you an evil, unbelieving heart, leading you to fall away from the living God.** Hebrews 3:7-8, 11-12

Forty years of wandering in the wilderness happened to the children of Israel because they drew back in fear and unbelief from following God and Moses into the Promised Land, their place of "rest." Have you been wandering, seeking rest, yet finding none? Our promised place of rest is "the peace of God, which surpasses all understanding"—the peace that Jesus gives us in any situation whenever we surrender our fears and our obedience to Him and abide in Him (Philippians 4:7). *There is no peace without complete surrender.* There is no abiding in rest without being willing to trust and obey (John 15:1-17). Sometimes we have to labor to enter that rest (Hebrews 4:11). Always we have to keep watch lest the enemy "draw us away" from our new life of trust and obedience (James 1:16). Our promised land is a life of abundant joy and peace lived in close relationship with Jesus Christ in this life and the next. Although heaven is promised to all who believe, God's Kingdom on earth is promised to those who engage the battle of fighting to exercise their faith.

> **"From the days of John the Baptist until now the kingdom of heaven has suffered violence, and the violent take it by force."** Matthew 11:12

A convincing temptation to doubt God's Word precipitated the Fall into sin. So convincing is the enemy's deception, that at critical points in our growth we will find it much easier to believe the lies that the enemy has sown into our lives, than the truths from God's Word that the Holy Spirit is seeking to teach us. Forewarned is forearmed! Let us

> *Faith is believing God is honest—true to His Word. Unbelief is not believing God's Word is true.*

never forget that the Word of the Lord is the effective instrument by which everything that now exists was created. All of creation is a testimony to the truth and power of God's Word to create and to sustain life (Genesis 1:1-3). It is impossible that God could ever speak forth a Word that would not be true—His Word is truth (John 17:17). He cannot lie (Numbers 23:19). Yet, there is one whose word should never be trusted. From the beginning God's Word has been contested by Satan. He seeks to "father" us into believing his lies, seeing from his distorted perspective and walking in his false ways.

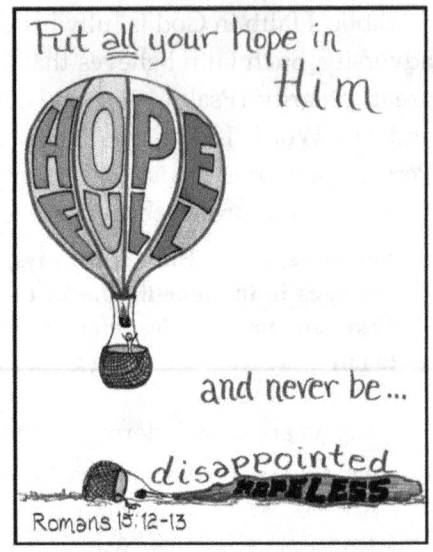

HOPE IN HIM

The joy that hope releases is what happens whenever our hearts are beholding by faith the unchanging reality of who our God is to us and who we are in Him. Hold fast to the One reality that never changers!

> "You are of your father the devil, and your will is to do your father's desires. He was a murderer from the beginning, and has nothing to do with the truth, because there is no truth in him. When he lies, he speaks out of his own character, for he is a liar and the father of lies." John 8:44

God seeks a people who will believe in His Word and serve Him in Spirit and truth (John 4:23). God's answer to the Fall was to cultivate a son of Adam who would believe God at His Word and therefore become the spiritual father to a nation of restored believers. In calling Abraham, God promised him great things which Abraham at first gladly believed (Genesis 15:1-6). Notice, however, that God did not make it easy for Abraham to go on believing the promises. The unexpectedly long delay between the promises and their fulfillment (with the birth of Isaac) severely tested Abraham's ability to believe God's Word. Just like Abraham, we too have been given magnificent, life-giving promises through God's Word. Some of these promises have to do with who He is to us; some have to do with who we are in Him; some have to do with what our life in God could become. Just as it was with Abraham, God's delays may make it hard to believe His promises. Sometimes they may seem impossible to believe at all. We may stagger in unbelief, but we must learn Abraham's way, who, "contrary to hope, in hope believed," if we are to reap the full life of faith offered to us and enter our Promised Land (Romans 4:18).

> By which he has granted to us his precious and very great promises, so that through them you may become partakers of the divine nature. 2 Peter 1:4

Unbelief Is Believing in Un-truth

There are two formidable challenges to everyone's faith: our own understanding and our feelings. We are not to lean on our understanding (Proverbs 3:5) or be led by our feelings (Romans 8:14). Trusting in God with our whole heart means the quality of our new life will depend upon our ability to find joy and peace *through our faith in God* even when our understanding can't understand and our feelings are kicking and screaming. That kind of believing in God is hard work at times, but this is the real work we are called to do.

> **Jesus answered them, "This is the work of God, that you believe in him whom he has sent." John 6:29**

Watch out for the deadly, deceptive "Ds": doubt, discouragement, despair and depression.

It was unbelief in the truth of God's Word that broke the world God created. Believing in untruth has been breaking hearts and breaking down lives ever since. Watch out for these deceptive, deadly "Ds": doubt, discouragement, despair and depression—they are all rooted in *active unbelief,* even if surrounded by *passive faith.* Jesus has come that we might know the truth. And by the truths He shows us and by the faith He gives us, we would be made free. However, for His truths to work for us, we often have to work very hard at believing them and become adept at casting down *all* unbelief. Even a tiny bit of unbelief can be sufficient to block the faith we are seeking to exercise from liberating our heart. However, fully believing the truth will *automatically* restore peace, joy, confidence in God and bright hope into our hearts.

> **So Jesus said to the Jews who had believed in him, "If you abide in my word, you are truly my disciples, and you will know the truth, and the truth will set you free." John 8:31-32**

Fortunately, we do not have to work at believing in God and His Word by will power and good intentions. No stronghold can be defeated in our own strength. God is gracious and willing to help us with our areas of unbelief. Be bold in confessing your distrust as the sin it is. Don't be afraid to admit to God how often unbelief may be ruling over you. He sees it clearly and loves you anyway! Unbelief in God's Word can block healing, keep us from receiving the blessings of God and prevent us from entering the Kingdom on earth, but it cannot separate us from His love (Romans 8:37-39).

Learn to let your every recognition of unbelief carry you in gratitude to your loving Father and then let His perfect love for you cast out your fears (1 John 4:18)—even where seeing your own unbelieving heart is concerned. Beware, therefore, of the way spiritual pride can blind you. The great difficulty is recognizing how unbelieving we may be at any given moment and then going to God with it (without fear or shame), rather than reacting in doubt, despair or denial. No one prayer can guarantee humility or ultimate victory, but the distraught father's prayer for his son's deliverance is a good beginning, "Lord, I believe; help [me overcome] my unbelief!" (Mark 9:23-24).

The Way to Freedom

The most difficult thing about getting free of unbelief is recognizing that it is working *on* you, since it feels so natural and seems like such a reasonable reaction given the circumstances. But we are called to the higher life of an active faith based on what is "unfelt" and unseen—the rock-solid promises of our God!

1) Be ready to pounce on any deflating or despairing thought, realizing that any loss of bright hope or confidence is not coming from your true self, but from a spirit of unbelief.

2) Take full responsibility for agreeing with it: Repent, renounce and carry it captive to Christ until you see something in Him that restores your trust and confidence in God.

3) Turn to the Father and release gratitude to Him that He loves and accepts you even when your faith is riddled with unbelief!

NOTES/JOURNAL

_____
_____
_____
_____
_____
_____
_____
_____
_____
_____

EXERCISE

Don't be a spiritual couch potato! Put Romans 8:28 to work for you.

We know that all things work together for good for those who love God, to those who are called according to his purpose. Romans 8:28 WEB

Consider a trauma of two years or more in the past (to have allowed time for grieving the pain). Then make a list of five ways in which God has been making it work for good in your life. Ask the Lord to open your eyes of faith. Go on! Give the Lord the benefit of the doubt—He says He is at work to bring good out of it.

The truth is that as long as we believe that God has allowed anything in our past to be working against our ultimate good, rather than for us, we will find it very hard to surrender to God in the present or trust Him for what He may allow in the future. Beat that weapon of the enemy into a plowshare (Mic 4:3)—let the pain of the past help you fight to become a full believer in His Word. Sow a believing faith over your past by taking the Step to Freedom of recognizing and repenting of unbelief (see Lesson 7).

Awful past experience:
_____

Five ways that awful past experience has actually been used by God to help me:
1) _____
2) _____
3) _____
4) _____
5) _____

DISCUSSION QUESTIONS

This is a group exercise in gaining eyes to see God's "hidden" work. Have someone in the group read 2 Corinthians 12:7-10—Paul's thorn in the flesh. Ask them to note why the thorn was given, what purposes it was serving and what Paul's response to it was. Now have them consider areas of weakness in their own lives—places where they are struggling and find themselves unable to gain the victory that they desire in their own strength. We tend to get "tunnel vision" in the struggle and lose sight of the grace that is all around us—and thereby lose the faith ability to live in that grace.

Ask one or two (who are willing) to share their area of weakness and struggle (briefly!). Do not allow anyone to try to fix that weakness by offering solutions. *Jesus didn't do that for Paul.* Jesus showed Paul how God's grace was working to sustain Paul by God's strengths (not Paul's). Follow His example. Have everyone look to see ways in which God might be working to cultivate spiritual growth through that experience. Then pray for everyone to learn to experience by faith the sufficiency of being held and helped by God's grace in the midst of struggle—and (only then) pray for the Lord's help to overcome or remove the problem areas.

MAIN POINTS

- Unbelief is a stronghold sown into the life of every believer.
- Believing is the active power of the life of faith—it is dynamic, not passive.
- Joy and peace come by the Spirit's power, when we believe truth is truth.
- The challenge is believing God's truth in the very situations that trouble us.
- Our feelings, understanding and circumstances do not declare truth to us.
- Biblical faith is believing God at His Word, betting your life He is right.

- Recognize unbelief as the *absence* of joy and peace. Confess it for what it is, repent and let God work to restore you to a living faith.

DIGGING DEEPER

Sometimes it helps to see the entrenchment of a stronghold—and unbelief is an unusually well hidden one—by the way other negative emotions gravitate around it. Remember, behind the negative emotions, the unseen tempters are at work to snare us. Let the Holy Spirit show you if you have entertained spirits related to unbelief.

1) Doubt that comes from a spirit of doubt is different from simply questioning or searching out a matter. This kind will "pounce" upon your feelings and throw you into a state of confusion—rendering you anxious and unable to resolve the question or situation that triggered it.

2) Intellectual pride esteems too highly one's own understanding and this can easily become an unwitting God blocker when up against His higher ways (Isa 55:8-9).

BRING THE HAMMER DOWN

The Magnificent Promise of Romans 8:28 assures us that God can and will bring a greater good out of anything the enemy intended for evil. Crush all doubt and self-pity, then feed on the sweet meat of redeemed life!

3) Religious spirits are very deceptive. Watch out for these. They will make you feel like you are full of faith, while stealing your joy and making you critical of others. You will be walking around with an invisible pulpit in front of you, or speaking like you wrote the Bible, making everyone run for cover.

4) Arrogance wants to have an opinion on everything and have it accepted by everyone.

5) Rebellion will not submit to the truth that God's Word is declaring whenever it conflicts with deeply held personal beliefs or strongly felt emotions.

6) Control would prefer to hold on to past understandings (even if they are proven to be wrong or unfruitful), rather than let go and let God's Word lead the way. Such control is fear-based, not Spirit-led.

7) Fear of all kinds is rooted in unbelief. Otherwise we would all relax and trust God—just as we were doing before a spirit of fear ambushed us.

SWORD AND SHIELD

Consider the Israelites as they doubted God's Word and wandered for forty years in the wilderness. Know anyone who has been in a dry place lately? Next, compare their journey of faith with Abraham's. Whose footsteps will you follow?

> To whom did he swear that they wouldn't enter into his rest, but to those who were disobedient? We see that they were not able to enter in because of unbelief. Let us fear therefore, lest perhaps a promise being left of entering into his rest, anyone of you should seem to have come short of it. For indeed we have had good news preached to us, even as they also did, but the word they heard didn't profit them, because it wasn't mixed with faith by those who heard. For we who have believed do enter into that rest. Hebrews 3:18-4:3 WEB

> That is why it depends on faith, in order that the promise may rest on grace and be guaranteed to all his offspring—not only to the adherent of the law but also to the one who shares the faith of Abraham, who is the father of us all... In hope he believed against hope, that he should become the father of many nations, as he had been told... No distrust made him waver concerning the promise of God, but he grew strong in his faith as he gave glory to God, fully convinced that God was able to do what he had promised. That is why his faith was "counted to him as righteousness." Romans 4:16-22

PRAYER FOCUS

Pride blinds us. The great difficulty is recognizing *unbelief* as the underlying problem and then going to God with it. No one prayer can guarantee humility, but this prayer is a good beginning.

Father, it is not my faith that saves me—I am being saved by Your calling, Your love, Your truth, Jesus' Blood, and the Holy Spirit's power. Forgive me for taking credit for having faith in You (for You alone opened my eyes) and for turning a blind eye to what I have not been believing (that You have already shown me to be true). I cast down all past pride and fear. I want to become able to see this hidden stronghold when it is blocking me. Help me to believe what You believe. I do believe, but please help me recognize and overcome my unbelief!

RENUNCIATIONS AND AFFIRMATIONS

Renounce any agreements with untruth; believe Jesus' *truth* as your new *way* of *life*.

Fear and bitterness are faith blockers. If you have anger with God, self or others it may keep you from being able to believe what you need to believe to get free. Fear, especially fear of punishment, of rejection or of abandonment by God, inflames unbelief, since fear makes it hard to believe that the saving truths about God's mercy could be true for you. Let this prayer sink into you.

Father, forgive me for my unbelief in the rightness and necessity of forgiveness. It is the true coin of your realm! Help me fully and freely receive Your forgiveness for ALL my sins and pass Your mercy on to everyone that has ever hurt me or wronged me. I also confess that in my heart of hearts I keep believing the lie that I will be punished, rejected or abandoned due to my sins and failings. You have not given me a spirit of fear. The Blood of Jesus fully covers me. Your love fully covers me. I utterly renounce all unbelief and chose to believe in You and in Your perfect love for me. Thank you for loving me even as I struggle with unbelief!

PUTTING FEET TO YOUR PRAYERS: STRETCH YOURSELF!

Stages of progressive faith in truths that you are discerning may include being shown what truth is, searching to see if that truth is true, beginning to hope or believe that that truth just might be true, then coming to know deep down that that truth really is true, and finally trusting your very life to it. To help you process truth from your head into your heart take these steps:

1) Confess the truth (God's truth) that you believe, even if you don't feel like it is true. You may need to repent of and renounce any lie/untruth you had previously believed. This step may require some really determined effort on your part. Do it out loud if need be. Let your spirit know you mean business!

2) Simply know that the truth you now are coming to believe is true. Rest in knowing it. Jesus said you will *know* the truth and the truth will set you free— He didn't say you will *feel* the truth.

3) Be upheld: As you relax into just knowing truth you eventually begin to feel the Spirit's lifting power helping you believe with your whole heart. Feelings follow knowing. Knowing follows believing (see Psalm 46:10).

Walking in the light is when you exercise faith to believe for freedom even under attack and keep pressing forward. This week persevere in believing one truth that God has been showing you through this lesson that you really need to hold on to better:

The truth God is showing me: _____

The scripture(s) that will help me believe it: _____

CHAPTER 14

DISCERNING THE ENEMY

The Stronghold of Accusation

If the Lord were the only "outsider" dropping thoughts into us, our lives would be so much simpler, but there is another kingdom speaking to us, seeking to bring us into agreement with its ways of thinking and acting upon the earth. One of the strategies of that other kingdom is to make its thoughts seem like our own thoughts or God's thoughts—so that wrong thoughts will go unrecognized. Therefore, there is a great need on our part to learn to *discern* these hidden ways of the enemy and to *recognize* his voice (the fourth Kingdom key). This stronghold of accusation comes early in this sequence of lessons on strongholds because the voice of the Accuser came on the scene early in the Garden and early in our own lives as well. Be on guard! To the one being deceived the condemning thoughts never seem like accusations suggested by an invisible enemy: They always seem like truth-telling about God, self or others coming from our own reasoning process.

Paul said that the Early Church was no longer "ignorant of his devices" concerning the enemy and his ways (2 Corinthians 2:10-11). We need to make sure those same lights have been turned on for us! For instance, the "voice" of the Accuser has both a content of accusing words and an oppressive tone in the way those thoughts are formed—an insistent pressure to tear down or beat down, but never to build up. The Spirit of the Lord does not speak in that way. Let your spiritual senses, as well as your intellect, become fine-tuned to recognizing and resisting this voice. This can only come with time as we are enlightened and aided by the Holy Spirit, but don't worry, you are certain to have plenty of opportunities for practice! The writer of Hebrews says that our discernment grows as our "senses", not just our minds, are trained by "reason of use."

> But solid food is for those who are full grown, who by reason of use have their senses exercised to discern good and evil. Hebrews 5:14 WEB

Accusation Separates and Condemns

Many incurable sicknesses are rooted in the areas of separation that accusation produces between God, self and others. Such "stress fractures" break down the body's health over time just as their physical counterparts do material structures in the natural world. Accusation is also a block to healing because it invariably leads to bitterness which blocks both healing and answered prayer (Mark 11:25). Speaking in a condemning way against the Lord's anointed servants also brings severe consequences (1 Samuel 24:6). Scratch the surface and you will likely find that accusations lie behind all of the deeply implanted false

> *Satan and his kingdom deceive, tempt, destroy, and accuse.*

beliefs which cause mental illness, addictions and stress related diseases. Clearly, this is a major realm of the enemy's operations.

Satan and his kingdom deceive, tempt, destroy *and accuse*. Every time the enemy seeks to tempt us into agreement with his ways by deceptive thoughts, he is also seeking to divide us from our sources of life and strength, and by so doing, destroy us. Accusation is dangerous precisely because it is so divisive—it is the enemy coming between us and God. Accusations isolate us by separating us from others and by drawing us away from the peace of Christ (James 1:14). The fruit of accusation can include doubt, confusion, turmoil, fear, suspicion, jealousy, bitter judgment, and a whole lot more. The Accuser divides by using *truth with a twist* in ways that are hard to recognize and seem very convincing. He works to separate us:

1) From God, His Word or His Person (Genesis 3:1-5; Job 1:9)

2) From our true self, as God see us (1 Corinthians 4:3-4)

3) From others, as God sees them (Genesis 3:11-13; Job 2:4; Zechariah 3:3; Luke 9:56)

Accusation and condemnation are the exact opposite of what God is doing through Christ. Paul says that God neither accuses,

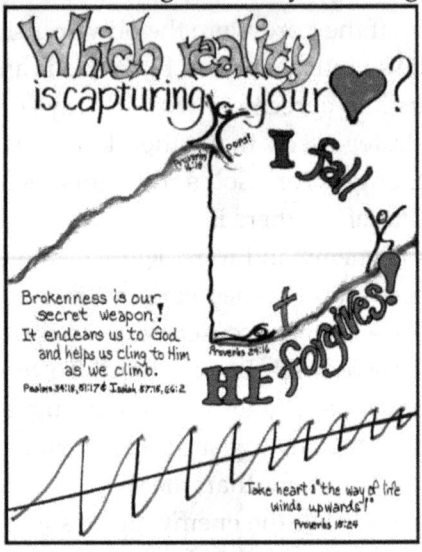

WHICH REALITY?

The Accuser wants us to focus on what is wrong, rather than what is gloriously right. Are your unwanted failings capturing your heart with greater love of God for His mercy, or sinking you into greater despair of self?

nor condemns us (Romans 8:32-35). His desire is for the one in sin to be gently restored (Galatians 6:1-2). Until death comes, there is always hope for restoration to God and separation from sins through repentance, grace and faith. We are meant to keep Jesus' hard won victory and heaven's hope-filled perspective in our hearts *towards everyone.* So let's settle this once and for all: Accusation and condemnation come from the enemy—not God. Satan measures out his criticisms and charges with just enough apparent truth to hook us—but he always twists our thoughts away from God's perspective of love and mercy. His activity is described as unrelenting and unceasing (Revelation 12:7-11). "Radio Satan" is always "on the air." We have to learn to detect it and change channels.

From Genesis to Revelation

Let's review how accusation got its start. Satan, whose name means "Adversary," began with accusations against God's Word in the Garden (Genesis

3:1-5). Adam and Eve were drawn away from trusting God and fell into separation from God and spiritual death along with it. Although they did not realize it, they now had a new father—the devil—whose nature entered them and whose own image and ways were beginning to distort the Image of God they carried (John 8:31-38). When the Lord returned to find them, He said something astonishing to Adam: "Who told you that you were naked?" (Genesis 3:11).[40] God's question to Adam was meant to open his eyes to see that the Accuser was still speaking to him, no longer through the snake, but through Adam's own thought processes. Under the pressure of inward condemnation, Adam accused Eve of being the reason he chose to sin. His words also carried a veiled accusation against God for giving Eve to him in the first place. Then Eve joined in by accusing the serpent, thus trying to shift blame from herself to the source of her temptation. By one fell swoop the Accuser succeeded in subverting humanity to do his work of accusation for him and they were *completely unaware of his instigations* (Genesis 3:9-13)!

Now zoom forward to see how accusation went global. Having established his kingdom through such slight devices of accusation in the Garden, the enemy handily expanded his operations to cover the earth. John on Patmos was given a vision of the Accuser as no longer being a lowly serpent, but a mighty dragon.

And the great dragon was thrown down, that ancient serpent, who is called the devil and Satan, the deceiver of the whole world—he was thrown down to the earth, and his angels were thrown down with him. And I heard a loud voice in heaven, saying, "Now the salvation and the power and the kingdom of our God and the authority of his Christ have come, for the accuser of our brothers has been thrown down, who accuses them day and night before our God.
Revelation 12:9-10

Notice that salvation, strength, Kingdom and power come when this formidable enemy is cast down. The choice is before us: Will we serve the Accuser or will we make a quality decision to cast down all accusations that try to rise up within us against God, self or others? Let the voice from the Garden become silenced. Turn off "radio Satan" and live in the Kingdom!

Recognize Accusing Thoughts

Accusation is a counterfeit of the true knowledge of God. It is a wrong use of genuine discernment. The Holy Spirit may indeed allow us to see sin in another person or one's self, but a spirit of accusation will seek to turn it into bitter judgments that bind the person to their sin and separate us from them. Learn to recognize the voice of the Accuser—the way self-condemnation speaks *to you* or the way offended self-righteousness seeks to speak *through you* to others. We are

---

[40] Teaching and insights stemming from "Who told you?" and accusation as a block to healing from Be In Health® teaching and materials, Dr. Henry W. Wright, Thomaston, Georgia, seminar notes, October 2000.

indeed called to discern good and evil (Hebrews 5:14), but one of the greatest evils is to accuse or judge another (Matthew 7:1-5). Seek to be aware of where your thoughts are coming from—always check the source. Godly thoughts come from God's Word, other people (speaking by the Spirit), the Holy Spirit and our renewed mind. Accusing thoughts come from the world, other people (speaking by the enemy), an accusing spirit or our un-renewed mind. Learn to discern.

We are meant to cast down "every high thing that exalts itself" against God (2 Corinthians 10:3-6). Accusation is a "high thing" because it puts us above others in judgment of them and because it rises up within us against God's clear command not to. Learn to discern and cast down all accusations against God (anger, unbelief, discouragement); against others (judgments, un-forgiveness, slander); against self (condemnation, shame, regret). Instead, join with Jesus in continual intercession (Hebrews 7:25). There is always room for one more on the Mercy Seat!

Discerning between conviction versus condemnation is also key to living a life of grace, since so much that we most immediately experience of sin is its indwelling presence with us. We don't want to live in denial, blind to our own faults nor do we want to live burdened by guilt and feelings of self-reproach, blind to the grace of God. How can you tell the difference between conviction by the Holy Spirit versus condemnation by the enemy? It takes a lot of trial and error to gain accurate discernment, but here are a few guidelines. Conviction shows us the problem and offers a way out; condemnation makes us the problem and seals the exits. Conviction is a gentle voice embracing us with quiet acceptance; condemnation breathes out threats of judgment and displeasure. Under conviction we may feel sorrow for those we have hurt; under condemnation we feel sorry for ourselves. Conviction leads to life; condemnation leads to death. The difference is dramatic, though often difficult to discern under the pressure of events. Don't give up and you'll get it!

> **I now rejoice, not that you were made sorry, but that you were made sorry to repentance. For you were made sorry in a godly way... For godly sorrow works repentance to salvation, which brings no regret. But the sorrow of the world works death.** 2 Corinthians 7:9-11 WEB

Conviction by the Spirit	**Condemnation by the enemy**
Always points to true guilt	Often heaps on false guilt
Knows grace exists	No grace exists
Contrition (sorry you sinned)	Feeling worthless, inept (sorry sinner)
Targets your sin (that was wrong)	Attacks your person (you are bad)
Explains, reasons, corrects	Accuses, condemns, reprimands
Illuminates your path	Darkens your understanding
Specific wrong is clarified	Fog of general wrongness sinks in
Brings repentance	Spreads confusion
Feels light and right	Feels heavy and wrong

May not be ready to repent, but you agree with truth.	May be willing to confess to anything, but you still can't get free.

Let's look at it this way: Repenting of true sins brings restoration and freedom from true guilt. Confess the sin (this requires faith in Christ's shed Blood) *and receive God's mercy*. On the other hand, resisting the accusations of the enemy produces freedom from condemnation. Confess the truth (this requires courage to live what you believe about your right standing with God through Christ) *and resist the devil*. See the difference? That's discernment!

If you are still in need of freedom, reconnect quickly and powerfully by taking the Hebrews 4:16 "elevator" to the top: Go boldly to the throne of grace, get the mercy you need to reestablish your heart, get grace to help you believe in the mercy, then stand against the Accuser.

Let us then with confidence draw near to the throne of grace, that we may receive mercy and find grace to help in time of need.
Hebrews 4:16

The Way to Freedom

Little progress can be made until godly discernment comes so prayer may be needed to recognize judgmental thoughts as being wrong! Also, because we reap what we sow, our accusations aimed against others will hinder our progress at becoming free from the pain of their accusations against us and of our own inward self-condemning thoughts. We must become committed to mercy—all the way around (Matthew 5:7, 7:2; Luke 6:38).

1) As you recognize your own accusing or condemning thoughts against others: Repent, renounce and carry those thoughts captive to Christ, interceding for them instead.

2) As you recognize the pain of accusations against you by others: Forgive them, carrying those thoughts and feelings captive to Christ until your focus on *His* love for you is restored.

3) As soon as you sense condemnation or feelings of unworthiness weighing you down: Go boldly to the throne of grace to receive the Father's mercy, then rebuke the Accuser!

NOTES/JOURNAL

_____
_____
_____
_____

_____
_____
_____
_____
_____
_____

EXERCISE

If someone offered you a poisonous snake, what would you do? Take it to your bosom and let it bite you? Or would you say, "No thank you, I don't shake hands with snakes!" Whenever we have listened to accusing words condemning us and putting us down, we had a choice: to let the words fall off of us, or to take them to heart and let them bite into us, infecting us with their poison.

God is not asking any of us to take into our own hearts the accusing words of others. His word to us is "I do not accuse you!" (see the Sword and Shield section). Make a list of things that people have said to you (that hurt you) in one column and the reasons in God why you do not have to believe those words or feel what the enemy wants you to feel.

Hurtful accusations I have received	Reasons in God for not holding on to them
_____	_____
_____	_____
_____	_____

DISCUSSION QUESTIONS

Have someone in the class read Revelation 12:7-11. Then ask the following three questions for them to explore in the text using their Biblical knowledge:

1) How does a serpent become a dragon? We are shown two prophetic images: one from the dawn of time and the other from the end of this age. In the first we are reminded of Satan as a serpent (deceiving only two people); in the second he is shown as a mighty dragon, which has deceived the whole world. How did that serpent become a dragon? Hint: How do babies grow? How do we keep expanding? Also see Isaiah 5:14 for an enduring image. The answers to questions 1 and 3 are at the end of the chapter.

2) What four great things will come to you, if you cast down the Accuser? Assuredly this is a prophetic picture of the whole earth's liberation from the Accuser. But is it not fair to say that if we make a quality decision to cast down the Accuser, these same four things will come to us? Have the group discuss a)

how it feels when they were filled with accusations (toward God, self or others)—were any of the four great things moving very strongly in them? What is it like for them when they are living "under the mercy," receiving and giving mercy? What does that feel like? How does life seem?

3) How is Satan accusing the brethren "day and night" to God? Is Satan actually in heaven haranguing God 24/7? In Job we are shown that Satan spends at least part of his time "going to and fro" across the earth (Job 1:7). Yet, Paul says that we wrestle against spiritual hosts of wickedness *in the heavenly places* (Eph 6:12). That certainly mean *over* the earth, but surely not within the highest heaven where God dwells (2Co 12:2)! Yet, Satan evidently enters heaven to demand to sift people at times (Job, Peter) or to accuse them even in God's presence (Zec 3:1-4). However, this is not the same thing as living continually in the very realm he detests! So how is he accusing the brethren *continually* right before God? Really dig into this before looking up the answer.

4) Now have the group pray in repentance for any and all agreements with the Accuser and purpose before God to cast him down the next time he starts twisting the truth or tries to use their tongues as a launching pad.

MAIN POINTS

- Accusing spirits seek to separate us from God, self and others by twisting the truth away from God's perspective of mercy.
- All accusing and condemning thoughts come from the enemy—not God.
- Listening to the enemy's accusations—as if it were their own voice—became "second nature" to Adam and Eve.
- We need to "check the source" to see who we've been listening to.
- Accusing spirits seek to turn our discernment of sin into judgment and condemnation for the person caught in sin.
- True discernment joins Jesus at the Mercy Seat interceding for sinners.
- As the Accuser is cast down Kingdom power and authority come to you.

DIGGING DEEPER

The gospel gives us a clear choice: We can live under law or under grace. Too small an idea of the Blood, the love and the mercy that cover us creates an often unrecognized inner compulsion to be covered by our own efforts to be righteous.

Living under Law	**Living under Grace**
Rising easily into judgment of others	Loving to intercede for them
Sinking easily in condemnation of self	Spring boarding from sin into Presence
Shocked that others don't get it	Surprised when they do

Covering up mistakes and errors	Honestly admitting them
Holding on to memory of failure	Untroubled by failure or shame
Trying so hard to be right (all the time)	Content just to trust and obey
Hard on self	A friend to self
Expecting too much of others	Delighted by any goodness

Surprisingly, the enemy seeks to train us to live *by the laws of God*, as well as the "law of sin." How can this be? Clearly, if we become subject to the law of sin we will be compromised by unrighteousness, but if we put our focus upon the laws of God, we risk becoming compromised by either self-righteousness or self-condemnation. Either way he has us sidelined. Very sneaky! God wants to train us to live by the new law of the Spirit—which only "works" by keeping our focus on Jesus (see Chapter 8).

There are only three conditions of righteousness:

1) Un-righteousness: not trying to live by God's laws. This is the typical snare of non-religious people.

2) Self-righteousness: trying to live by God's laws, but in one's own strength. This is the typical snare of religious people. The best way to recognize this pattern in oneself is by:

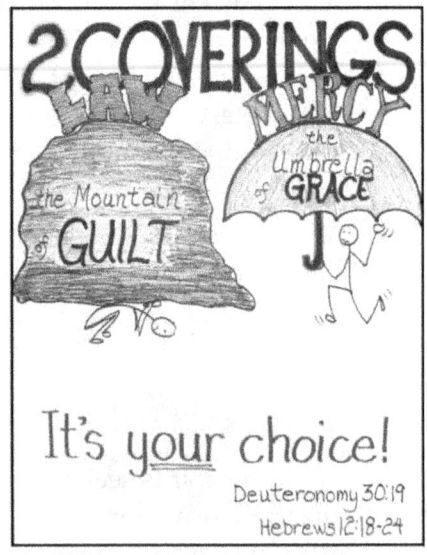

CHOOSE YOUR COVERING

Every day God offers us the all-inclusive covering of His mighty grace forged by the Blood. Or we can try to keep the Law perfectly, get everything right in our own strength and live frustrated with ourselves when we don't.

    a) **Stress levels**: Worry, tension and anxiety always indicate a lack of confidence in the grace of God as our covering; we are trying to live by "trusting" Self instead!

    b) **Judgment levels**: Because we are working so hard at being right, we naturally fault those who aren't matching up with our "progress."

3) God's righteousness is very different. It fulfills God's laws by living in the Spirit—the new way of life offered to us by the gospel of grace (Gal 2:20). God's righteousness works in us and through us as we surrender, trust and follow (allowing His Spirit to lift us and lead us). His righteousness reaches out to cover, love and pray for anyone caught in a sin or offense. Self-righteousness, on the other hand, always takes offense and judges.

Little children live with God's kind of righteousness. They need a "tutor" to lead them back to the law whenever they depart from being in the Spirit, but they do not need anyone to teach them how to live as little children. They get that from the Lord as they live with trust, love and openness in their hearts—the way it is meant to become for us (Mt 18:3). The new life "operates" on:

100% grace: God covers us and surrounds us with everything we need.
100% surrender: We trust whole-heartedly to the grace given us.
100% guidance: We submit entirely to His leadership and flow in His Spirit.

SWORD AND SHIELD

The Accuser loves to twist the Word. Learn to straighten out your own thinking in these all important matters and take your stand against accusation by these Words of Truth. (See also Isa 50:7-9; Ac 13:38-39; Ro 4:5-8; 5:1-10; 5:18-19; Eph 1:6.)

There is therefore now no condemnation for those who are in Christ Jesus.
Romans 8:1

Who shall bring any charge against God's elect? It is God who justifies. Who is to condemn? Christ Jesus is the one who died—more than that, who was raised—who is at the right hand of God, who indeed is interceding for us. Romans 8:33-34

PRAYER FOCUS

Since we reap what we sow (Gal 6:7), we need to first repent of and resolutely cast off any pattern of accusing others. Then we will be in a position to receive grace for living under greater freedom from accusations and condemning thoughts within ourselves (Mt 5:7, 7:2; Lk 6:38).

Father, help me truly repent of all the accusing thoughts I have cherished towards others and all of the hurtful accusing words I have spoken. Surely, as much as I have felt the pain of accusation by others, I know that others have been hurt by me. Forgive me and break the power of what I have done in agreement with the Accuser and help all those get free of any pain I have caused. Grant that I would become an intercessor for, not an accuser of others. Enable me to become a grace giver!

RENUNCIATIONS AND AFFIRMATIONS

Renounce any agreements with untruth; believe Jesus' *truth* as your new *way of life*.[41]

Father, I renounce _____ (Bitter judgments, Bitterness...) in the generations of my fathers and I repent of having walked in it myself. I repent of my own sin of

---

[41] Renunciation list modified from Be In Health® teaching and materials, Dr. Henry W. Wright, Thomaston, Georgia, seminar notes, October 2000.

_____ (Holding someone to his or...). *Forgive me and break its power over me and off my generations.*

Bitter judgments
Holding someone to his or her past
Holding a record of wrongs
Refusing to accept a person who changed
Refusing to believe a person *may* change
Inner vows never to be like someone

Bitterness (coming out of accusation)
Being easily hurt and offended
Making judgmental and cutting remarks
Having a critical spirit, rejecting others
Indifferent to others, hardness, apathy
Negative view of people in general

Self-seeking
Competition (I must win to be OK)
Envy and jealousy
Comparison of myself to others
Comparison of others to myself
Perfectionism, driven to achieve

Suspicion
Mistrust and fear
Prejudice and bigotry
Paranoia: worried what others say
Quick to believe the worst of a person

Division
Focusing on other's weaknesses
Spreading strife and misunderstandings
Gossip and listening to gossip

Self-condemnation (hidden pride)
Self-accusation, self-blame, self-shame
Feelings of unworthiness and insecurity
Embarrassment, self-consciousness

Blame-shifting
Accusing others but excusing myself
Blaming another for my problem
Denying responsibility for my own sin

PUTTING FEET TO YOUR PRAYERS: STRETCH YOURSELF!

What would it be like to go through the day with positive thoughts filling your mind? Well, here is a practical way to begin: Just consider how much of the day is spent thinking about people we know. Let's begin there! Make a list of the people you think about the most. Now write beside their names a list of their positive qualities. Begin rehearsing these when the thought of them comes to mind—and then thank God for those qualities. Jesus says, bless and do not curse! This not only dismantles the work of the Accuser, it also builds love.

Persons I often think of	**Their positive qualities I want to dwell upon**
_____	_____
_____	_____
_____	_____

Answer to Discussion Question 1: The Accuser has grown to dragon size by feeding upon us! Just as hell is "enlarged" by lost souls, so too the enemy's reign on earth is extended by anything and everything that we do not surrender up to God in trust and/or obedience in thought, word, or deed (Isa 5:14). Answer to Discussion Question 3: Is it not through those who are seated with Christ in heavenly places who perpetually have the ear of the Father and are being listened to by Him day and night (Eph 2:6)?

CHAPTER 15

FREEDOM THROUGH FORGIVING

The Stronghold of Bitterness

In the previous chapter we exposed the "hidden" work of the enemy to divide us from God, others and even from ourselves—by accusations that turn us from God's way of mercy-giving love. Accusations seek to create division and separation over issues of hurt and offense and then hold it all in place by means of un-forgiveness. So what is God's answer? *Forgive!* How much, how often, how thoroughly? As much as needed, as often as needed, as thoroughly as needed—to fully release your heart. The truth is a childlike heart of joy is waiting for all of us on the other side of fully forgiving the very ones who the enemy used to rob us of our joy. God really wants to turn the tables on the enemy, but He needs us to work with Him, not against Him. *Un-forgiveness in all of its forms is an agreement with Satan, not God.* It not only hardens our hearts (separating us from peace and joy), but it also damages our bodies (through the stress response). These strongholds have to be torn down if we ever want to live a grace-filled life and become champion grace givers like our glorious Lord!

Bitterness Is Not Your Friend

Bitterness holds in place a host of deadly emotions. Many people have testified that being bitter is like drinking poison and hoping the other person will die. Thanks to modern medical science we now know that grudges really do terrible things to our bodies, as well as to our relationships. Choose to get well rather than to get even. The writer of Hebrews warns that if we have a root of bitterness it will trouble us and defile many others through their contact with us.

> **Strive for peace with everyone, and for the holiness without which no one will see the Lord. See to it that no one fails to obtain the grace of God; that no "root of bitterness" springs up and causes trouble, and by it many become defiled.**
> Hebrews 12:14-15

Bitterness is a very damaging stressor to the body, directly leading to illness. However, unforgiveness also keeps trauma from being healed and that adversely affects our health as well. Un-mended trauma of the past always increases the levels of anxiety and fear we carry which, like bitterness, are very harmful to health. The pain of an unforgiven offense is "warning" us that God and others can't be trusted, keeping us "on guard" and fear-filled. Bitterness is also a block to healing because God has written that He will not release the extra measures of mercy we need or answer prayer if we don't show mercy (Luke 6:37-38).

> **"Whenever you stand praying, forgive, if you have anything against anyone; so that your Father, who is in heaven, may also forgive you your transgressions. But if you do not forgive, neither will your Father in heaven forgive your transgressions."**
> Mark 11:25-26 WEB

Bitterness is not your friend. Learn to carry it captive before it carries you captive (2 Corinthians 10:3-6). The high thought of bitterness is saying to God, "My law of not forgiving is better than Your law of mercy." Fall completely out of agreement with its thoughts and feelings, before what begins as a seed of hurt or offense grows into a stronghold of nightmarish proportions. Bitterness never stays where you put it, rather it seeks to grow and spread. It wants to take over your life. There are at least seven stages of bitterness, an ascending order of descent into darkness: unforgiveness (not letting go of hurt), resentment ("re-feeling" old offenses; keeping a record of wrongs), retaliation (getting even by criticism, passive aggressive behavior), anger and wrath (sudden upsurge toward the other person or down upon oneself), hatred (detesting, despising, strong disliking, hardness, apathy), violence (wanting to see harm come to another), and murder (with the tongue, or in the heart, or by criminal act; wishing them dead).[42]

Resisting the Stronghold

There is massive power released when forgiveness is combined with actively believing God's promises of redemption. Forgiving others truly releases the pain and weight of wrong off of us, but we may still feel saddened by the loss we experienced. To help us recover a rightful sense of fullness, God has given magnificent promises of the restoration He intends. Notice, however, that the promise of all things being made to work for our good is restricted to "those who love God," which by Jesus' definition means those who obey Him (John 14:15). To fully reap the benefits of restoration we have to choose to obey God's command of *full forgiveness*. This is a great and gracious incentive for releasing the past into His Hands:

> **We know that all things work together for good for those who love God, to those who are called according to his purpose.** Romans 8:28 WEB

Recognize and resist the temptation to judgment. God separates us from our sins (see Chapter 5), but judgment *binds* our spirit with bitterness and *blinds* us to our own prideful and unloving hearts. The Holy Spirit gives discernment about sin so that we won't walk in the dark, not knowing good from evil or right from

---

[42] Teaching and insights concerning this sevenfold progression of bitterness and bitterness as a block to healing from Be In Health® teaching and materials, Dr. Henry W. Wright, Thomaston, Georgia, seminar notes, October 2000.

wrong. With proper discernment we can pray for people who are sinning and help them regain their freedom by speaking the truth in love. The enemy, however, desires to turn discernment into judgment. Such bitter judgments are the nature of Satan's kingdom, not God's.

Forgiveness is necessary for our own hearts. The truth is no one is ever trapped in their pain by the sins of others. We are entrapped by our own sin of bitter judgments. We actually imprison our own hearts. Forgiveness brings release! It is a major key to the Kingdom of God (see Chapter 3). We are to loose sinners from their sins and bind the enemy. Sadly, when believers bind sinners to their sins, we unwittingly loose the real enemy and advance his kingdom—first in us, then into the world around us as we spread the poison. Turn the key that sets captive hearts free!

What Forgiveness Is Not

Compare these six common misconceptions to your own beliefs.

1) It is *not* a feeling: Forgiveness is a choice, an act of the will, not a feeling. We cannot control our feelings, but we can control how we choose to respond despite our feelings.

2) It is *not* glossing over: Forgiveness does not pretend the offense was not as bad as it really was. It does not turn a blind eye to real faults. It sees sin as sin and then forgives the person.

3) It is *not* nursing the fond memory: Real forgiveness does not keep score, hold grudges, or build walls. It is necessary to watch our boundaries, but not to build walls on them!

4) It is *not* a reward: Christian forgiveness is not something earned by being sorry or by efforts to change. The less deserved it is, the more it is Christlike, mercy-based forgiveness.

5) It is *not* a divine pardon: Forgiveness is not letting the other person "off the hook"; it is taking them off our hook and putting them in God's hands for redemption. Trust Him!

6) It is *not* blindly trusting: Forgiveness creates no obligation to trust the offender. Jesus trusted Himself to no one, but He lived in forgiveness and love with everyone. He still does. Aren't you glad He forgives you, even though He can't trust you never to betray his love? Let's learn to do likewise.

So what exactly does forgiveness involve? Forgiveness means being open to loving and even liking the other person, accepting them just as they are—just as we would desire to be accepted and loved if we were them. It means releasing them, setting them free, letting them go, letting them be themselves and setting our own hearts free in the process. *Forgiveness is giving your pain and the injustice to God and trusting Him with it.* It will always liberate you!

Five Biblical Motivations to Forgive

Try these motivations for leverage, they really work.

1) Your own freedom: Unforgiveness brings torment by binding hurt, hardness and heaviness to our hearts (Matthew 18:34-35). It also generates fear and insecurity and it is a block to receiving answers to prayers, even prayers for healing.

2) They don't know what they are doing: Because Jesus said it, we know it's true. Let it work for you (Luke 23:34). Everyone who sins has been deceived by an invisible enemy.

3) Humble yourself: See Jesus dying on the cross for you and it is easier to release others (Matthew 18:33). See your own sin of bitterness for what it is and you will immediately be humbled.

4) Get compassion for them: God looks past the sin to see the wounds. Do likewise (2 Timothy 2:24-26). Everyone who sins came into the world as an infant just wanting to be loved. Something went wrong.

5) Let Jesus gain the inheritance He died to receive—forgiveness for all sinners: He wants *everyone* forgiven and in heaven.

The Way to Freedom

Usually it is not difficult to discern when we are holding hurt or a hardened heart against someone, only to release the "death grip" we may have on them for the hurt or offense. But avoidance of dealing with past pains and doing the hard work of forgiving is a very real threat to ever gaining our true freedom. Be determined! If you break a hard job down, it's easier to do. Really go to work with these ten steps and they will work for you. Bring the five motivations in and power up! Set your will to agree with God and let Him take your heart on a pilgrimage to new life.[ii] If at first you don't succeed, don't give up. The Lord loves to reward those who persevere. You really can do this—with His help.

1) Seek grace: Ask God to help you by the power of His Spirit to make a real commitment of your will to do His will. If you really want to obey Him, then He will empower you.

2) Acknowledge the pain: Sin hurts. God grieved for you and has grieved with you, but comfort alone will not heal you.

3) Ask God to forgive them: Really mean it. He already does, but you need to express it and set His mercy in motion.

4) Ask God to catch the thief and make him pay: Commit the real enemy (Satan's kingdom) to God for His justice.

5) Ask God to forgive you (for judging them): Believe that He has and be ready to share with them the grace you just received.

6) Choose to forgive them: Pray it and say it by an act of your will; put your heart in it: "By an act of my will, I choose to release you from all my bitter judgments…"

7) Choose to forgive yourself (for prolonging the pain): Accept it. Release the pain. Command the "tormentors" to go.

8) Choose to believe God's promise of redemption is for you (Romans 8:28): Rejoice in restoration and blessings to come.

9) Pray for them: Pray for them to receive all of the blessings you would like God to bestow on you.

> *Turn the key that sets captive hearts free: forgive all for all.*

10) Thank God by faith for His wisdom and goodness in what He allows: Re-surrender and resubmit to His leadership.

God is seeking a people after His own heart—a people willing to keep their hearts open and loving, no matter what the cost. Don't pass up this opportunity to become a grace giver. It begins as an act of the will. Feelings follow. Experience the peace and release of finally letting go. Say *Yes!* to life.

NOTES/JOURNAL

_____
_____
_____
_____
_____
_____
_____
_____
_____
_____

EXERCISE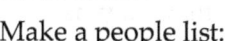
Make a people list:

1) Ask God to reveal any areas of bitterness still remaining in your life—people you have never forgiven as well as those you have tried to forgive but haven't *fully* forgiven. When you think of them does your heart tighten, get heavy, or feel numb? Add them to the list!

2) Forgive all from the heart, not as a feeling, but as an act of the will. Make a resolute decision to forgive them and let them go. Release them and let God deal with them. If you have truly forgiven them, the pain will no longer be there in your heart and you will no longer want justice or vengeance—even when you see them or think of them. You will be free!

3) Pray for them the good blessings that you would wish God would shed upon you. If you can't do this you haven't fully forgiven them. Doing this will help you to release true forgiveness.

Individuals to forgive

Mother/Father	Family members	Others in authority
Brother/sister	Teachers/coaches/bosses	Friends/enemies
Husband/wife/children	Pastors/spiritual leaders	Anyone for anything

People I need to forgive

_____   _____   _____
_____   _____   _____
_____   _____   _____

DISCUSSION QUESTIONS

Does anyone have personal knowledge of a disease that began because something "unforgivable" happened to them or someone they knew or of a disease that ended when forgiveness was released? Let psychological illness (soul dis-ease) count as a disease.

It helps to see the gravity of this error by the negative example that really bitter people give us as a warning. Seeing their wretchedness becomes part of our own motivation for doing the hard work of forgiving. Perhaps someone could share such a story of a person no one in the group could possibly know, but whose life was tragically wrecked by their un-forgiveness. Then pray extravagant grace down upon that person to help them get free.

Since we defeat the enemy by the word of our testimony (Rv 12:11), this is a very appropriate time for people to share stories of how they had to do some forgiving in a hard place and the way in which it set their own life free. But be watchful: If anyone dwells too long on what was done to them, they may need to do more forgiving. Invite them into a prayer to release the past more fully.

MAIN POINTS

- Un-forgiveness is both a root of illness and a primary block to healing.
- Jesus commands us to forgive absolutely everyone for any sin against us.
- Bitterness has seven levels—it can grow from a seed of unforgiveness into vengeance and murder.
- Forgiveness has at least five motivations—from selfish (enlightened self-interest) to selfless. Use them all!
- The "tormentors" come when we don't forgive fully from the heart.
- The key of forgiveness releases us as well as others—work the ten steps.

DIGGING DEEPER

A barren tree and a stump—an image of the forgiveness process.

1) By an act of your will choose to cut the tree down. The enemy will oppose this. Do it anyway.

2) With each return of old feelings, cut through the trunk. The enemy will accuse you of having failed at forgiving—he works both sides of the street! Keep on doing it anyway.

3) Eventually you will work through the leafy branches and feel full forgiveness—remembered pain is gone!

4) The stump that trips you up later is the question that "stumps" us: Why did God allow it? Release Him also. Trust His love and wisdom—even when you can't understand it. Believe His promises of restoration.

ROOT OF BITTERNESS

There is a process to doing the work of forgiving and it can be as hard as cutting down a tree, hauling off all the branches, then digging up the stump. It doesn't always happen just by saying the words. Set your will to do it!

Who to forgive? We need to spread it around evenly wherever it is needed.

1) Others: most frequently. A prayer that rarely gets answered: "God don't let anyone offend me today, I don't have time to deal with it." In fact even where learning to forgive others is concerned, practice makes perfect.

2) Self: not nearly as easy as you might think. Unless you have low expectations of yourself, a weak conscience, or a great hold on grace, it can be very hard to *fully* forgive yourself.

3) God: Don't underestimate the need for this. If God is all-powerful and all-loving (which He is), then the pain of what He allows can be a very real hurt or source of offense to us. The Father is absolutely innocent of any evil or wrong-doing, but our hearts may be holding hurt or un-forgiveness and need to release Him from any bitter judgments we may have been carrying.

4) Nature: rare, but real. Events, animals and objects that we may have associated with pain or trauma all may need to be released by forgiveness.

SWORD AND SHIELD

So many scriptures command forgiveness—the Lord must really want us to get this! He actually sees *not forgiving* as a form of *hating* (1Jn 2:9-11; 3:14-15; 4:20-21).

> "And forgive us our debts, as we also have forgiven our debtors. And lead us not into temptation, but deliver us from evil. For if you forgive others their trespasses, your heavenly Father will also forgive you, but if you do not forgive others their trespasses, neither will your Father forgive your trespasses." Matthew 6:12-15

> Then Peter came up and said to him, "Lord, how often will my brother sin against me, and I forgive him? As many as seven times?" Jesus said to him, "I do not say to you seven times, but seventy times seven." Matthew 18:21-22

> "Then his lord called him in, and said to him, 'You wicked servant! I forgave you all that debt, because you begged me. Shouldn't you also have had mercy on your fellow servant, even as I had mercy on you?' His lord was angry, and delivered him to the tormentors, until he should pay all that was due to him. So my heavenly Father will also do to you, if you don't each forgive your brother from your hearts for his misdeeds." Matthew 18:32-35 WEB

> "Judge not, and you will not be judged; condemn not, and you will not be condemned; forgive, and you will be forgiven; give, and it will be given to you. Good measure, pressed down, shaken together, running over, will be put into your lap. For with the measure you use it will be measured back to you." Luke 6:37-38

PRAYER FOCUS

Get your heart ready. The first stage in gaining victory is recognizing the spiritual problem and then allowing yourself no excuses, but being willing to take full responsibility for having it. The second stage is praying for God to help you with it—casting the burden on Him to do it in you and through you and for you. The third stage is coming into obedience to the part that the Lord shows you that you need to do. Let your prayer focus be on stage two: asking God for help and strength to obey Him now that you realize you will *have* to forgive.

Lord, make me willing to be made willing to obey you fully from the heart. Help me want to want what You want (forgiveness) and hate what You hate (un-forgiveness).

Review the five motivations and these affirmations against holding bitterness.
- I would rather be free (on the inside), than bitter.
- I will set free anyone I have to in order to get free.
- What was done to me is nothing compared to what bitterness has been doing to me all along.
- I am not bound by the past—only by my bitterness about it.
- Whatever my reasons are for being bitter, they are not as good as freedom is going to feel.
- I will turn the key of forgiveness and walk away.
- I will just give it to God and leave it all behind.
- I will walk away from the ruined place and let God be the one to restore it.
- If I have to start my whole life all over, just to walk away from bitterness, it will be worth it in order to live with an un-bitter heart.
- Why should I complain or be bitter about all of the past years of carrying the pain, because the truth is that I bound the pain of my hurt to myself though bitterness.

RENUNCIATIONS AND AFFIRMATIONS
Renounce any agreements with untruth; believe Jesus' *truth* as your new *way of life*.[43]

Father, I renounce ___ (Bitterness, Related spirits) in the generations of my fathers and I repent of having walked in it myself. I repent of my own sin of ___ (Unforgiveness, resentment...). Forgive me and break its power over me and off my generations. I choose to forgive _____ and release him/her from all my bitter judgments. I am giving _____ to You along with all the pain and injustice for You to redeem. I trust You with it all. Thank You for forgiving me for being so unforgiving!

The seven degrees of bitterness

1) Unforgiveness	4) Anger	7) Murder by tongue, heart desire
2) Resentment	5) Hatred	(wishing them dead)
3) Retaliation	6) Violence	or actual deed

---

[43] Renunciation list modified from Be In Health® teaching and materials, Dr. Henry W. Wright, Thomaston, Georgia, seminar notes, October 2000.

Related spirits

Self-pity	Accusation	Shame, blame	Envy/jealousy
Rebellion	Rejection	Cursing	Gossip, slander
Fear	Death	Suicide	Strife, hostility

PUTTING FEET TO YOUR PRAYERS: STRETCH YOURSELF!

Really go to work with these ten steps and they *will* work for you. Review what forgiveness *is* and *is not*, bring the five motivations in and power up! Set your will to agree with God and let His truth take your heart on a pilgrimage to new life (Ps 84:5). Turn the key that sets captive hearts free!

1) Seek grace: Ask God to help you by the power of His Spirit to make a real commitment of your will to do His will. If you really want to obey Him, then He will empower you.

2) Acknowledge the pain: Sin hurts. Sin is injustice. It is wrong. It grieves God and us.

3) Ask God to forgive them: really mean it. He already does, but you need to express it.

4) Ask God to "catch the thief": Commit the real enemy (Satan) to God's vengeance.

5) Ask God to forgive you (for judging them): Believe He has and gratefully receive it.

6) Choose to forgive them: Pray it and say it by an act of your will; put your heart in it.

7) Choose to forgive yourself (for prolonging the pain): Accept it. Release the pain.

8) Choose to believe God's promise of redemption is for you (Ro 8:28). Rejoice in it.

9) Pray for them—all of the blessings you would like God to bestow on you (Job 42:10).

10) Thank God by faith for His wisdom and goodness in all He allows and re-surrender entirely to His leadership over your life.

That's a lot of steps—and some are as tough as nails! Are you ready for a short cut? Here it is if you can do it: Picture yourself letting the unforgiveness go out of your heart into God's Hands with this prayer:

Father, I'm giving the hurt, the offense, the sin, the injustice and this person to You and trusting You with it all. I trust You with why You allowed it and with what You will do to bring about redemption and restoration.

Still having a hard time letting go? That probably means that your heart has become a "fist" refusing to open to grace: Use the five motivations to pry your "spiritual fingers" free. There is one for each finger! Walk your heart once again through the truth of the motivations (page 160), the descriptions (page 159) and the affirmations (page 165). As you take the steps, pray for God's grace to conquer all your resistance to giving grace. Don't give up and you will be surprised and delighted how God's grace comes to your rescue along the way!

CHAPTER 16

MENDING THE BROKEN HEART

The Stronghold of Trauma

Almost everyone knows what it is like to carry the wounds of unhealed traumas of the past. Like the physical cuts and bruises that we try to shield from further damage, these are memories that we don't want to touch on in conversation or can only talk about very carefully because so much pain still remains. Some things have happened, large or small, that hurt us and broke our trust with God, self or others. As long as there is pain in the memory, our heart is still broken by those incidents and the distrust and fears that assail us have reason to remain.[44] Unhealed trauma will always make our world seem unsafe to our emotions.

Ironically, the safest life to have is not one that can't be broken by painful events but one which is quickly restored by releasing full forgiveness to others and steadfastly trusting in God despite the pain God allows. Don't believe me? Then ask Jesus. It is the way that He lived; it is the Way He is asking us to follow (Matthew 10:24). Every harrowing passage through the cross of unwanted pain will always carry us into a resurrection of New Creation life— if we do not lose hope (see The Disciple's Cross in Postscripts). God never afflicts us with trauma— He doesn't author evil—but He will use it to grow a heart in us like that of Jesus. *Isn't that what we really want?* To become more like Him. In the end we will all be thanking God for the suffering that prepared us for a greater "weight of glory" (2 Corinthians 4:17)—why not learn how to enter into heaven's perspective now?

What Are Traumas?

For the purpose of this series, trauma is considered to be any event of the past from which we are still carrying pain, broken trust, and/or unresolved negative emotions. Consider these definitions of trauma taken from *Webster's College Dictionary*[45]

1) A body wound or shock produced by physical injury, as from violence or an accident.
2) Psychological shock or severe distress from experiencing a disastrous event outside the range of usual experience, as rape, military combat, or an airplane crash.
3) Any wrenching or distressing experience.

Traumas often become doors through which the enemy enters to plant distortions of the truth and to bind the heart with bitterness, fear and soul-killing

---

[44] For this excellent definition of a broken heart: Art Mathias, Wellsprings Ministries of Alaska, seminar notes, January 2006.
[45] Random House, *Webster's College Dictionary* (New York: McGraw-Hill, 1991).

messages. These wounded areas can grow into strongholds (Chapter 11)—areas of our flesh that are well-fortified against the life of the Spirit and are hard for us to overcome. Traumatic events of childhood, such as illness, accidents and abuse may also have been points of entry for evil spirits. Traumas engender a legacy of fears that follow us into adulthood: phobias, dreads, our characteristic set of semi-irrational dislikes and anxieties as well as bitter feelings of regret, resentment and shame. Lies the enemy has planted hound us throughout life, such as: "You're not wanted; you're no good; you'll never make it." Additionally, we tend to define ourselves by what has happened to us in the past, rather than by the new identity and the bright future that God says is ours forever.

We always have a choice how we will respond to each moment or event in life. The enemy takes unfair advantage of our innocence and ignorance to subvert the choices we make, but they are still *our* choices. Without sufficient knowledge of God and His ways we may have reacted in a wrong manner to what was done to us. This is "only natural" (allowing fallen nature to guide us) and all too common. Yet, such ungodly reactions to trauma are what bring the curse upon us. When trauma happened we may have taken on fear and un-forgiveness (our sins) and this binds the past to us and compounds the pain and spiritual darkness resulting from the trauma (our consequences). We may have reacted in ignorance of God's ways, but we are still responsible for decisions we made, attitudes we formed, any acting out we did, or any inner vows we may have made. Thankfully, there is real hope! We have a God who knows how to deliver us out of *all* our afflictions. His ways really work—as we learn to cooperate.

> *Many are the afflictions of the righteous, but the Lord delivers him out of them all.*
> Psalm 34:19

Many are the afflictions of the righteous, but the Lord delivers him out of them all.
Psalm 34:19

Preliminary Steps towards Healing

Jesus is a mansion builder in our soul, yet many live in the dungeon of what should be their mansion—locked in a dark room with terrible memories, devastated by trauma, bound by bitterness. It's rightly said by A.A. that we are as sick as our secrets—for darkness is the enemy's domain.[46] Tragically, the very things we hide from God and others are the things He wants to heal. If we truly want to be free, we will have to honestly and openly deal with past trauma so that the root of fear, hurt or bitterness can be removed, and make ourselves trusting

---

[46] A.A. *Alcoholics Anonymous* (New York: Alcoholics Anonymous World Services, Inc. 2001) 59. Quotation frequently cited in reference to Step 4: "Made a searching and fearless moral inventory of ourselves."

and vulnerable to those God would use as instruments of His healing. We will have to risk exposing our wounds to the Light of Christ in the presence of the people He appoints (discerning who to trust). But not all at once! Think of issues like tissues in a box and let the Lord pull them out one at a time. God wants to mend your broken heart as time goes on, but you have to give Him all of the pieces. Hold nothing back.

It was prophesied of the Messiah that He would mend broken hearts. At the start of His ministry Jesus read from this text of Isaiah in which that promise had been given (Luke 4:18-19). This ministry of Jesus has never ended. He still comes to heal the brokenhearted.

> **"The Spirit of the Lord God is upon me, because the Lord has anointed me to bring good news to the poor; he has sent me to bind up the brokenhearted, proclaim liberty to the captives, and the opening of the prison to those who are bound; to proclaim the year of the Lord's favor."** Isaiah 61:1-2

To pursue our freedom we will have to learn how to recognize the thoughts of trauma. Usually we are aware of the traumatic events of our past, but sometimes we can live in unconscious denial, having lost touch with the reality of how much we were hurt. Because we have been given free will, if we do not freely choose to bring our wounded places to the Lord, He will not be in a position to mend them. Hence, it is important that we keep ourselves sensitive to what the Holy Spirit may want to show us. Traumas may be carried by us in three main ways:

1) Painfully obvious: Often we are aware of the traumatic events of our past and still carry them with us like raw wounds that throb with pain whenever we think back upon them. We have carried them so long that it seems like we have been permanently damaged by them—but that is a lie of the enemy. God can and does heal even the deepest traumas.

2) Partially buried: Some traumas are so painful that we shove them down and spend a lot of mental energy keeping them submerged. Some of the worst traumas are forcefully forgotten until present events bring memories to the surface or trigger the powerful negative emotions they contain.

3) Hidden in plain sight: There are other events that we have glossed over so thoroughly that they no longer seem to bother us, but it spills out of us in conversation through stories we keep repeating (Matthew 12:34-35). Or we may feel fine until someone begins to pry and poke into these memories. The emotions that come out of us are the best indicators of what is still hidden in our hearts (Proverbs 23:7).

Five Ways God Heals Trauma

There are five main ways that God heals trauma. Note that these are not automatic. They all require a good deal of cooperation on our part, including knowledge (recognition of the trauma) and motivation (a persevering desire to see it mended). If it were otherwise, everyone would be free. We need to become determined to aggressively seek the freedom from the past and entry into His Kingdom that God wants to give us (Matthew 11:12). Carry your traumatic experiences into these five proven ways of mending:

1) Our tears: There is a blessing on those who carry their grief to God and give it to Him. Think of tears as liquid prayers. God listens to what our hearts are crying out to Him when we grieve. The One who loves us also deeply feels our every wound and has already carried our grief and sorrow to His chosen place of redemption at the cross (Isaiah 53:3-4). In the Sermon on the Mount Jesus said that there is actually a blessing on those who mourn—God promises to comfort us (Matthew 5:4). Comfort means that the pain is eased, even lifted.

Not all grieving, however, carries this blessing upon it. We can grieve in an ungodly way if we allow ourselves to mourn as those without hope (1 Thessalonians 4:13). It may not be easy at first, but all of us can learn to grieve over past losses and still maintain a heart of faith that knows God is listening to our cry and will use our tears and prayers to mend our hearts and restore bright hope to our future.

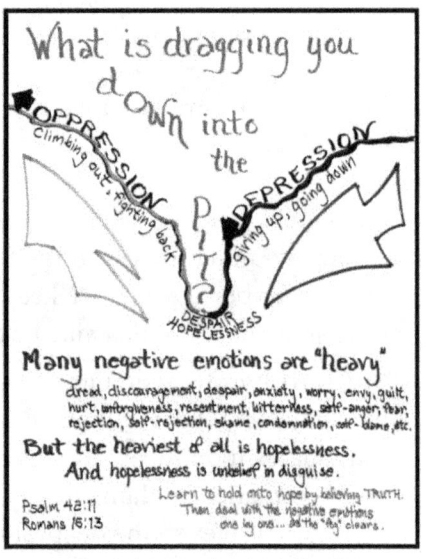

THE PIT OF DEPRESSION

For those under assault there is a difference between oppression and depression. Letting go of hope slides us deeper into the pit. By refusing to let go of hope we are learning how to overcome—and climbing out!

2) The prayers of others: Help is promised if we bring trauma to others for prayer. James tells us that we must confess to one another if we want to be healed. This is especially true of emotional wounds. Embarrassment, shame and blame come from the enemy who seeks to use them to keep us from exposing our wounds to the Light of Christ. This is why it is so important to be willing to be open, honest and vulnerable with close Christian friends we can entrust with our hearts. God wants to use the Body of Christ as an instrument of healing. This keeps us humbled and dependent upon one another and it also helps rebuild the trust in others which trauma damaged.

> **Therefore, confess your sins to one another and pray for one another, that you may be healed.** James 5:16

3) Forgiveness: Giving grace always clears the way for prayers to be answered and life to be restored. Forgiveness is absolutely necessary (Mark 11:25-27). It is even more important for our healing than learning how to release our tears to the Lord or confess to our friends because unforgiveness is the number one block to seeing our prayers answered (Chapter 15).

4) Believing truth: The promise of total restoration is a true godsend (Zechariah 9:12; Joel 2:25). A fully restored life would not be possible without this gift of love. It means that the Lord has purposed to overturn anything the enemy has done to rob us (whether it was the result of our own sin or someone else's) and bring about a greater good so that our joy in Him can know no bounds. Once you unite your faith to the truth of what He has promised you, the Holy Spirit ignites a believing heart inside you. Such *living* faith produces joy in you over what is now coming your way, rather than sorrow and regret over your losses. The challenge is to get it all out of your heart and fully place it in His Hands. Only then is He free to work on what you have given Him and can release to you His own joy over what you now entrust Him to accomplish (Chapter 13). Why keep holding on to what you cannot repair? Give it to Him in complete confidence that His Word is true and that He will fulfill it.

> **And we know that for those who love God all things work together for good, for those who are called according to his purpose.** Romans 8:28

5) Divine intervention: Dreams, visions, healing of memories, visitations and prophetic words are supernatural operations of the Holy Spirit which we can position ourselves to receive by worshipping and fellowshipping in environments where such manifestations are welcomed and encouraged.

Full healing of trauma is possible! No trauma has been fully healed if it still hurts to remember any part of it, or if patterns that began after the trauma happened are still continuing. Yet fully forgiving all who need to be forgiven and fully receiving forgiveness where we need it brings us to the place where there is no pain attached to any of the memories. Jesus heals the brokenhearted!

The Way to Freedom

Deeper wounds from trauma often call for a longer journey of cleansing and healing. Don't despair! There is much growth all along the way towards the final resolution and lifting of the pain. Like the pangs of childbirth, the pain of the recovery process will always appear "slight" once you come out on the other side, basking in the freshness and delight of new life.

1) First, become willing to face the pain, praying for faith that God really can take you through to the other side where healing abounds and for the strength to go the distance with Him.

2) On your own or with the help of a trusted spiritual friend, do the work of fully forgiving *from the heart* anyone who hurt you or sinned against you.

3) Take full responsibility for any acting out you did: Repent, renounce and carry those unloving ways captive to Christ, falling totally out of agreement with any false beliefs as well.

4) Turn to the Father and release gratitude to Him that He loves you and fully intends to overturn every evil with a greater good!

NOTES/JOURNAL

_____
_____
_____
_____
_____
_____
_____
_____
_____
_____

EXERCISE

The following list may help you recognize and remember traumatic events that have happened to you. Pray as you go over it to see if the Holy Spirit desires to bring anything to remembrance. Pray over what He reveals. Go back to the earliest memories and work up to the present—early memories often carry the root issues. Not all of these are for dealing with now, just for understanding them better in light of the teaching you have received. Make a list of the main events that have impacted you.[47]

Conception (unwanted)	Accidents and injuries	Broken dreams
Birth process	Illness and medical	Broken heart
Early fears or abuse	Rejection and bullying	Grief and loss
Separations, moves	Conflict with others	Witnessing violence
Parent's death, divorce	Abuse of authority	Experiencing violence

Traumas I have experienced

_____   _____   _____

_____   _____   _____

---

[47] Trauma list modified from Be In Health® teaching and materials, Dr. Henry W. Wright, Thomaston, Georgia, seminar notes, October 2000.

DISCUSSION QUESTIONS

We all know people who have never gotten over the terrible things that have happened to them—and it keeps ruining their lives in the present. The longer anyone carries pain and damage the harder it is for them to believe that they have a life they could want.

Nevertheless, our Invincible Savior says with supreme confidence that on that Great Day when we finally meet Him face to face, He will wipe every tear from our eyes (Isa 25:8, Rv 7:17; 21:4)—making everyone glad to have had the life they had, even after their chance to enjoy it down here is over! How will He do that? By the same five ways He uses down here with anyone who will let Him. To build hope and faith over this have people share on each of the five ways that they have seen God use for healing in their own life or that of someone they know.

1) **Tears**—even tears alone can do the mending. Whose tears has He already wiped away, leaving peace and gentle restoration in their wake?
2) **Full forgiveness.** If no one has this testimony, go back and redo Lesson 15!
3) **The prayers of others** that God has used to do His mending.
4) **Believing with a full heart of faith** the hope giving promises of God (Ro 8:28).
5) **Supernatural interventions**, especially revelations of His glory (2Co 4:16-18).

MAIN POINTS

- Traumatic events are often door points for the enemy to enter and oppress.
- Unhealed traumas generate ungodly beliefs, bitterness and fears.
- To be healed, we have to become willing for God to mend us on His terms.
- There are five main ways God heals trauma—time alone is not one of them.
- God uses tears, forgiveness, the counsel and prayers of others, active believing and the supernatural ministries of His Spirit.
- As long as there is still pain in the memory forgiveness is not yet complete.
- If a sense of loss or regret remains, believing His promise is incomplete.
- We can be fully mended from emotional trauma! Restoration is real!

DIGGING DEEPER

1) Ask God to show you one trauma from the Exercise list (page 172) that He would like to work with you on at this time. Put it on the form below. It will set a pattern for mending the other ones.

2) Fill in the names of anyone you may need to forgive (yourself and God included).

3) Ask God to show you where any doors may have been opened for the enemy to come in and oppress you through false messages (insecurity, rejection, shame) or ungodly reactions you may have had (promiscuity, un-forgiveness, rebellion). Write them down.

4) Finally, write down the truths from God's Word that you will need to *whole*-heartedly believe for your heart to be restored to wholeness.

5) Now go to work praying with the Holy Spirit's help. Enlist the help of a friend if needed.

Traumatic event _____
Person(s) to forgive _____
Ungodly reaction(s) to repent _____
False message(s) to renounce _____
Truth(s) to believe _____

SWORD AND SHIELD

The Lord completely understands the depth of our wound from trauma and doesn't want it to be just glossed over—He wants His peace restored into every hurting heart!

> **Let my prayer come before you; incline your ear to my cry! For my soul is full of troubles, and my life draws near to Sheol. I am counted among those who go down to the pit; I am a man who has no strength.** Psalm 88:2-4 [Be very honest with him in prayer about your pain.]

> **The sacrifices of God are a broken spirit; a broken and contrite heart, O God, you will not despise.** Psalm 51:17 [He is drawing near to you when you are hurting.]

> **But this is a people plundered and looted; they are all of them trapped in holes and hidden in prisons; they have become plunder with none to rescue, spoil with none to say, "Restore!"** Isaiah 42:22 [But God does!]

> **"I have seen his ways, but I will heal him; I will lead him and restore comfort to him and his mourners, creating the fruit of the lips. Peace, peace, to the far and to the near," says the Lord, "and I will heal him."** Isaiah 57:18-19

Meanwhile there is a brighter side to affliction and it is the good work that the Lord is doing to help us gain and grow through all of our unwanted pain (Jas 5:11).

> **Before I was afflicted I went astray, but now I keep your word.** Psalm 119:67

> **It is good for me that I was afflicted, that I might learn your statutes.** Psalm 119:71

> **So we do not lose heart. Though our outer nature is wasting away, our inner nature is being renewed day by day. For this slight momentary affliction is preparing for us an eternal weight of glory beyond all comparison, as we look not to the things that are**

seen but to the things that are unseen. For the things that are seen are transient, but the things that are unseen are eternal. 2 Corinthians 4:16-18

PRAYER FOCUS

Pray through the list you made in the Exercise section.

1) Forgive God, self and others using the ten steps in the previous lesson if needed. Remember the five motivations: They will help you get over the hurdle.

2) Repent for any acting out you did. God is full of grace and mercy, so don't hold anything back—and don't make excuses either! The fuller the confession (which includes taking full responsibility for your sins), the greater the victory.

RENUNCIATIONS AND AFFIRMATIONS

Renounce any agreements with untruth; believe Jesus' *truth* as your new *way* of *life*.

The enemy uses trauma to sow strongholds built upon lies. Remember: Some wounds need to be washed repeatedly to get infection out. Keep at it!

1) Renounce any false messages. Fall totally out of agreement with the enemy's perspective on your life that he tried to feed you. Yes, the world is unsafe, but your universe is incredibly secure: You have a God who loves you and who is always with you (it was a lie no One was there and no One cared) and He has promised to overturn every evil done to you and make it work for your ultimate good (it was a lie that you were "permanently damaged"). Choose to refuse to carry shame and blame over anything that you have put under the Blood. Break any inner vows you may have made.

2) Ask the Lord to forgive any unbelief you may have over the truths from His Word you need to believe (especially Romans 8:28) and confess the truth until you actually begin to believe it *from the heart*. Leave no room for self-pity— believe His promises! It is time to bring the hammer of His Word down on the trauma. (Review the "Hammer" illustration on page 144.)

Father, You have given me this promise of total redemption so it must be true; You have commanded me to forgive everyone so that must be what needs to happen for my life to be healed and restored. I choose by an act of my will to forgive the people in my past who have hurt me or wronged me, including myself. I release them from all my bitter judgments and give them to You for You to redeem. I also repent of my unbelief in Your Word and now choose by an act of my will to believe that the promise of Romans 8:28 is true for me—that greater good will come out of my past than all of the pain and loss the enemy sowed into it. I choose to believe in You!

PUTTING FEET TO YOUR PRAYERS: STRETCH YOURSELF!

It is hard to go forward carrying the past with us. One of the hardest things to let go of are broken dreams. Because the dream gave us hope and vision for our future, we can't imagine how our life can work out now that it is broken beyond our ability to repair it. But our Father is the giver of every good gift and He is never at a loss for new dreams to give us—dreams of a restored life, a fresh start. It could go like this:

Plan A. The dreams God gave led us out into life with hope-filled hearts.

Plan B. Somehow the dream became broken—by someone's sin or events beyond our control. This blocks the path forward. We become sodden with regrets and spend a lot of time trying to redeem things ourselves. But there is no going back because the dream can't be mended—certainly not by us. How can our life ever recover?

Plan C. Great news: The Lord is willing to meet you right where you are with a new path and new dreams to go with it (Jer 29:11). All you need to do is forgive anyone who needs to be forgiven (yourself included!), give the broken dream(s) back to the Lord, and then ask Him for the new dream(s), believing that you will receive them. What will the new life be like? You will have to trust Him and follow Him to

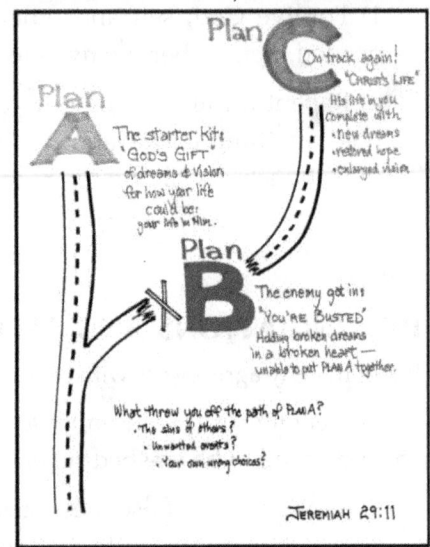

PLANS A, B AND C

Our Father is never at a loss for new dreams to give us—dreams of a restored life and a fresh start. Give Him whatever was broken, forgive all, surrender all, and stand ready to walk into a bright future following Jesus!

find out! Sweet dreams will come as you rest your heart on the promise of His power, love and planning ability always working for you (Pr 3:5-6; Ro 8:28-39).

CHAPTER 17

ACCEPTED IN THE BELOVED

The Stronghold of Rejection

Traumatic experiences can begin to sow feelings of rejection within us, especially if these were sins of verbal, physical or sexual abuse directed against us. In fact every sin against us is a form of rejection, even the well-meaning, conditional love of parents and teachers who put their approval of us on a performance basis. Even perfect love must at times reject behavior and attitudes that are not right, but never the person we are deep down, the person who is always loved by God. To be rejected (for who we are) by the looks, words or deeds of others is a tremendously painful, traumatic experience.

Many people—the shy, the perfectionists, the exhibitionists, the high achievers—organize their whole lives around trying to avoid rejection by others, while seeking to gain their approvals. The math on this is terrible: Have you noticed that ten approvals can be easily wiped out by one rejection? Sadly, the pain of *possible* rejection keeps millions hiding their true self from others (even from God), running from real intimacy, love and life into the safer, shallow waters of meaningless relationships and purposeless lives. Rejection is an ugly stronghold in the land promised to us that must be brought down!

The Antidote for Rejection

Begin wrapping your heart and your life around this astounding truth: Our Father will never reject or forsake us. From before the worlds were created He has loved us and desired us. *We are secure in Him.* This is the antidote for any rejection we feel. The Father's total and unalterable acceptance is the FACT upon which the joy of our new life is based: Because of His great love for us, He sent Jesus to the cross to atone for all of our sins and has even given His Spirit to help us believe in the grace He wants us to receive.

> **Blessed be the God and Father of our Lord Jesus Christ... According as he hath chosen us in him before the foundation of the world... Having predestinated us unto the adoption of children by Jesus Christ to himself... wherein he hath made us accepted in the beloved.** Ephesians 1:3-6 KJV

People, on the other hand, can and will reject and forsake us. Rejection by others is extremely painful to experience whenever we are secretly looking to other people to declare our worth to us. However, if our hearts had been established in God's love for us, as Jesus' was, we could have handled the pain of rejection every bit as well as He did. Fortunately, it is never too late to learn! Let the pain of rejection that you have experienced drive you to fastening your heart on what *God* says about you, not on what *people* say. God's view of you is the truth that will set you free. Learn to fall out of agreement with the compelling power of the enemy's beliefs about you. Learn to resist the lion's roar and the serpent's venom!

Considering what rejection is made of, it is no wonder that it is so painful to feel. So, what is rejection?[48] These are its major parts:

1) It plays an integral role in all mental and emotional illness, since it is very damaging to our sense of self.

2) It is a terrible lie. There may be sin in us worth rejecting, but we are not sin and are never meant to be rejected (Chapter 5).

3) It is a sin against us. God has commanded everyone to love and accept us as He does. He commands you to love and accept *all* of them, right? They are under the same command.

4) It is an evil spirit—one that delights to feel and express rejection in us and towards others.

5) It becomes *our own sin* of unbelief in God and idolatry of others, whenever we agree with it.

Did you get that last point? The sin of receiving rejection and agreeing with it is the real source of all the pain. The pain of being rejected hurts when it hits us, but holding on to it allows the torment to continue, like a "death-grip" on an exposed electric wire that was touched *while being improperly grounded*. We need to learn how to let go *and* get better grounding (Eph 3:16; Col 1:23)!

> *Rejection is a sin against us, but it becomes our sin when we agree with it.*

Rejection can also opens doors for the enemy to bring even more pain and problems upon us through the fear of man and through self-rejection (see Lesson 18). How little did we realize that in seeking people's approvals, we were subtly being trained by an unseen enemy in the ways of *idolatry*. By trying to get our worth affirmed through others, rather than through God, we began making other people's opinions into a god to us. Have we become "addicted" to approval by others? Thank God, this is not held against us (2 Corinthians 5:19) and we can begin to find freedom by recognizing sin as sin and turning from our idolatry of others' opinions to instead live by what God declares about us.

Turning from that false god will leave us sorely lacking a sense of worth unless we can stir our faith to truly trust in and rely upon the acceptance our Father is giving us every moment of the day. It is here that we may encounter another problem—our *unbelief* in God. In any moment we could have joy, confidence, and assurance of acceptance imparted to us by our loving Father, but He gives it through our faith in His Word and not very often as a feeling. Faith is like an electric tool—it does little good unless it is plugged into a "live" electrical current.

---

[48] Teaching and insights about these five components of rejection from Be In Health® teaching and materials, Dr. Henry W. Wright, Thomaston, Georgia, seminar notes, October 2000.

We need to plug what we believe about God into the current of a living faith. To do this we may first have to confess that the sin of unbelief has been capturing our heart and learn to walk by faith, not feeling.

The truth is that the pain of rejection, as terrible as it is, can actually help us if we learn to let it turn us away from the wrong direction we keep trying to go with our hearts. All along, our hearts were only meant to be "plugged in" to God. The pain of rejection is like touching a hot stove. Let's learn the lesson and turn away from what burns us and live by what gives life.

The Secret Snares of Rejection

There is a "secret knowledge" that snares us. Rejection plays into a painful inner sense that already makes us feel insecure—the knowledge of sin dwelling within us. Even as children we may have known that something was wrong on the inside, though we would likely not have been able to articulate it. The terrible truth about our fallenness is that for our sins and separation from God, we should all ultimately be rejected. Our sinfulness actually deserves hell—the ultimate rejection. Yet, this truth of who we are *apart from Christ* is meant to be swallowed up by the greater truth of the gospel: Jesus suffered rejection and abandonment by God on our behalf so that we would *never* have to experience it. The gospel liberates us from the torment of rejection—if we believe it with our whole heart.

Unchecked by a living faith, rejection creates unhealthy defense mechanisms. These failed coping strategies are ways of the fallen nature we may have used to defend ourselves against rejection when it happened to us, whether it was real or imagined. We may have been only half-aware or completely unaware of what we were doing—no doubt it seemed the best way to handle it at the time. Nevertheless, these ungodly patterns now imprison us behind walls that keep the lovely, New Creation side of ourselves from emerging. Did any of these strategies gain a strong hold on you?

1) <u>Withdrawal</u>: Retreating like a turtle into its shell in order to avoid rejection. <u>Remedy</u>: Believe God for His acceptance of you, keep your eyes on Him and stay in the game.

2) <u>Anger and hatred</u>: Rejecting others when hurt by rejection. <u>Remedy</u>: Forgive everyone from the heart and you won't be carrying around so much anger.

3) <u>False identity</u>: Searching for an identity other than who we are in Christ. <u>Remedy</u>: Trust and obey Jesus so that the Holy Spirit can unfold your true personality, the one that is "hidden" with Christ in God (Colossians 3:3).

4) <u>Perfectionism</u>: Trying to avoid possible rejection by becoming "bullet proof" against criticism. <u>Beware</u>: If you live by the approval of others, you will "die" by their disapproval. Put differently, the law of ego is "what goes up, must go

down." <u>Remedy</u>: Fasten your heart to the grace and love that God covers you with, living under *His* leadership, not your own demands.[49]

Rejection often leads to self-rejection, a deceptive and very destructive snare. Spirits of self-rejection want you convinced that you are unworthy, unacceptable, unlovable, and that's why you're being rejected. No! Rejection is *always* the other person's sin, not yours. In listening to and agreeing with it you open yourself up to hating and rejecting yourself. The more you reject yourself, the more you become afraid that God and everyone you meet will also reject you. This amplifies the pain and the problem. Soon you may be feeling rejected *even when you aren't*.

Never forget the truth from Ephesians that your Father loved you long before He created you. You are no accident! He made you someone He can and does love wholeheartedly. Let *that* reality capture your heart—not the opinions of sinful mortals (even yourself). You are fully accepted, totally unique, unconditionally loved and forever embraced. You won the "spiritual lottery." By grace alone you are destined to live in endless joy. God's mind is made up! He wants you! So, don't listen to the whispers of a spirit of rejection or let it cast a shadow on God's feelings for you. You are an awesome work of His Hands and Heart (Psalm 139:14-15).

Jesus and Rejection

Jesus knows what rejection is. He experienced rejection as a man for our sake throughout His life, His ministry and especially in His dying. At the cross He felt the full force of rejection first come *against* Him (as He was rejected and sentenced to death) and then *enter* within Him (as our sins and their rightful punishment came upon Him). He was made to *be* sin so that we could be freely given right standing with God and *never* be rejected. He bore it all at the cross in His innermost being—He knows how awful it feels and how deadly it is. He fully sympathizes (Hebrews 4:15).

> **He was despised and rejected by men; a man sorrows, and acquainted with grief; and as one from whom men hide their faces he was despised, and we esteemed him not.** Isaiah 53:3

Jesus also bore the rejection of the Father. In the final moments on the cross His mournful cry of dereliction revealed that He was experiencing the full penalty of sin that was due to us—the utter abandonment by God to death, separation and judgment upon sin Matthew 27:46). He spared us from *ever* having to experience that ultimate agony.

---

[49] Teaching and insights about these four coping strategies from Be In Health® teaching and materials, Dr. Henry W. Wright, Thomaston, Georgia, seminar notes, October 2000.

Spirits of rejection lie against the truth. They want you to feel rejected, unworthy, inferior and insecure. The truth is that you have very real spiritual enemies who despise you and who will always seek to make you feel rejected, but you don't have to think what they think or feel what they feel. You can learn to rest your heart in God who will never abandon you or reject you.

> For He [God] Himself has said, "I will not in any way fail you *nor* give you up *nor* leave you without support. [I will] not, [I will] not, [I will] not in any degree leave you helpless *nor* forsake *nor* let [you] down (relax My hold on you)! [Assuredly not!]" Hebrews 13:5 AMP

Learn to stop touching the hot stove of letting others declare to you your worth (turn from the idolatry of others). Put your whole heart into what He says He sees when He looks your way (seek to defeat all unbelief). The first step to freedom from any sinful pattern is recognizing the sin or the evil spirit that needs to be dealt with as not being the real you and then dealing with it accordingly. You are already accepted and saved by God, so don't take no for an answer. Say "No!" to thoughts of rejection instead. Jesus is God's "Yes!" to you (His Name is *Yeshua* in Hebrew).

The Way to Freedom

Usually the pain of being rejected is easy to recognize as someone's sin against us, but the reality of our own sinful grip on those feelings of rejection is much harder to see and comprehend. Defeating feelings of rejection requires dedication to God's truth.

1) In the midst of the painful feelings, begin declaring forgiveness for the person who rejected you, repenting of the idolatry of putting their opinion about you above God's.

2) Repent for taking the message of rejection to heart, carrying those thoughts captive and, repenting of unbelief until you recover faith that God's acceptance of you is all you really need.

3) Turn to the Father and release gratitude to Him that He loves you perfectly and accepts you always—*just as you are!*

NOTES/JOURNAL

_____
_____
_____
_____

EXERCISE

Learning to recognize how rejection impacts us needs to go hand in hand with realizing that it is a *lie* that we took too much to heart and believed in to our own hurt. As you go down the check list, rejoice that rejection is *not true* about you (from heaven's perspective), even if you still feel that it is. Fall out of agreement with past patterns and past beliefs. God will work with you to help your feelings change as you work with Him to change your beliefs!

Have you believed these lies? They all come from a spirit of rejection! *Renounce them!*

___ Feeling like you cannot get over what people have said about you or to you.
___ Feeling like you will never be able to measure up or be good enough.
___ Feeling that no one loves you, no one really cares, not even God.
___ Feeling like you don't belong in any group, or that you are less than human.
___ Feeling that no one can love you, or that even you can't love yourself.

Have you noticed these behaviors? They came from fearing rejection. *Reject them!*

___ Being afraid to look other people in the eyes; holding your head down.
___ Avoiding people, preferring to be alone, constantly finding fault with others.
___ Excessive introspection, excessive attention to your words and appearance.
___ Never letting anyone get too close; wanting attention, but easily embarrassed by it.
___ "Branding" yourself through physical appearance to feel unique and special.

Dr. Henry W. Wright of Be In Health teaches that a spirit of rejection comes equipped with a "scrambler" which twists what people say or do to make it seem like you are being rejected even when you aren't.[50] That "scrambling" is not really coming from you, but from the spirit of rejection that you are entertaining. Good communication usually defeats the "scrambler." However, excessive feelings of shame or self-defensiveness won't allow you to clarify through honest and open communication what the other person really meant or intended. Because of fear or hurt you may find yourself going immediately into anger and rejection of self or rejection of the other person. As long as the "scrambler" can deceive you, it can snare you and keep you in turmoil. Fortunately, *being aware of this pattern* will help you guard against it as you pray and seek God to overcome it.

---

[50] Teaching and insights about "the scrambler" from Be In Health® teaching and materials, Dr. Henry W. Wright, Thomaston, Georgia, seminar notes, October 2000.

DISCUSSION QUESTIONS

Have the group consider these ten possible sources of rejection in childhood. Is it any wonder that so many people have had to develop some kind of coping strategy to deal with the pain?[51]

___ Growing up without a father's love	___ Generational patterns
___ Coming from an unwanted pregnancy	___ Undesired gender at birth
___ Child of adoption	___ Child of unmarried parents
___ Competition for love of parents	___ Divorce/blended families
___ Death of a parent when a child is young	___ Verbal, sexual, or physical abuse

Now, ask the group to discuss the coping strategies cited in the lesson: withdrawal, anger and hatred, false identity, and perfectionism. What are the drawbacks to each one? Why don't they work? How do they hurt us? What are the reasons why we keep using such failed strategies? In addition to the prayer steps (repentance of carrying rejection and confession of the truth about our total acceptance), what practical steps could help break these habits?

Discuss the applicability of the four A's: "Because of a lack of Affection, I sought Achievements in order to gain Approval so that I could feel Accepted." Repeat this faith statement as a group prayer: "I can finally rest secure in the Father's unending affection for me and His acceptance of me."

MAIN POINTS

- Our Father will never reject us—His love and acceptance of us is perfect.
- It is a sin against us—God has commanded everyone to love and accept us.
- It is a devastating lie—there may be sin in us, but we are not sin.
- It is a key element of psychological illness—damaging to our sense of self.
- It becomes *our* sin (unbelief in God; idolatry of others) when we agree with it and take it to heart.
- It is an evil spirit, one that delights for us to feel the very feelings we hate.
- It draws power from a "secret truth": Something *is* wrong in us (sin).
- Apart from Jesus we would all be ultimately rejected; yet because of Jesus we who believe in Him will be totally accepted!
- Let the pain of rejection push you into fully agreeing with The Father's view of you—live covered and shielded by His acceptance of you.

---

[51] Sources of rejection list is modified from Be In Health® teaching and materials, Dr. Henry W. Wright, Thomaston, Georgia, seminar notes, October 2000.

DIGGING DEEPER

The bigger the bush or the sapling, the deeper we have to go in our digging to finally "uproot" the plant that we no longer want growing in our yard. One section at a time may have to be exposed so that the axe can be "laid to the root" (Mt 3:10). This same principle applies in the spiritual life. Since rejection is usually so stubbornly rooted in our hearts, we may need to go after it section by section.

One powerful root to rejection is fear and fear may have many supporting feeders. The fruitful question to ask is "what am I really afraid of?" Find what those deep-seated fears are, *face them*, and then carry them captive to Christ, holding them against the light of His Word, His character and His promises until you see something in Him that starts removing the dark power from that fear.

What am I really afraid of...

...when strangers seem to reject me?

_____

...when people close to me say hurtful things?

_____

...when I don't get things just right?

_____

...when my appearance isn't perfect?

_____

SWORD AND SHIELD

Learn to take a stand on what God says about who you are in Him—and then keep standing! No one says this will be easy, only that it really works if you work it. Standing firm on the truth of scripture is what even Jesus did in the face of strong temptation. We are not greater than He (Mt 10:24-25). Let's do it His way!

> "Yet the Lord had a delight in loving your fathers, and He chose their descendants after them, you above all peoples, as it is this day." Deuteronomy 10:15 AMP

> But Zion said, "The Lord has forsaken me; my Lord has forgotten me." "Can a woman forget her nursing child, that she should have no compassion on the son of her womb? Even these may forget, yet I will not forget you. Behold, I have engraved you on the palms of my hands; your walls are continually before me." Isaiah 49:14-16

> For thus said the Lord of hosts, after his glory sent me to the nations who plundered you, for he who touches you touches the apple of his eye. Zechariah 2:8

"Teaching them to observe all that I have commanded you. And behold, I am with you always, to the end of the age." Matthew 28:20

Therefore, if anyone is in Christ, he is a new creation. The old has passed away; behold, the new has come. 2 Corinthians 5:17

Blessed be the God and Father of our Lord Jesus Christ, who has blessed us in Christ with every spiritual blessing in the heavenly places, even as he chose us in him before the foundation of the world, that we should be holy and blameless before him. In love he predestined us for adoption through Jesus Christ, according to the purpose of his will, to the praise of his glorious grace, with which he has blessed us in the Beloved. Ephesians 1:3-6

PRAYER FOCUS

Rejection wants you to feel rejected, unworthy, insecure. The truth is that you have an enemy who hates and rejects you, but you can learn to rest your heart in God who will never leave you, forsake you, or reject you. Put your whole heart into believing what He says He sees when He looks your way!

Father, forgive me for holding out my heart to other people to declare my worth to me. You have declared Your unending love for me and my eternal worth to You by sending Jesus to the cross. Forgive me for letting other people's opinions matter to me more than Your own. I repent of and renounce all rejection I have ever taken on. It is not about what they did or said—it is all about my unwitting sin of holding on to it—and letting them be god to me. By an act of my will I am taking my heart back from others and giving it to You. May I only desire to see me through Your eyes. Thank You for Your steadfast love and acceptance. My heart is safe under the covering of Your perfect love and Your promise to never leave me or forsake me.

RENUNCIATIONS AND AFFIRMATIONS

Renounce any agreements with untruth; believe Jesus' *truth* as your new *way of life*.[52]

Father, I renounce ___ (Abandonment, Accusation…) in the generations of my fathers and I repent of having walked in it myself. I repent of my own sin of ___ (Fear of abandonment…). Forgive me and break its power over me and off my generations.

Abandonment	Rejection	Self-rejection
Fear of abandonment	Rejection by others	Unhealthy need for love
Pattern of abandoning	Rejection of others	Unhealthy need for

---

[52] Renunciation list is modified from Be In Health® teaching and materials, Dr. Henry W. Wright, Thomaston, Georgia, seminar notes, October 2000.

others	Self-rejection	approval
Fear of commitment	Self-hatred	Unhealthy need for identity
	Condemning spirit	
Self-salvation		False or fabricated personality
Driven-ness to achieve	**Accusation**	
False burden bearing	Accusation by others	Insecurity, inferiority
False responsibility	Accusation of others	Inability to receive love
Rescuing, co-dependency	Self-accusation	False humility, shyness
Perfectionism	Critical spirit	
People pleasing		**Self-pity**
	Fear	Depression
Rebellion	Fear of failure	Spirit of heaviness
Control	Fear of man	Deep hurt and wounding of the spirit
Manipulation	Fear of rejection	
Unbelief in God's acceptance	Fear of other's words, attitudes	Hopelessness, despair
		Unbelief in God's promises
Discontentment	Fear of speaking	
Complaining	in public	Sympathy seeking

PUTTING FEET TO YOUR PRAYERS: STRETCH YOURSELF!

Here are some tips for struggling free of the "cocoon" of rejection. It is not easy, but it is do-able with God's help. One day we will get those lovely "butterfly" wings of faith and float high above the contrary winds of other people's opinions, if we keep persevering in the right direction now. Let's overturn the fiendish activity of rejection!

1) Pray through the steps of repentance outlined in these exercise and in Chapter 7. This will enlist the aid of the Lord in helping you bring the stronghold down.

2) Stay in the game. Commit to being faithful in your relationships (unless physical or sexual abuse is involved): You cannot change them, but you can let their ways bring helpful changes to you. You are there to learn to love them, accepting them as they are!

3) Don't run from possible scenarios of rejection; don't let shyness or the fear of man stop you from doing what you know in your heart God would want you to do. No one gets free by hiding from the problem. Stay vulnerable.

4) Persevere. Of course rejection hurts! But let the pain of rejection keep pushing you into God's Heart—that is where your heart needed to be all along.

5) Behold Him! Make sure you begin each day basking in the bright Son-shine of Your Father's love! Hold fast to the great truth of your complete safety in Him (see Chapter 10).

CHAPTER 18

LOVE THYSELF!

The Stronghold of Self-Rejection

In the previous chapter we explored the emotional damage that rejection by others can cause and the effective remedy that Jesus brings us through faith in His revelation of our Loving Father who will never reject or forsake those who desire His salvation. Not knowing our true security in God, when others rejected us (by thoughts, words or deeds), the power of that pain may have carried us into rejecting ourselves. The truth is that unless we truly believe in our heart of hearts that it is a great, good thing to be who we are *just as we are*, we have been robbed of a major part of our glorious inheritance in Christ. Did you know that Jesus actually expects us to love and accept ourselves—*just as He does*? Why else would He take proper love of self as a standard for how we are to love others?

> **And he said to him, "'You shall love the Lord your God with all your heart and with all your soul and with all your mind.' This is the great and first commandment. And a second is like it: 'You shall love your neighbor as yourself.'"** Matthew 22:37-39

These words of Jesus carry a curious fulfillment. We are to love our neighbors *as* we love ourselves. But what if we don't love ourselves? Not loving ourselves will limit and set obstacles to truly loving others. And it happens in this way: If I am angry with myself, it will spill out onto others as frustration with them. If I haven't learned to receive mercy for myself over my brokenness, I will become judgmental of others. If I cannot entrust my life to God, I will tend to become fearful for and controlling of the ones I love. If I am critical towards myself, I will tend to be critical of others. This cycle goes on and on because the sad truth is that even though we try to manage it, make up for it and cover it up, we can only truly love others as we truly love ourselves. So, let's learn to give grace to ourselves, *rightly* love ourselves in Christ and become grace givers to others!

A Worthwhile Life Lesson

Worthwhile life lessons don't come easily. For many of us the ultimate challenge of the truly converted Christian life is learning to love the sinner and hate the sin. Would you believe that to help us God has assigned a problem-prone sinner to each one of us? By "sneaky" design He has placed in all our lives someone for us to get to know intimately, someone whose weaknesses, failings and stupidities cause us no end of trouble. Yet, we are fully expected to learn how to love that sinner unconditionally, while still holding a perfect hatred for all the sins. Look no further, that sinner is you! You the sinner is joined at the hip to you the New Creation—*oh my God!* It's time to come to conversion about the gospel applied to ourselves. To see how much work may be needed, take this test to determine how well you give grace to yourself. Can you apply 1 Corinthians 13:4-8 (the "love" chapter) to yourself?[53]

___ Are you harder on yourself than on others? Do you berate yourself?
___ Get angry with yourself easily? Depression counts as self-anger!
___ Are there things about yourself that you dislike and can't accept?
___ Are there things in your past that you just can't forgive yourself for?
___ How do you talk to yourself when you have done something stupid?

If you answered yes, why would you think treating yourself this way is normal? It may be common like a cold but it is not a healthy normal.

Accepting the "Unacceptable"

There are many things about us that God is at peace with, but which we still fear and hate. In fact He seems to be in no hurry to make change come in these areas. Not being reconciled to God about these things can keep us striving against ourselves. Complete self-acceptance is the grace-filled starting point for entering into God's good plans for our life. Provided that we have repented where necessary, He is always the One who completely accepts us just as we are and is willing to lead us into new life. *We are the holdouts who cannot accept our lives as they are and resist living on His terms.* Make sure you can accept all nine of these things about yourself *without reservation*. God already does! Become fully reconciled to the God who is already reconciled to you.

We implore you on behalf of Christ, be reconciled to God. 2 Corinthians 5:20

1) Past hurtful events: We need to see that the Father grieved over pain and injustice coming into our lives, but God is a realist. He has had to accept that all manner of pain had to be allowed because free will is allowed. So God grieves, but He is also ready, willing and able to lead anyone

GOD'S ACCEPTANCE

God's acceptance of those who are in Christ is so complete that He is always ready to meet us where we are *just as we are* with the embrace of His perfect love. Fully accept your life and meet Him where He meets you!

---

[53] Love suffers long and is kind; love does not envy; love does not parade itself, is not puffed up; does not behave rudely, does not seek its own, is not provoked, thinks no evil; does not rejoice in iniquity, but rejoices in the truth; bears all things, believes all things, hopes all things, endures all things. Love never fails.

into a life in which evil is overturned and made to work for good. Such living begins on the other side of acceptance. At the very least accept that it happened and be willing to go on with God. Even better, vigorously thank God by faith for all you have been through.

2) Failures, wrong choices: No one wants to fail and make wrong choices, but we all do. God allows us to experience failure in order for us to learn from our mistakes things we evidently could not learn by the truths He has shown us. He will never reproach us; instead He will help us gain and grow. The only one who really fails is the one who doesn't keep trying, the one who doesn't persevere (Revelation 3:10). Don't live with a fear of failure: Repent, receive grace, push delete and get going again!

3) Weaknesses/foolishness: Because we receive so much affirmation from others over our strengths, we often tend to concentrate our efforts there and build a sense of self-worth around things we do well. Let your perspective shift on this one. Our strengths are God's gifts to us; trusting Him with our weaknesses is our gift to Him. For most of us it wasn't our strengths that brought us to Christ, but our weaknesses. Our weaknesses grow our prayer life, increase humility in us and compassion for others, and remind us to depend upon God for his help. His strength and grace are perfected in us through the very weaknesses we despise (2 Corinthians 12:9-10). Don't try to be weak, but when you see your weaknesses, choose to look upon them as "tutors" and "spiritual guides" leading you closer to Christ (Galatians 3:24).

4) Lack of knowledge: We often seek knowledge out of a misguided desire to cover ourselves by being right. But it is not knowledge that covers us, it is Jesus' Blood and God's love. It is not knowledge as information that saves us, it is knowing God in trust and intimacy. The humble truth is that we are hugely ignorant of both the world of information and the vast Infinity that is God. Let pride take the hit: Admit your boundless ignorance as a finite, fallen creature, then acknowledge that you know One who will never fault you for it, but will graciously share His wisdom with you (James 1:5). We are learners for Life!

5) Family heritage: It's too late. God made the call and didn't consult you. Take it on faith that God chose your heritage for reasons of the blessings—not the curses—that are in your generations and the divine purposes that will fulfill your life (Acts 17:26).

6) Present limitations: At times we probably have all hated our limits, whether of age, intelligence, appearance or abilities. God will likely grow us beyond many present limits as we pray and seek His will, but in the meantime come to peace and acceptance about limits that are allowed to remain in our lives as we wait on God for growth (Isaiah 40:31).

7) Personality and patterns: This is tricky because if you are reading this book you may want some of your personality and patterns changed so that the New Creation life can come forth—never buy into an aspect of Self as being the real you if it doesn't match up with Jesus *in you*, right? (Good you're learning!) But what we don't want is to hold our breath as we wait for those changes to come. For example, if shyness has been a personality pattern, confess it as the fear of man, then cast the burden of freeing you from it on the Lord and take your peace back. Then the next time shyness tries to rise up inside of you be prepared to fight to not let it stop you and eventually it will lose its grip. Put the burden of changing you on the Lord.

8) Your fallen nature: You didn't ask for it. It is not even your fault that you have it. It is in you because of Adam's sin. That's why it's called *Adam's* nature. God isn't asking you to get rid of it—Paul never got rid of his. In fact God has no plan to remove it *down here*: It comes off when we die. While we live it serves a good purpose by keeping us humble and dependent upon Him, grateful that we are covered by the Blood and by the love, and less prideful towards others. What He is saying is this: "Just, don't get dressed up in it and walk in that old nature!"

9) Physical appearance: The truth about physical appearance is that anyone who has truly put on Christ (in love and delight) has such inner beauty shining out of them that it never fails to transform even the most ordinary countenance. A heart fully yielded to Christ is the best "make up" in the world and all it costs in this context is casting down vain concerns about how we look outwardly (1 Peter 3:3). God looks deep inside and loves us. Let's learn to do it His way.

The Battle Is Over Believing Truth

Son or daughter of Adam, "Who told you that you were naked?" (Genesis 3:11). We, too, may feel exposed and vulnerable in our fallenness, but our God is covering us! Are you listening to what God's Word says about you or are you listening to your feelings, your understanding, your circumstances, or your past failures? Learn to let God alone be your source of truth and every contrary thought be recognized as a lie, *even if it comes from you* (Romans 3:4). Self-rejection is a double snare, because if I reject myself or my life, I am also rejecting the One who created me and is redeeming me. I may be completely unaware of this dynamic, but if I hate my life, I'm saying in effect that the Lord is doing a sloppy job of leading me towards the joy He has promised. That cannot be! God knows what He is doing and His ways of leading us are saturated with His wisdom and love. We simply must learn to admit that we don't have the proper perspective and then choose to see the whole of our life through God's eyes. Heaven's perspective on your life is the one you want (Psalm 139:14).

into a life in which evil is overturned and made to work for good. Such living begins on the other side of acceptance. At the very least accept that it happened and be willing to go on with God. Even better, vigorously thank God by faith for all you have been through.

2) Failures, wrong choices: No one wants to fail and make wrong choices, but we all do. God allows us to experience failure in order for us to learn from our mistakes things we evidently could not learn by the truths He has shown us. He will never reproach us; instead He will help us gain and grow. The only one who really fails is the one who doesn't keep trying, the one who doesn't persevere (Revelation 3:10). Don't live with a fear of failure: Repent, receive grace, push delete and get going again!

3) Weaknesses/foolishness: Because we receive so much affirmation from others over our strengths, we often tend to concentrate our efforts there and build a sense of self-worth around things we do well. Let your perspective shift on this one. Our strengths are God's gifts to us; trusting Him with our weaknesses is our gift to Him. For most of us it wasn't our strengths that brought us to Christ, but our weaknesses. Our weaknesses grow our prayer life, increase humility in us and compassion for others, and remind us to depend upon God for his help. His strength and grace are perfected in us through the very weaknesses we despise (2 Corinthians 12:9-10). Don't try to be weak, but when you see your weaknesses, choose to look upon them as "tutors" and "spiritual guides" leading you closer to Christ (Galatians 3:24).

4) Lack of knowledge: We often seek knowledge out of a misguided desire to cover ourselves by being right. But it is not knowledge that covers us, it is Jesus' Blood and God's love. It is not knowledge as information that saves us, it is knowing God in trust and intimacy. The humble truth is that we are hugely ignorant of both the world of information and the vast Infinity that is God. Let pride take the hit: Admit your boundless ignorance as a finite, fallen creature, then acknowledge that you know One who will never fault you for it, but will graciously share His wisdom with you (James 1:5). We are learners for Life!

5) Family heritage: It's too late. God made the call and didn't consult you. Take it on faith that God chose your heritage for reasons of the blessings—not the curses—that are in your generations and the divine purposes that will fulfill your life (Acts 17:26).

6) Present limitations: At times we probably have all hated our limits, whether of age, intelligence, appearance or abilities. God will likely grow us beyond many present limits as we pray and seek His will, but in the meantime come to peace and acceptance about limits that are allowed to remain in our lives as we wait on God for growth (Isaiah 40:31).

7) Personality and patterns: This is tricky because if you are reading this book you may want some of your personality and patterns changed so that the New Creation life can come forth—never buy into an aspect of Self as being the real you if it doesn't match up with Jesus *in you*, right? (Good you're learning!) But what we don't want is to hold our breath as we wait for those changes to come. For example, if shyness has been a personality pattern, confess it as the fear of man, then cast the burden of freeing you from it on the Lord and take your peace back. Then the next time shyness tries to rise up inside of you be prepared to fight to not let it stop you and eventually it will lose its grip. Put the burden of changing you on the Lord.

8) Your fallen nature: You didn't ask for it. It is not even your fault that you have it. It is in you because of Adam's sin. That's why it's called *Adam's* nature. God isn't asking you to get rid of it—Paul never got rid of his. In fact God has no plan to remove it *down here*: It comes off when we die. While we live it serves a good purpose by keeping us humble and dependent upon Him, grateful that we are covered by the Blood and by the love, and less prideful towards others. What He is saying is this: "Just, don't get dressed up in it and walk in that old nature!"

9) Physical appearance: The truth about physical appearance is that anyone who has truly put on Christ (in love and delight) has such inner beauty shining out of them that it never fails to transform even the most ordinary countenance. A heart fully yielded to Christ is the best "make up" in the world and all it costs in this context is casting down vain concerns about how we look outwardly (1 Peter 3:3). God looks deep inside and loves us. Let's learn to do it His way.

The Battle Is Over Believing Truth

Son or daughter of Adam, "Who told you that you were naked?" (Genesis 3:11). We, too, may feel exposed and vulnerable in our fallenness, but our God is covering us! Are you listening to what God's Word says about you or are you listening to your feelings, your understanding, your circumstances, or your past failures? Learn to let God alone be your source of truth and every contrary thought be recognized as a lie, *even if it comes from you* (Romans 3:4). Self-rejection is a double snare, because if I reject myself or my life, I am also rejecting the One who created me and is redeeming me. I may be completely unaware of this dynamic, but if I hate my life, I'm saying in effect that the Lord is doing a sloppy job of leading me towards the joy He has promised. That cannot be! God knows what He is doing and His ways of leading us are saturated with His wisdom and love. We simply must learn to admit that we don't have the proper perspective and then choose to see the whole of our life through God's eyes. Heaven's perspective on your life is the one you want (Psalm 139:14).

There is one who hates you and will never cease from faulting you and putting you down. You don't have to listen to him! Neither do you have to listen to yourself. It is a devious form of pride *in us* that demands perfection *from us*—never the Lord who knows that we can "do nothing" apart from the grace He supplies (John 15:5). Such striving grew out of a fear of displeasing others and a wrong image of the Father. Trying to be perfect, or to always be right, is the vain belief that we can cover ourselves with our own good intentions and best efforts—a modern form of works righteousness. This inevitably feeds frustration which can then become very damaging to our physical health by producing the auto-immune diseases.[54] Somehow self-rejection sends a message to our immune system that we are the enemy it needs to attack.

Beware also of how self-rejection is held in place by self-pity. Self-pity only wants to wallow in what has been wrong; it never wants to climb out of the morass of the past. It has been called "the super-glue of hell."[55] Why waste time on those lies? Being saved by God through Christ means that we are of all people *not to be pitied*; we have a God who saves, delivers, prospers, heals and provides—all according to our real needs being watched over by His love and wisdom for us.

Are you prepared to recover your life from all past agreements with the enemy's invisible kingdom? You have to be willing to fight to be free, but your God will train you for the battle! (Psalm 18:34). Live according to your future not your past—God is not going to quit working with you until you are as full of joy over your life with Him as He is (John 15:11, 16:24):

> *I am not what I was. I am not what I will be. I am being changed from glory to glory. And God is loving me full throttle all along the way!*[56]

The Way to Freedom

The difficult thing to recognize about self-rejection is that you are always the person God wants you to be and that you—in your right mind—would want to be, if only you had His perspective. Don't let your pain, problems and sins tell you otherwise!

1) Recognize every thought or feeling of self-rejection, self-frustration, or self-condemnation as coming from the enemy—not God and not the true you.

---

[54] Art Mathias, PhD, *In His Own Image* (Anchorage, AK: Wellspring Ministries of Alaska, 2003), pp. 25, 44.
[55] Teaching and insights about self-pity as the "super-glue from hell that binds us to our past" and the relationship of self-rejection to the auto-immune disorders from Be In Health® teaching and materials, Dr. Henry W. Wright, Thomaston, Georgia, seminar notes, October 2000.
[56] From the "Unloving Spirit" cassette series, Be In Health® teaching and materials, Dr. Henry W. Wright, Thomaston, Georgia, 2000.

2) Take full responsibility for agreeing with it: Repent, renounce and carry it captive to Christ until you see something in Him that restores your confidence that God's mercy, loving plans and the promise of Romans 8:28 are all for you!

3) Turn to the Father and release gratitude to Him that He loves and accepts you even when you don't. Then cast that devil out!

NOTES/JOURNAL

___
___
___
___
___
___
___
___
___
___

EXERCISE

Write down your "victim" story—all of the worst things you wish had never happened to you by other's sins or your own. Make it as bad and bleak as you can, but be succinct! File stuff by title or you will need many more pages. Be sure to write down the things that the enemy gets you to agree with when you hit the end of your rope and your self-talk is at its worst. Then recognize the source as demonic and break all agreements with this ungodly thinking.

___
___
___
___

Now write down your "responsibility" proclamation! You can take 100% responsibility for what is going on, because even the part that belongs to the others in the past, you have been building on ever since. Those events were the "raw material," but you have been the builder. Then tell the truth with prophetic declaration. Shout it out if you need to: This is a battle for your soul's orientation. Will you see yourself *as you are really are*, a person with all of the resources and love of heaven surrounding you (as an overcomer), or will you stay dispossessed and un-empowered (as a victim)—living way below your true inheritance in Christ? Here is a sample proclamation from Lance Wallnau.[57]

The truth is I'm an anointed spiritual (man or woman) whom God has assigned with an uncommon assignment and supernatural favor to learn things in the crucible of life so that I come out sharper, stronger, more equipped and better. I've got promises over my life that right now are working for me and years of sowing that right now are paying off. I am closer to the breakthrough I need than I have ever been before. This will be the best year of my life.

_____
_____
_____
_____

DISCUSSION QUESTIONS

Have the group take the test applying 1 Corinthians 13:4-8 to themselves. Ask them to score it on a 1-10 scale with 1 being hardly ever and 10 being all the time.

_____ Are you harder on yourself than on others? Do you berate yourself?
_____ Do you get angry with yourself easily? Depression counts as self-anger!
_____ Are there things about yourself that you dislike and can't accept?
_____ Are there things in your past that you just can't forgive yourself for?
_____ Do you talk down to yourself when you have done something stupid?
Total: _____

A score of five signifies a person full of grace or someone in deep need of honesty!

1) Now ask those who are willing to discuss their scores about their self-talk and self-attitude. The enemy is pushed back whenever we see a) a problem area that we had previously unrecognized and b) realize that we are not the only one struggling with that problem.

2) Have the group tell stories they have heard of famous people who had "everything going for them" and yet who nevertheless could not find peace with themselves. The point of this exercise is to see that abilities, charisma and success do not ensure self-acceptance.

3) Now ask on what basis can we all hope to arrive at total self acceptance. Is it possible to fully accept yourself if you don't have the abilities, charisma and success you have desired? Why and why not?[58]

---

[57] Lance Wallnau, *Killer Sheep Marketing*, seminar notes on the exercise and the final quotation: MorningStar Ministries Conference, Charlotte, NC, January 2009.
[58] Answer: of course it is! Because of Who our God is to us—but get them to talk over what this means and how it applies. And a very lovely thing is the way God helps us gain abilities, charisma and successes once we have come to self-acceptance.

MAIN POINTS

- We are to love, forgive and accept ourselves as fully as God does—and still recognize and hate the sin that we see.
- We can only love others as we love ourselves—our hearts truly need to be converted, fully applying the gospel of grace to ourselves.
- We love God to the extent that we receive the revelation of His love for us.
- Any un-love towards self, blocks our ability to believe and receive God's love, as well as that of others.
- Stop hating and fearing the nine "unacceptable" things about yourself.
- Self-pity is the hellish glue that binds you to self-rejection and past hurts.
- You have to fight to get your life back, but God will be loving you and helping you every step of the way.
- It really is a great good thing to be who you are in Christ. Choose to believe it and reject any thought or feeling that doesn't agree with this truth.

DIGGING DEEPER

Remember the exercise on fear in the Digging Deeper section of the previous chapter? We need to ask the same question—*what am I really afraid of*—in order to get at the root issues behind why we have such a hard time accepting certain things about ourselves. None of the nine "unacceptable" things stand in the way of God's perfect acceptance of us. Why are we so bothered by them?

It would be great if we could just look at a list like this and say, "OK God, if this is what I have to accept about me, you've got it!" and be done. But for most of us our hearts need to hear compelling reasons for letting go after years of entrenched opposition to grace. Make no mistake about it—these issues are "grace killers" in our lives. So let's go for the grace offered us. First, ask the fruitful question: What is it about this that makes me so afraid to accept myself? Then write down the answer in God that will help you let it go.

This scares me because…	God's truth that helps me
1) Past hurtful events	
2) Failures, wrong choices	
3) Weaknesses/foolishness	
4) Lack of knowledge	

5) Family heritage

_____   _____

6) Present limitations

_____   _____

7) Personality and patterns

_____   _____

8) Your fallen nature

_____   _____

9) Physical appearance

_____   _____

SWORD AND SHIELD

We are covered by a Great Love. Beloved, you just can't be more loved than this!

> "As the Father has loved me, so have I loved you. Abide in my love. If you keep my commandments, you will abide in my love, just as I have kept my Father's commandments and abide in his love." John 15:9-10

> "For the Father himself loves you, because you have loved me and have believed that I came from God." John 16:27

> "I in them and you in me, that they may become perfectly one, so that the world may know that you sent me and loved them even as you loved me." John 17:23

> In this is love, not that we have loved God but that he loved us and sent his Son to be the propitiation for our sins. 1 John 4:10

> We love because he first loved us. 1 John 4:19

PRAYER FOCUS

Time's up: Accept these "unacceptable" things about yourself. They aren't going away and life really won't get much better until you do! Go over each grace killer individually and make sure you are making real peace in your heart and mind with God and yourself about it. Let your prayer be:

Father, since you accept this about me, I choose by an act of my will to break agreement with all of my fear and hatred for ____ being in my life the way it is, and I choose to fully accept it about myself because you do.

As you do each one, check it off. But make sure you pray it through thoroughly.

__ Past hurtful events	__ Failures, wrong choices	__ Family heritage
__ Present limitations	__ Personality and patterns	__ Your fallen nature
__ Lack of knowledge	__ Weaknesses/foolishness	__ Physical appearance

RENUNCIATIONS AND AFFIRMATIONS

Renounce any agreements with untruth; believe Jesus' *truth* as your new *way of life*.[59]

Father, I renounce ___ (Self Bitterness, Pride...) in the generations of my fathers and I repent of having walked in it myself. I repent of my own sin of ___ (Bitter with self...). Forgive me and break its power over me and off my generations.

Self Rejection	**Pride**	**Need for approval**
Bitter with self	Self exalting	Perfectionism
Self condemning	Self-debasing	Attention getting
Angry self-talk	Willful, stubborn	Competition,
Self-hatred	False piety	Comparison
Suicide attempts		Insecurity
	Self-punishment	Inferiority
Self-pity	Excessive self denial	Fabricated personality
Selfishness	Self-sabotage	Idolatry/imitation of others
Self-absorbed	Self-mutilation	Self-consciousness
Victim mentality	Purging, bingeing	Worthlessness

PUTTING FEET TO YOUR PRAYERS: STRETCH YOURSELF!

Unloving attitudes against ourselves block the Holy Spirit given ability to express or receive love. ***The truth is it really is a great, good thing to be you—*** because of who He is to you and who you are in Him. He believes it and you can too! So, forgive self, renounce self-rejection and agree with God! Make the following faith confession your own declaration of freedom, confessing it by faith as an act of your will. Repeat this out loud as often as you need to and as loudly as you may need to until you really believe it:

Because of my Father's perfect love for me, His never-ending mercy for me, the future and hope He has for me, and His commitment to bring good out of everything that has ever happened or will ever happen to me, ***it really is a great, good thing to be me!*** *I therefore choose to fully forgive myself and accept myself—just as He does. And I will fight to take my life back from all unloving attitudes against myself. I may have had a bad beginning, but I am going to have a great never-ending!*

---

[59] Renunciation list is modified from Be In Health® teaching and materials, Dr. Henry W. Wright, Thomaston, Georgia, seminar notes, October 2000.

CHAPTER 19

GODLY CONTENTMENT

The Stronghold of Envy

Not receiving a fullness of assurance that we are loved, that we belong and that our lives therefore hold great meaning and purpose, leaves us prey for the undercutting work of envy and jealousy. Envy and jealousy scream out: "They are getting what I need and deserve!" Sure it is black-hearted, but it is also revealing of a deep seated pain and an invisible reality: All of us have been robbed. None of us are getting what we desperately need and were meant to have. The enemy came in through Adam's sin and stole from every child what God desired them to receive, even from the moment of conception. All of us were blocked at birth by Adam's nature from knowing in the depth of our spirits that we are totally loved, fully forgiven, completely accepted by our grace-giving Father. The spiritual "umbilical cord" that was meant to connect us to God's loving heart was severed by the Fall.

This deep void cannot be fully filled even by the best of parents and fairest of treatment and it leaves all of us exposed to the temptations of envy and jealousy. New birth through faith in Christ restores the missing connection, but old emotional habits are hard to break. We who believe in Christ are inheritors of riches beyond our wildest dreams (Ephesians 1:11-18; Colossians 1:12; 1 Peter 1:4). However, we may still be held captive by the old feelings of deprivation and former patterns of striving to get "our fair share." St. Francis is credited with saying that he who expects nothing "can enjoy everything."[60] That may well be true, but only if he (or she) has first dealt with the stronghold of envy.

The Superior Power of Contentment

Godly contentment is our graced antidote for the poison of envy and jealousy. Whenever this stronghold seeks to snare you, quickly search out Jesus to restore your sense of contentment as His well-beloved child. Paul says that godly contentment was something that he gained as he grew. We can learn it too.

Not that I am speaking of being in need, for I have learned in whatever situation I am to be content. I know how to be brought low, and I know how to abound. In any and every circumstance, I have learned the secret of facing plenty and hunger, abundance and need. Philippians 4:11-12

Contentment is actually great gain. It brings with it the peace which "surpasses all understanding," a peace that is truly out of this world (Philippians 4:7; John 14:27). It removes fruitless and disturbing anxieties and replaces them with a

---

[60] G. K. Chesterton, *St. Francis of Assisi* (Garden City, NY: Image Books, 1957), p. 75.

gentle fullness. Contentment is safe to desire because we can never have too much of it.

> Now there is great gain in godliness with contentment, for we brought nothing into the world, and we cannot take anything out of the world. But if we have food and clothing, with these we will be content. But those who desire to be rich fall into temptation, into a snare. 1 Timothy 6:6-9

The Destructive Power of Envy and Jealousy

Envy and jealousy, on the other hand, keep us stirred up and dis-contented. These spirits keep us thinking about and noticing what others have and what we don't have. Why should this seem so natural? Isn't the Holy Spirit always at work inside of us to help us notice what others don't have (so we can serve them) and what we do have (so we can be thankful and rest contented)? Why is the voice of the enemy so much easier to hear? Are we that well practiced at listening to our enemy? We need to be much more discerning about which spirit is directing our perceptions. Any upsurge of envy means that we are definitely being robbed of something that we deserve to have, but what the thieves are actually stealing is none other than our godly contentment!

Envy is destructive of our bodies. Bone marrow is crucial to a healthy immune system, but envy weakens it. On the other hand a sound heart is a grateful heart—it gives life to the body.[61]

> **The life of the body is a heart at peace, but envy rots the bones.** Proverbs 14:30 WEB

Envy is also destructive of the Body of Christ. Much of the strife and conflict in the church comes from jealousy among the members. It is difficult for anyone to be advanced by God or to become especially gifted without envy being set loose to destroy the fellowship. This holds everyone back.

> **What causes quarrels and what causes fights among you? Is it not this, that your passions are at war within you? You desire and do not have, so you murder. You covet and cannot obtain, so you fight and quarrel.** James 4:1-2

Getting to the Root of the Problem

Envy and jealousy grow out of three roots we would do well to pray against: covetousness, pride and bitterness.

---

[61] Teaching and insights about the relationship of envy to the immune system and the role of coveting, pride and comparison from Be In Health® teaching and materials, Dr. Henry W. Wright, Thomaston, Georgia, seminar notes, October 2000.

Root #1) Covetousness (James 3:14-17): To covet is to long for or lust for something that is not yours. Covetousness always wants more—and it wants it right now. Never content with present blessings, it sets us at enmity with others and with God (James 4:1-4). It is a form of idolatry, since it places things before God and keeps us focused on *getting something from* God, rather than *giving ourselves to* God. As soon as our heart covets something, even a blessing or a spiritual gift, we are putting it ahead of our relationship with Christ and we begin losing our entry into the Kingdom, for that is only supplied to those who seek the Kingdom *first* (Matthew 6:33). Consequently, the Kingdom's peace, joy and power slip through our fingers when we grasp to gain an idol rather than the Lord (Ephesians 5:3-5).

> **Put to death therefore what is earthly in you: sexual immorality, impurity, passion, evil desire, and covetousness, which is idolatry.** Colossians 3:5

Root #2) Pride (1Timothy 6:3-5): Pride tries to gloss over or fill in the awful sense of not really having what we needed of love and acceptance. As a covering pride cannot help but bring us into conflict with others through competition or comparisons meant to prove to ourselves as well as to others that we are not inferior. We must come off seeming superior at least in our eyes or dissatisfied pride become jealous of their gifts and abilities.

> *There are three roots to envy and jealousy:*
> 1. *Covetousness*
> 2. *Pride*
> 3. *Bitterness*

Root#3) Bitterness (James 3:14-16): Bitterness towards others makes us resentful when they do well or receive blessings. We hate it that they are being shown favor instead of discipline. Self-bitterness, on the other hand, can make us feel that we haven't received what we needed or deserved—and that can lead into self-pity. Either way, if bitter envy is in the heart it is something truly demonic—give it no place!

Beware to compare! When we don't get what we want, we may look around and compare ourselves to others, wanting what they have. You can't win at this: Always some have less, and some have more. Trust God to be measuring out what blessings are truly right and needful for you (and for others) and keep your eyes on Him.

> **Not that we dare to classify or compare ourselves with some of those who are commending themselves. But when they measure themselves by one another and compare themselves with one another, they are without understanding.**
> 2 Corinthians 10:12

Let's get something straight: Our Father does not play favorites or show partiality (Acts 10:34-35; Romans 2:11). Amazingly, the Father doesn't even love Jesus more than He loves you!

"I in them and you in me, that they may become perfectly one, so that the world may know that you sent me and loved them even as you loved me." John 17:23

Our Father is a great provider (Matthew 6:33; Psalm 37:3-5; Psalm 73:25). The devil plays long and loudly upon our litany of wants, but God faithfully goes about supplying our needs. What's more, He Himself is our "exceedingly great Reward" (Genesis 15:1). Be on guard: Envy will never remind you how great a provider your Father is, so ask the Holy Spirit to keep reminding you, and run back to rest contented in your Father's perfect love and loving plans for you—at the first twinge of envy.

> *Our Father is a great Provider.*
> *He is also our exceeding Great Reward!*

Keep your life free from love of money, and be content with what you have, for he has said, "I will never leave you nor forsake you." Hebrews 13:5

Practical Help to Practice

To work at defeating the root of covetousness, try these five practical steps for increasing your trust in God's provision:

1) Tithing. "Returning" the tithe is a faith journey that frees us from being controlled by thinking we are our own providers and opens our eyes to see God's sustaining Hand.

2) Why stop with the tithe? Let "offerings" carry you beyond the tithe. Give at His promptings and watch how God works to keep the river of blessing flowing through you to others.

3) Why just give money back to Him? By a strange twist whenever we realize that nothing "belongs" to us, everything can be seen as a gift (1 Corinthians 3:21-23).

4) Letting what He provides guide. Learn to let what He actually provides guide your decisions about what you can afford and show you where He draws the line between what we need and what we desire.

5) Practice gratitude for what has already been given. This turns our world around and fills even the seemingly emptiest cups as the "sacrifice" of thanksgiving opens our eyes to see all He already is giving (Jeremiah 33:11; Hebrews 13:15). St. Augustine prayed, "You have given so much to us. Give us one thing more, a grateful heart."[62]

Here is the best practical step of all for defeating envy and jealousy: As soon as you begin feeling envious of another's blessing, vigorously thank God for His provision to them. Get really good at affirming others in their spiritual gifts and at

---

[62] St. Augustine of Hippo (354-430 AD), *The Confessions*.

celebrating their victories with them. This totally disarms the enemy (envy), and opens the way for the Lord to extend blessing to you.

Waiting upon the Lord also grows contentment. Many of us have become so accustomed to "instant gratification" as a way of life in the modern world that we easily overlook the value that the scriptures place upon waiting. Waiting on God is a huge subject in the Bible: It includes active faith, bright hope and lively expectancy, combined with patience and perseverance. Without an ability to wait upon the Lord to make the fullness of His provision manifest, we are prey to being captured by envy and jealousy over what we don't have that others do—*in the moment*. However, with this faith ability in place we are actually told that we can possess our souls by patience (Luke 21:19). Simply by learning patience we can be uplifted, rather than crushed, by whatever is going on in our lives (see also Psalms 27:14 and 130:6; Micah 7:7). We can learn how to live for God's Better Day, which He is always leading us towards, on the other side of present troubles or short comings.

> **But those who wait for the Lord** [who expect, look for, and hope in Him] **shall change** *and* **renew their strength** *and* **power; they shall lift their wings** *and* **mount up** [close to God] **as eagles** [mount up to the sun]; **they shall run and not be weary, they shall walk and not faint** *or* **become tired.** Isaiah 40:31 AMP
>
> **From of old no one has heard or perceived by the ear, no eye has seen a God besides you, who acts for those who wait for him.** Isaiah 64:4
>
> **The Lord is good to those who wait for him, to the soul who seeks him. It is good that one should wait quietly for the salvation of the Lord.** Lamentations 3:25-26

There is a great joy in the world of things and in the operation of spiritual gifts, but it is not found in what we can get for ourselves by our own striving. True joy is found in what we see the great God of heaven actually giving to us freely out of His love and care. From this flows endless and deep satisfaction. Everything can come to be seen as a gift of love—both what God provides as well as what He withholds. Through that accurate vision there are such *treasures* of contentment, security and love as to fill even the emptiest of hearts.

The Way to Freedom

Envy and jealousy are thieves that get us chasing in the wrong direction, trying to grasp after blessing, rather than allowing God to bestow all good things in His good time. The tricky part is learning to remember how good godly contentment felt only moments before envy showed up and snatched it from us!

1) Be honest about every false or wrong desire "to grasp" after something you've not yet been given and recognize every twinge of envy as stealing your peace and godly contentment!

2) Take full responsibility for agreeing with it: Repent, renounce and carry it captive to Christ until you see something in Him that restores your confidence in God's provision for you.

3) Turn to the Father and release gratitude to Him for His loving plans to lead you step-by-step into your true inheritance!

NOTES/JOURNAL

___

EXERCISE

Write down three things that have most frequently or powerfully provoked you to envy or jealousy of others. Then pray and ask the Holy Spirit to show you what it was that you really wanted or what it was that you felt so deprived of that you became envious of another's blessing. Finally, seek the Lord for what it was that you were not trusting about God the Father. He is a perfect Provider, but His ways of providing do not always include giving us what we want, or believe we need, right when we desire to have it.

What I wanted and didn't get   **What it was that I really needed or was looking for**
1) _____   _____
2) _____   _____
3) _____   _____

The event shows me I was not trusting God to be my perfect Provider in this way:
1) _____
2) _____
3) _____

DISCUSSION QUESTIONS

Ask for a show of hands: How many in the group were told not to be envious of their brothers or sisters or playmates? How many were shown how not to feel envy? Typically we were given "the law" concerning correct and forbidden behaviors, but few of us were given the saving grace of being shown how to get free of the compelling negative emotions we were told not to express. This often leads to disguised ways of expressing the negative emotion anyway—for as Jesus said, what lies in the heart is the real source of sinful behavior (Mt 15:19; Mk7:21).

1) So, just for grins, what has the group noticed of the disguised (more socially acceptable or just plain sneaky) ways that envy and jealousy still seek to find expression in church or the workplace? What are some of the obvious ways?

2) Now, let's take these reflections and consider what a child could have been shown or taught that would have helped their heart get free of the influence of envy/jealousy? Consider that if a wise and understanding adult had been with us any time our heart suffered hurt or loss in childhood, we could have actually grown greater trust in God and forgiving love for the people around us—rather than have learned failed ways of coping on our own.

3) What does this show us to do with our hearts now—when envy seeks to rise?

MAIN POINTS

- Envy and jealousy are the opposites of godly contentment.
- Envy and jealousy grow out of coveting, pride and bitterness.
- Covetousness always wants more; it is a form of idolatry about things.
- Pride constantly compares to others to prove we are not inferior.
- Bitterness makes us resentful of the blessings of others.
- Beware of comparison to others—there is no wisdom in it.
- Our God is a great Provider—He faithfully supplies what we really need.
- Let the first sign of envy cause you to quickly return to trusting in your Father's promises of faithfulness to you.

DIGGING DEEPER

Let's take a closer look at waiting—if you have the time to spare! The scriptures actually promise us that if we learn to wait—if we cultivate the virtue of patience—we will "possess" our souls. What a concept! Envy and jealousy stay focused on what we didn't get or are afraid of losing, but *waiting* will "get" us the most important thing of all—a liberated, joyful soul. Patience is worth getting!

By your steadfastness *and* **patient endurance you shall win the true life of your souls.** Luke 21:19 AMP

But let endurance *and* **steadfastness** *and* **patience have full play** *and* **do a thorough work, so that you may be** [people] **perfectly and fully developed** [with no defects], **lacking in nothing.** James 1:4 AMP

Here are even more paeans of praise to the virtue of patience which "waits" upon God and looks to Him for everything needed.

And we desire each one of you to show the same earnestness to have the full assurance of hope until the end, so that you may not be sluggish, but imitators of those who through faith and patience inherit the promises. Hebrews 6:11-12

Behold, we call them blessed who endured. You have heard of the patience of Job, and have seen the Lord in the outcome, and how the Lord is full of compassion and mercy. James 5:11 WEB

Though you have not seen him, you love him. Though you do not now see him, you believe in him and rejoice with joy that is inexpressible and filled with glory, obtaining the outcome of your faith, the salvation of your souls. 1 Peter 1:8-9

SWORD AND SHIELD

There are many scriptural examples of envy and jealousy.

- Cain (which means "to get" or covet) was envious of Abel (Ge 4:3-5).
- Haggar's conception produced envy in Sarah (Ge 21:9-11).
- The Philistines envied Isaac for his wealth (Ge 26:12-16).
- Joseph's brothers envied him (Ge 37:3-11; Ac 7:9).
- Korah's rebellion grew out of his envy of Moses and Aaron (Nu 16:1-3; Ps 106:16-18).
- King Saul became envious of David's successes and favor with the people (1Sa 18:8-9).
- The chief priests delivered Jesus to Pilate because of envy (Mk 15:9-10).

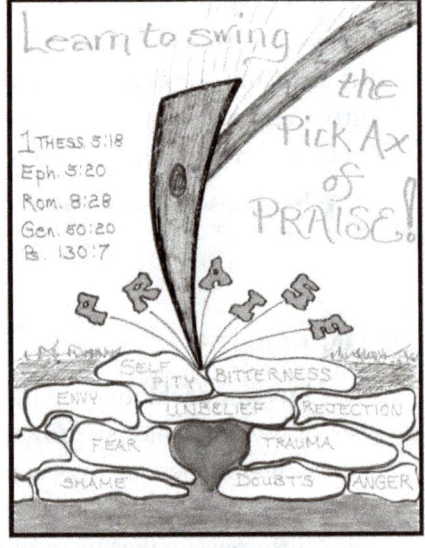

THE PICK AX OF PRAISE

Thanking God in all things radically shifts our perspective and liberates our heart. It takes a firm resolution to learn how to swing the pick ax of praise, but for those who do, fountains of living water are released!

God's antidote for envy/jealousy is *resting content* with His plans and provision.

Godly Contentment

> Not that I am speaking of being in need, for I have learned in whatever situation I am to be content. I know how to be brought low, and I know how to abound. In any and every circumstance, I have learned the secret of facing plenty and hunger, abundance and need. I can do all things through him who strengthens me. Philippians 4:11-13

> Now there is great gain in godliness with contentment, for we brought nothing into the world, and we cannot take anything out of the world. But if we have food and clothing, with these we will be content. 1 Timothy 6:6-8

> Keep your life free from love of money, and be content with what you have, for he has said, "I will never leave you nor forsake you." Hebrews 13:5

Scriptures confirm to us that our Father is an excellent provider.

> Trust in the Lord, and do good; dwell in the land and befriend faithfulness. Delight yourself in the Lord, and he will give you the desires of your heart. Psalm 37:3-4

> "Therefore do not be anxious, saying, 'What shall we eat?' or 'What shall we drink?' or 'What shall we wear?' For the Gentiles seek after all these things, and your heavenly Father knows that you need them all. But seek first the kingdom of God and his righteousness, and all these things will be added to you." Matthew 6:31-33

God's ways (of providing) are not always what we might expect.

> "For my thoughts are not your thoughts, neither are your ways my ways, declares the Lord. For as the heavens are higher than the earth, so are my ways higher than your ways and my thoughts than your thoughts." Isaiah 55:8-9

> "Yet the house of Israel says, 'The way of the Lord is not just.' O house of Israel, are my ways not just? Is it not your ways that are not just?" Ezekiel 18:29

PRAYER FOCUS

There is a great joy in the world of things and in the operation of His spiritual gifts, but it is not found in what we can get for ourselves by our own striving. True joy is found in what we see the sovereign Lord of heaven actually giving to us freely out of His love and care. From this flows endless and deep satisfaction. Everything can come to be seen as a love gift—both what the Father provides as well as what He withholds. And in that vision there are sufficient treasures of contentment, security and love to fill even the emptiest of hearts. Let us pray:

> *Father, forgive me wherever I have doubted Your goodness or wisdom in how You have provided for me throughout my life. Forgive me wherever I have sought Your Hand of blessing and failed to seek Your Face of love. Forgive me wherever I have measured Your love by my lack, rather than by the cross where You Yourself willingly suffered loss for my sake. I see Your love now and I cast myself fully and freely upon Your wisdom in what You choose to provide and what You choose to withhold. Let it all work to bring me to that place of incomparable joy where I finally see all elements of my life—even the "missing" ones—as loving gifts from My Beloved.*

RENUNCIATIONS AND AFFIRMATIONS

Renounce any agreements with untruth; believe Jesus' *truth* as your new *way* of *life*.[63]

Father, I renounce ___ (Covetousness, Bitterness...) in the generations of my fathers and I repent of having walked in it myself. I repent of my own sin of ___ (Idolatry, Materialism...). Forgive me and break its power over me and off my generations.

Covetousness	**Not trusting God**	**Pride**
Idolatry of possessions	Jealousy (love relationships)	Competition, comparison
Material security	Unbelief that God will provide	Superiority, inferiority
Greed, love of money		Selfishness, self-seeking
Wanting more	Discontent with present provision	Ambition, vanity
Bitterness	Envy of another's provision	**Possessiveness**
Unforgiveness	Fear of loss of control	Grasping (striving to get)
Resentment	Strife, rivalry, division	Control, manipulation
Retaliation	Fear of losing people	Always wanting more
Vengeance	Fear of losing things	Status conscious

PUTTING FEET TO YOUR PRAYERS: STRETCH YOURSELF!

Once you have done the repentance and the prayers, the best practical step of all for defeating envy and jealousy is to stir yourself to move in the ***exact opposite direction*** from the way spirits of envy or jealousy want you to go. Therefore, at the slightest feeling of envy when someone is being praised or promoted instead of you, or is displaying their possession of something you wish you had, *immediately* begin thanking the Lord for blessing them. Keep *vigorously* praising God for loving them until you sense a victory growing inside. This totally disarms the enemy (envy and jealousy), and opens the way for the Lord to extend blessing to you!

---

[63] Renunciation list is modified from Be In Health® teaching and materials, Dr. Henry W. Wright, Thomaston, Georgia, seminar notes, October 2000.

CHAPTER 20

EXPOSING THE DARKNESS

The Stronghold of the Occult

At this point in the series we have come to a stronghold that is unlike all the others in that it doesn't grow out of the ordinary interactions of people and events, but is constructed by points of direct contact with spiritual darkness. For some people this will be a lesson of little consequence—they have been blessed to have walked a path free and clear of trespassing into the occult domain. For others their immersion into the "depths of Satan" (Revelation 2:24) has been so devastating (whether of their own volition or forced upon them by others) that this chapter may seem like a pop gun, when what they need is a canon.

For many of us, however, contact with this realm has been by dribs and drabs: A little here, a little there, and the infiltration into our lives through the generations before us may hardly have been noticed in its effects upon us. Indeed, this is a domain that prefers to remain hidden in that half-light where curious or spiritually hungry souls go to find "something more" in the way of spiritual life and experience—not necessarily wanting evil, but drawn towards things beyond the pale of orthodox Christian faith. By posing as legitimate spiritual experience the New Age has made huge inroads into Western culture. The spider knows how to make the web all but invisible to the unsuspecting fly it seeks to catch. The enemy is a deceiver! One pastor said deception is like falling asleep: You don't know you are asleep until someone tries to wake you.[64] Let spiritual darkness be exposed for what it is and we will all wake up and seek the safety and freedom our Lord offers.

The Occult Realm Identified in Scripture

The occult is an entry point for the enemy. Like trauma the occult can open doors for the enemy's kingdom to enter and oppress us, but unlike trauma we may not have been aware of anything obviously wrong in our times of contact with it. Nevertheless, scripture shows that transgressing upon the occult is serious; in the Old Testament the penalty for it was nothing less than death and no sacrifice could atone for it (Exodus 22:18-20; Leviticus 20:6-8, 27). As New Testament believers we do not war against flesh and blood in this way, but Israel's example clearly shows us that we are not to be compromised by any involvement with the occult—we must keep it out of our lives.

> *Four main forms the occult takes:*
>
> *1) Worship of false gods, idolatry.*
> *2) Forbidden knowledge of the future.*
> *3) Forbidden contact with the dead.*
> *4) Forbidden access to spiritual power.*

The occult, like unforgiveness, is also a major block to healing. Until our contact with it is put under the Blood, it gives the

---

[64] Pastor Wade Trimmer, Grace Fellowship of Augusta, GA during a sermon in 2006.

enemy the legal right to bind and torment us with the curse of the law, since we let him lure us away from God's protection. The occult realm is a false god that seeks both worship (to become our heart's desire and daily focus) and service (to get us acting according to its desires). You don't have to love evil to worship and serve it; all you have to do is simply begin desiring the things it presents, thinking they are good. Then it's got your focus. Soon it gets you.

In ancient times, high places were sites where idol worship took place. Under our covenant prideful beliefs are the new high places where the Lord may be rejected in favor of that which is false (Exodus 20:3-6; 2 Corinthians 10:4-6). That is why this concealed realm needs to be exposed! *Webster's College Dictionary* defines the occult as "hidden from view."[65] The occult is anything that exalts itself against the knowledge of God or obscures the knowledge of God. This broad definition could apply in general to all of the operations of Satan's kingdom, but the occult, more narrowly and traditionally defined takes four main forms in scripture:

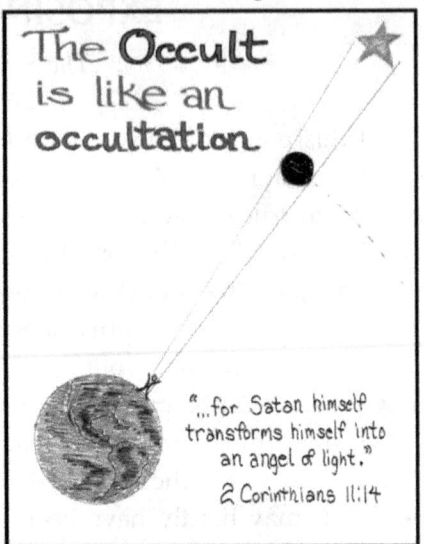

THE OCCULT COUNTERFEIT

Like a planet crossing in front of a star, the occult counterfeits true spiritual power and light (truth). Beware of spiritual claimants that look good, appear to be full of light, boast of great power, but hides the One True God.

1) Worship of false gods: idol worship, false religions, cults (Exodus 20:3; Deuteronomy 5:7).

2) Forbidden ways of seeking knowledge of the future: astrology, fortune telling, prognostication (Isaiah 47:13; Daniel 2:2; Matthew 24:11).

3) Forbidden contact with the dead: séances, mediums, Ouija (Leviticus 19:31, 20:6; Isaiah 8:19, 19:3).

4) Forbidden ways of seeking to access spiritual power: witchcraft, sorcery, shamanism (1 Sammuel 15:23; 2 Kings 17:17, Acts 8:9; Galatians 5:20).

The occult counterfeits genuine spiritual power and light (truth). In astronomy a planet that crosses in front of a star is said to cause an "occultation," meaning that the star is hidden from view. This gives us a perfect picture of Satan's counterfeiting activity.[66] Just as a planet reflects the sun's light, but has no fire of its

---

[65] Random House, *Webster's College Dictionary* (New York: McGraw-Hill, 1991).
[66] Teaching and insights about the occult analogy from astronomy from Be In Health® teaching and materials, Dr. Henry W. Wright, Thomaston, Georgia, seminar notes, October 2000.

own, so too the enemy seeks to draw our attention by a deceptive display of occult knowledge and power, while obscuring the wisdom and power that come through the One True God and his servants. Do not expect this kingdom to exhibit its dark side very often. Spiritual darkness prefers to disguise itself as light—at least in terms of attracting unsuspecting "flies" (us!) into its web. We would hardly walk into such a trap if we could see the evil on the other side (Proverbs 7:23; 14:12). This "occulting" activity of Satan is described in scripture. As you read these texts try to discern the false religion that has spread around the world which began with the visitation of "an angel of light" to an unwary soul.[67]

> *For even Satan disguises himself as an angel of light.*
> 2 Corinthians 11:14

And no wonder, for even Satan disguises himself as an angel of light. 2 Corinthians 11:14

But even if we or an angel from heaven should preach to you a gospel contrary to the one we preached to you, let him be accursed. Galatians 1:8

Temptations of the Occult

There are two main temptations of the occult. These are the "flesh hooks" that the tempter uses to snare the unwary.

1) Knowledge. The spirit behind it tempts with. Divination is the act or practice of trying to foretell the future by occult means. The cults also seek knowledge, claiming a superior and secret wisdom or way of salvation, but it doesn't come from God or the Bible.

> **Now concerning things sacrificed to idols: We know that we all have knowledge. Knowledge puffs up, but love builds up. But if anyone thinks that he knows anything, he doesn't yet know as he ought to know. But if anyone loves God, the same is known by him.** 1 Corinthians 8:1-3 WEB

2) Power. The spirit behind it tempts with control (1 Samuel 15:23). Witchcraft and sorcery seek to make things happen by the power of the mind, special talents or natural elements. It is a form of control—a rebellion against God's order or authority. Sorcery uses spells to control others or events; witchcraft uses objects. Both rely upon demons to do the real work.

> **Samuel said, "Has the Lord as great a delight in burnt offerings and sacrifices as in obeying the voice of the Lord? Behold, to obey is better than sacrifice, and to hearken than the fat of rams. For rebellion is as the sin of witchcraft, and stubbornness is as idolatry and teraphim (household good luck images)."** 1 Samuel 15:22-23 AMP

Sorcery is a translation of the Greek word *pharmakia* used in Galatians 5:19 to describe one of the works of the flesh. This is the root for pharmaceuticals, our

---

[67] Mormonism began when Joseph Smith was visited by the angel Moroni and shown a "different gospel."

word for prescription drugs. There is a subtle caution here that habitual use of medicines without going to God and/or without dealing with sin can become a dependency that is occult in nature because it obscures God. Dependency on prescription drugs can easily become a way of trying, be it knowingly or unknowingly, to bypass the curse of illness by not seeking to get right with God about what may be wrong in our hearts that is causing the physical problem (review Chapter 1).[68]

Be alert to signs and symptoms of occult penetration. The thoughts of the one being deceived become increasingly negative and are drawn to an unhealthy interest in the "dark side" of life or of things in general. The mind becomes confused, "foggy," blanks out easily, loses strength to think things through rationally and logically. Fear intensifies. A person is often bound to past occult contact in fear and/or pride. Other signs may include hatred of God, rejection of God's Word, inability to hear God and an inability to stay awake in church or when reading scripture.

The power of an occult experience to entrap people is built upon the temptation to believe in one's own experience and perspective above God's Word. *Powerful deception comes from the way the occult spirits make the truth claims seem real.* The connection is made by means of a subjective experience which conveys "authority" or credibility to the truth claim of the practice—whether it is a "spooky" feeling from ghosts in a house reputed to be haunted, or facts spoken during a séance that only the deceased could know, or crystal ball predictions that sometimes come true. If the final arbiter for the one becoming deceived is their own experience, *rather than the Bible*, the "spider's web" has not been set in vain. Like modern retailers, the enemy is a master at giving out "loss leaders," bits and pieces of knowledge or supernatural encounters, in order to get you to buy into what he wants to sell you. Then the real merchandising (the selling of your soul) begins. One occult activity, no matter how slight it seems, can easily lead into many other practices. Don't buy the lies! God desires that we choose life by avoiding that which He calls evil (Deuteronomy 30:11-19).

Principles for Balanced Discernment

Keeping in mind C. S. Lewis' caution about becoming either too dismissive of or too obsessed with this realm (Chapter 4), we will want to have some sound principles of balance and discernment concerning occult contact. Consider the following for starters:

1) It is heart attachment to any wrong thing or habitual sin which evil spirits use to subvert our focus and cause us to perish—not the "flirtation" of momentary temptations.

---

[68] Teaching and insights about the occult connection to pharmaceutical abuse from Be In Health® teaching and materials, Dr. Henry W. Wright, Thomaston, Georgia, seminar notes, October 2000.

> "But if your heart turns away, and you will not hear, but are drawn away to worship other gods and serve them, I declare to you today, that you shall surely perish." Deuteronomy 30:17-18

2) Agreement with any occult activity or belief opens doors. In terms of active transgression, it does not matter if we acted in ignorance or innocence or deliberately. The lines are clearly drawn between the two kingdoms—any trespass is a very real transgression. Nevertheless, even as He holds us accountable, the Lord in His love for us looks upon the heart and may choose to cover with His protection what we have touched in ignorance (Proverbs 17:9).

> **Hatred stirs up strife, but love covers all offenses.** Proverbs 10:12

3) The devil is an extreme legalist and will seek to use any touching of the occult, any trespass into his territory, to activate the curse of the law—the negative consequences of our disobedience. It is wise to renounce all contact with the occult that you suspect you, or your past generations, may have made.

> **Take no part in the unfruitful works of darkness, but instead expose them.** Ephesians 5:11

4) Dependence upon any created thing is a form of idolatry. Are you hooked on it? Are you defending your involvement with unreasonable intensity?

> **Jesus answered them, "Truly, truly, I say to you, everyone who commits sin is a slave to sin. The slave does not remain in the house forever; the son remains forever. So if the Son sets you free, you will be free indeed."** John 8:35-36

5) There are "gray areas" of legitimate, honest disagreement about what is forbidden for us "to touch," because the scriptures are *suggestive* of application, but not always *definitive*. Paul's word in Corinthians on eating meat sacrificed to idols shows us a position of grace in a "gray area" of their day—leaving conviction to the individual's conscience about matters of possible legal defilement.

> **So then each of us will give an account of himself to God. Therefore let us not pass judgment on one another any longer, but rather decide never to put a stumbling block or hindrance in the way of a brother. I know and am persuaded in the Lord Jesus that nothing is unclean in itself, but it is unclean for anyone who thinks it unclean.** Romans 14:12-14

6) The furthest reach of our liberty and God's covering grace are summed up in the phrase, "To the pure all things are pure" (Titus 1:15). However, we should always be willing to check the assumed purity of our motives. Just because we think something is harmless doesn't mean it is or that our reasons for being involved with it are aboveboard. Do not be deceived!

> **There is a way that seems right to a man, but its end is the way to death.** Proverbs 14:12

The Way to Freedom

Depending upon previous levels of involvement, gaining freedom from the occult can be simple or extremely laborious, especially if traumatic events took place. These steps are for light to moderate involvement with occult activities. Every chapter in the book will be needed where more severe penetration occurred.

1) Recognize, repent and renounce any involvement in occult activities by family members or ancestors, putting it under the Blood of Christ and breaking the curse in Jesus' Name.

2) Take full responsibility for any contact or involvement with occult activities you may have had: Repent, renounce in the same manner, carrying every activity captive to Christ.

3) Turn to the Father and release gratitude that there are no sins and no powers on earth that can separate you from His love!

NOTES/JOURNAL

_____
_____
_____
_____
_____
_____
_____
_____
_____
_____

EXERCISE

Consider carefully these questions to prompt your recall of any possible trespasses into occult territory.[69] Then take what you discern into the Prayer Focus and Renunciations sections.

1) Divination (seeking knowledge especially of the future from forbidden sources): Have you ever had your fortune told, followed your horoscope, had a tarot card reading, played with a Ouija board, consulted a medium or numerologist, or engaged in automatic handwriting?

---

[69] Modified from a list by Christian Healing Ministries, Jacksonville, FL, website download, 2009.

2) Spiritualism (seeking contact with the forbidden spiritual realm, including the dead): Have you ever attended a séance, practiced Transcendental Meditation or Yoga to enter an "altered state", been involved with mind-control, ESP or hypnotism, communicated with apparitions that were not of God, or worshipped at a pagan shrine or temple?

3) Witchcraft (seeking power from forbidden sources): Have you ever been involved in casting spells, practiced white or black magic, used voodoo, sought healing from a spiritualist, shaman or witch doctor, used a charm or amulet for protection or good luck, studied books on the occult with a view to use, practiced table-lifting, levitation or astral travel?

4) Devil worship (Satanism and false religions): Have you ever attended or belonged to a coven, attended a Black Mass, made a promise or pact or blood covenant with Satan, been a victim of Satanic Ritual Abuse (SRA), or attended witchcraft or voodoo services, or worshipped the gods of false religions or New Age gods?

5) Contact with objects (by ones' own initiative or that of others): Do you have objects or books in your possession that have associations with the occult?

6) Membership and relationships (we receive generationally and sexually from others): Have you, an ancestor or an intimate in sexual relationship been a member of the Masons (including all of its branches) or other cults (such as Christian Science, Scientology, Mormons, Rosicrucianism, etc.), or been involved with witchcraft, pagan religions, or the occult?

7) Activities (ones that may lead to oppression by the occult spirits): Have you ever been bound to substance addiction, sexual sins including pornography, drug trips, "hard rock" music, read or viewed comics, books and movies with demonic content, played games of an occult nature, believed in superstitions or been fascinated with the "dark side"?

DISCUSSION QUESTIONS

The point of this discussion is to pull the veil of secrecy off of this area of the enemy's work. Many people do not believe that the occult realm is real—and the enemy loves to have it so. Be careful, however, not to go into fear or excessive interest: Our God is far more powerful and fascinating! Close with a prayer for the Father to forgive, cleanse and cover the group wherever they have transgressed His boundaries.

- Why is this area (the occult realm) so interesting?
- Why do you suppose that God is so adamant about closing it off to us?
- How do you discern if you have encountered real spiritual darkness?

- How did occult contact feel? How else would you describe it?
- Did it affect your thoughts as well as your feelings?
- Have you had family members or friends involved in the occult?
- Did they ever realize that they had transgressed and seek to get free?
- Have you ever tried to talk someone out of being involved in the occult or a Christian or non-Christian cult?

MAIN POINTS

- The occult is a block to healing and a door point of entry for evil spirits.
- Unlike the shock of trauma, contact with the occult is not always noticed.
- The enemy is a legalist who brings a curse upon those who have transgressed by crossing over into his territory.
- The occult is a counterfeit way of "secret" knowledge and forbidden power; cults are counterfeit ways of salvation.
- The two major temptations of the occult are knowledge (pride) and control (power).
- The New Age is a mixture of "old" occultism and eastern mysticism.

DIGGING DEEPER

Carefully review the occult list in the Renunciations section. There is no need to be in fear about the occult. Pray and read over the items on the sheet. As you pay attention, if the Holy Spirit convicts you of contact, then repent. If your conscience is not quickened, then wait upon further clarification. Don't feel you have to renounce something in a "gray" area. Such areas of legitimate, honest differences in discernment among Christians are marked with an asterisk.* If it doesn't seem to have touched you in a negative way or be something the Holy Spirit is convicting you about, then keep your peace. However, beware if you are angered: Occult spirits will strenuously defend themselves against conviction and exposure!

SWORD AND SHIELD

The scriptures show us the seriousness and futility of involvement with this realm.

> "When you come into the land that the Lord your God is giving you, you shall not learn to follow the abominable practices of those nations. There shall not be found among you anyone who burns his son or his daughter as an offering, anyone who practices divination or tells fortunes or interprets omens, or a sorcerer or a charmer or a medium or a wizard or a necromancer, for whoever does these things is an

abomination to the Lord. And because of these abominations the Lord your God is driving them out before you." Deuteronomy 18:9-12

Occult practices described and condemned in scripture.

Exodus 7:11-12	2 Kings 21:5-6	Jeremiah 10:1-3	Acts 16:16-18
Exodus 20:3-4	2 Kings 23:5-6	Ezekiel 13:20	Acts 19:19-20
Exodus 22:18	Isaiah 2:6, 8	Ezekiel 21:21	Romans 1:22-25
Leviticus 19:26, 31	Isaiah 8:19-20	Daniel 2:27-28	1 Corinthians 10:21
Leviticus 20:6-7, 27	Isaiah 19:3	Micah 5:12	Galatians 5:19-21
Deuteronomy 18:9-14	Isaiah 47:9, 12-13	Acts 8:9-11	Revelation 16:14
1 Samuel 28:6-12	Isaiah 57:13	Acts 13:6-11	Revelation 18:2

PRAYER FOCUS

Father, thank You that You have both the power and the loving desire to cleanse me from all of my transgressions in these areas. Jesus, thank You for the Blood that You shed which is my liberation and the enemy's doom. Holy Spirit, thank You for working to lead me into all truth by removing the veil of deception that blinded me in the past. I ask for and gratefully receive all of Your ministry to me in this area. Please continue in every way to lead me out of darkness into Your glorious Kingdom of Light!

RENUNCIATIONS AND AFFIRMATIONS

Renounce any agreements with untruth; believe Jesus' *truth* as your new *way* of life.[70]

Father, I renounce these occult practices in the generations of my fathers and I repent of having walked in them myself. I repent of my own involvement with or contact with _____. Forgive me and break its power over me and off my generations.

Am. Indian ceremonies, cultic items
Angel worship
Apparitions, ghosts, poltergeists
Astral projection, aura reading
Astrology, horoscopes, zodiac signs
Buddhism: Zen and other forms
Cartoons, comics, movies, video games
  displaying horror, porn, violence
Chanting, mantras, incantations
Charms: horseshoes, rabbit's foot
Christian Science (Mary Baker Eddy)

Mormonism
Martial arts*: Tai chi, karate, judo,
  yoga, kungfu, aikido, tai kwan
Masons, Shriners, Eastern Star,
  Rainbow Girls, DeMolay
New Age thinking, symbols
Occult music and books
Ouiji™ boards
Pagan religions
Pornography
Psychic reading, psychic portraits

---

[70] Renunciation list is modified from Be In Health® teaching and materials, Dr. Henry W. Wright, Thomaston, Georgia, seminar notes, October 2000.
*An asterisk denotes a "grey area" of legitimate disagreement among Christians: see Digging Deeper

Clairvoyance, clairaudience, mental telepathy, ESP
Conjuration, channeling, mediums
Crystal balls, crystals
Cultural pagan ceremonies
Course of Miracles, Unity Church
Déjà vu
Demonic rock music
Divination: tarot, fortune telling, tealeaf reading, handwriting analysis, palm reading, I Ching, numerology, false prophecy, Kabala
Drug and alcohol abuse
Familiar spirits: necromancy, séances, table tapping, mediums
Fetishes, power objects
Hinduism, gurus, Eastern philosophies
False prophets (Nostradamus, etc.)
Hypnotism, self-hypnotism
Islam, Black Moslem teachings
Jehovah's Witness, Watchtower
KKK, racism, ethnic hatreds
Magic: white, black, stage magic*
Reincarnation
Rosicrucianism
Satanism, Satan worship
Science fiction addiction: excessive interest in UFO's*, aliens*
Scientology (Dianetics; L. Ron Hubbard)
Secret brotherhoods, blood oaths
Sorcery, pharmakia* (excessive use or dependence upon pharmaceuticals)
Spiritism, spirit guides
Statues of idols: including glorifying artists, sports heroes, movie stars
Superstitions: fear of black cats, wishing on a star, walking under ladders, Friday the 13th
Unitarian teachings
Voodoo
Wart charming
Water-witching, geomancy
Wicca, witchcraft, spells, warlocks, witches
Witchcraft/rebellion in the home or church

PUTTING FEET TO YOUR PRAYERS: STRETCH YOURSELF!

Sometimes it is necessary to do a house cleansing. Go through the rooms asking the Lord to show you if there are things that you have collected or were given to you that need to be cast out. Try not to become legalistic, but seek to discern with His help what dishonors the Lord you now serve. If it is clearly from the dark side, don't sell it to some poor unsuspecting soul—burn it or trash it. That's what the early church did.

Also many of those who were now believers came, confessing and divulging their practices. And a number of those who had practiced magic arts brought their books together and burned them in the sight of all. And they counted the value of them and found it came to fifty thousand pieces of silver. So the word of the Lord continued to increase and prevail mightily. Acts 19:18-20

While you are at it, do a house blessing. Go through the same rooms dedicating them to the Lord and welcoming His Spirit to fill your home with peace. Often people will make the sign of the cross over doors and other openings with oil or water that has been blessed by a simple prayer of consecration committing the oil or water to the Lord for His purposes.

CHAPTER 21

FEAR NOT!

The Stronghold of Fear

What are you afraid of? OK, maybe you aren't afraid of anything. Let's put it this way: Are you anxious, do you experience dread over certain events, are you weighted down with concerns, are you chronically worried, stressed out, or shy around people? Like so many others, perhaps you avoid speaking in public, or want to run from times of conflict and confrontation? All these are forms of fear. As such they stand in the way of the life Jesus wants to live in us. Jesus is the Fearless One who has overcome the world, the flesh, and the devil, and is bringing to us the perfect love of the Father so that we too can become overcoming ones and live valiant lives, trusting our God even in situations of peril.

> *Fear is:*
> False
> Evidence
> Appearing
> Real

Fear is therefore a mighty stronghold that the enemy seeks to build in every believer to quench faith, stymie love and turn us away from the challenges of our high calling. Fear is built upon the other strongholds we have been studying: unbelief in God's perfect love is the root to all fears; accusation makes us feel cut off and condemned; bitterness binds the pain of the past to us; unhealed trauma makes our world feel very insecure; rejection sends frightful messages to our heart; self-rejection blocks us from believing that God really can love us; envy insists that others are getting a better deal; and occult involvement always brings massive amounts of fear. No wonder that fear is something of an emotional pandemic! Fortunately for all of us, the Lord has great remedies!

Two Forms of Legitimate Fear

There are two kinds of fear that are good and helpful: godly fear and fear awareness of immediate danger. Even so, we need to beware—both of these can quickly turn into the wrong kind of fear.

1) Godly fear is respect, honor and acknowledgment of who God is. It is a healthy awareness that God holds us accountable for our choices. On the other hand, being afraid of God, or of what God may do, or of what God may allow, or of what God may ask of us comes from the enemy.

2) Fear awareness of immediate danger enables us to deal with trouble and rescue the situation. Science has identified this as the "flight or fight" response of the General Adaptation Syndrome (review Chapter 1) and we need it to gear our bodies up for immediate action. This can quickly become "bad fear" if a) we are paralyzed or panicked and cannot act decisively or b) there is no real response we can make because we are being alarmed by imagined or future dangers, not immediate, life-threatening ones. This kind of fear response keeps most people living stressed up and breaks down health like a hammer.

Apart from these two good types of fear, all other forms are due to not trusting God. The critical issue is heart-trust in God.

You keep him in perfect peace whose mind is stayed on you, because he trusts in you. Trust in the Lord forever, for the Lord God is an everlasting rock. Isaiah 26:3-4

An Anatomy of Fear

If you want freedom you need to know that fear is a spiritual issue—not a personality problem. Watch this progression carefully. It will help you recognize and renounce any agreements with fear you may have. Remember, the enemy tempts us with very persuasive ideas, images and impressions. Stand on God's truth just as Jesus did when he had to face down the Tempter (Luke 4:1-13).[71]

1) Fear is the opposite of love. Just as perfect love casts out fear, so too "perfect fear" casts out love. Fear closes us in on Self (our old nemesis), activating selfishness, self-centeredness and above all self-protectiveness. Faith and trust open us and enable us to actively care for others and for things beyond ourselves in the self-less way of love (1 John 4:18-19).

2) Fear is little faith or no faith. Jesus upbraided the disciples for having little faith and no faith when they became worried about their daily needs (Matthew 6:25-34) and afraid during the storm at sea (Mark 4:35-40). We might have thought such concerns were normal, but the gospel shows us instead that it is "illegal" for a follower of Christ to fall into fear in any of its forms.

3) Fear is the opposite of faith. Fear works in the same way faith does but in the opposite direction. Faith looks past the problem of the visible reality to see its solution in the invisible reality of God and therefore becomes the substance in us that God uses to fulfill His purposes (Hebrews 11:1). Fear looks at the visible problem, ignores the invisible Savior, and becomes the substance the enemy uses to fulfill his plans for us. Job lamented that what he feared came upon him (Job 3:24-26). Fear is false protection—it actually brings trouble our way.

4) Fear is spiritual blindness. It keeps us from seeing with our eyes of faith. It minimizes what God can do, "shrinks" us as His vessels and magnifies what the enemy is doing. Fear "giganticizes" the problem (Numbers 13:30-33).

5) Fear is actually a sin. Fear is distrust in God, rooted in the sin of unbelief, for whatever is not of faith/trust in God is sin (Romans 14:23).

---

[71] Modified from a list by Pastor Ed Kelly: Be In Health® teaching and materials, Dr. Henry W. Wright, Thomaston, Georgia, seminar notes, October 2000.

6) Fear is spiritual bondage. It enslaves us and carries us captive to the enemy's mindset (Romans 8:15).

7) Fear is an evil spirit (2 Timothy 1:7). Spirits of fear enjoy pressing their own fearfulness upon us. They delight in using fear to derail our lives and destroy our health. They are liars and bullies who never tell you *the whole truth*—otherwise you would quickly go back to trusting God as you were before they showed up.

As Paul wrote to timid Timothy, it was not God who gave us "a spirit of fear" (and broke our faith connection to Him). What God gives us is "power, love and a sound mind" (2 Timothy 1:7). Note that we have a choice to make: We can have either fear *or* power, love and a sound mind. We cannot have it both ways! Even the presence of a little stress can begin robbing anyone of confidence in God, feelings of love and soundness of mind (thinking clearly, remembering readily). On the other hand, reconnect your faith with confidence in God's power, love and wisdom and see how quickly fear is sent packing.

> *For God hath not given us the spirit of fear; but of power, and of love, and of a sound mind.*
> 2 Timothy 1:7 KJV

Finding Freedom from Fear

There are many effective ways of getting free from the power of fear—try these out in addition to the steps of Chapter 7.

1) Receive: Let perfect love cast out fear. Work on renewing the true Image of God in your heart. God is love and real love is of God (John 4:16). Keep your thoughts fixed on who God really is (Isaiah 26:3). Believing in His perfect love casts fear out (1 John 4:18-19). Meditate upon His love expressed for you at the cross. Open your heart and receive His love by faith.

2) Believe: God's Word undercuts the power of fear. Remember that we build faith by staying in the Word (Romans 10:17). Saying scripture over and over has power to slowly push back the attack of fear. Believing scripture has awesome and immediate power once it becomes a living and life-giving Word to you. Truth must be touching your heart and your spirit to really bring inward release and freedom. Take your stand on the truth as Jesus did. Stoutly resist the temptation to fear.

3) Resist: Don't let fear stop you. Keep obeying despite your fears; don't give ground to the enemy. Refuse to let fear push you around or shut you down. Resist it (James 4:7-8). Taking decisive action ("just do it") defeats a lot of fears. Once you have finally struggled through the trial despite your fears, the same fears will have less power over you in future trials.

4) Rebuke: Prayers of command can cast out fear. Call a friend who can do spiritual warfare.

5) Love: Loving will release fears from your heart. Start with friendly animals and work up to friendly people. Whenever love fills your heart, fear becomes an outcast.

6) Rejoice: Laughter releases the grip of fear (Proverbs 17:22).

7) Surrender: Let a willingness to die to Self release you from fear (Luke 9:23-25). If we are harboring a fear of death, other fears will always defeat us—this one has to be dealt with first. A willingness to suffer, even die, for Christ defeats most fears, since the fear of death is the root of all fears (Hebrews 12:14-15). When we don't care what happens so long as His good will for us will be done, we slip out of the snare of many fears. The overcomers of Revelation 12:11 loved not their own lives even in the face of death. Just as in warfare between nations, "surrendering" to the Lord always brings peace and release, restoring His Kingdom's reign in our hearts (Isaiah 30:15).

8) Pray: Put your fears to rest as you release your concerns to God. Cast your cares on Him by praying concerns out of your heart and into His Hands. Keep carrying it to Him until you really do let it go (Philippians 4:6-7).

9) Discern: Learn to recognize the voice of fear (the way it presses upon you) and stop listening to it (Hebrews 5:14).

An Ongoing Battle

Oddly enough the best time to start trusting God is when you are caught in fear. Jesus used a storm-tossed and windswept sea to offer His first "class" in walking on water (Matthew 14:25). He waited for fear to strike His disciples *before* challenging them to trust Him. The Psalmist would have approved. Note that the repeated use of "will" indicates a deliberate choice.

> **When I am afraid, I will put my trust in you... In God I put my trust. I will not be afraid. What can flesh do to me?** Psalm 56:3-4 WEB

The very best way to get free of persistent fear is by the six steps to freedom laid out for you in Chapter 7. Along the way to victory you will "see" a threefold progression of understanding: Faith becomes seeing, seeing becomes believing and believing becomes resting in confidence.

1) Jesus has overcome the world—He will always be victorious. This is the "seeing stage" as faith opens our eyes to see Jesus as the answer because of what He has done and can do.

> **"In the world you will have tribulation. But take heart; I have overcome the world."** John 16:33

2) We overcome through faith in Him, not through faith in ourselves. Our faith in God's love and power is what overpowers our fear—one battle at a time. This is the "believing stage": We work hard at believing that what we see in Him is true.

> **For everyone who has been born of God overcomes the world. And this is the victory that has overcome the world—our faith. 1 John 5:4**

3) Our heart becomes established as we make progress at more continually beholding God's perfect love for us and His power to give us victories. This is the "resting stage": We trust Him enough to stay centered and surrendered most of the time.

> **There is no fear in love, but perfect love casts out fear. For fear has to do with punishment, and whoever fears has not been perfected in love. We love because he first loved us. 1 John 4:18-19**

Faith lifts and leads; fear presses and prods. Fear focuses on the thing feared—never on God. Learn to recognize when you are in fear and deal with it first, then you will be able to work with the problem it represents and receive the Lord's guidance and help much more readily. Ask the fruitful question: "What am I really afraid of?" Find it and deal with it! It is actually an act of faith-fullness to confess our fears as unbelief and sin. Our Father loves an honest conversation, even if it is about our failings.

> **Let us then with confidence draw near to the throne of grace, that we may receive mercy and find grace to help in time of need. Hebrews 4:16**

Naming fear as sin begins the process of repentance and restoration to trust. As we do this we enter into fellowship with the Father about the truth of our situation. The problem is not with God—in what He has allowed—it is with our inability or unwillingness to trust Him with it. Now that we are talking it over with Him, we can draw strength from our relationship. So let us go boldly to the throne of grace and obtain mercy, then re-discover that His grace really is sufficient to help us in our time of need (2 Corinthians 12:9).

The Way to Freedom

Some fears are easy to see; others are much harder to recognize—we have lived with them for so long that they seem normal and natural: "Of course I'm stressed, look at my situation!" The key is to focus on recovering the lost trust in God.

1) Be willing to recognize *any loss of peace* and any advent of stress as temptations coming from a spirit of fear—unless some other negative emotion is clearly predominating (such as anger).

2) Take full responsibility for agreeing with fear, losing peace and becoming "stressed": Repent, renounce and carry it captive to Christ until you see something in Him that restores trust.

3) Turn to the Father and release gratitude to Him that His perfect love is always able to cast out your fear!

NOTES/JOURNAL

___

EXERCISE

Job lamented that what he feared came upon him anyway (Job 3:25). Sometimes we act as if holding on to a fear will protect us. Sometimes we just bury our head and pretend it is not out there. A better way is to ask the fruitful question: What am I really afraid of? Then hold that deepest fear up to the Light of Christ until you find something in Him that answers it.

For instance: What is the worst thing that could happen to you? That you would die? Well, in that case you would go to heaven. So why are you so afraid? Or is it that you would lose a loved one? God forbid that it should happen, but if it did, Jesus would be right there to comfort you and lead you (if you let Him) to the other side of grieving where you would experience a resurrection of your life on earth. But living in fear of losing someone will rob you of your life on earth now. See how this works? Make it work for you!

The thing I greatly fear	What I need to see in Jesus to let that fear go
_____	_____
_____	_____
_____	_____

DISCUSSION QUESTIONS

Fear is such a prevalent enemy and it can take so many forms. Not everyone has known what it is like to live with dread, panic or phobias. On the other hand, anxiety and worry are like the common cold and flu bugs of the spiritual life. We never tire in winter of swapping knowledge about our favorite remedies, so take some time now to share what helps you combat the common contagion of fear.

- What do you do when you are afraid? Who do you call? Where do you go?
- What "natural remedies" work best? Example: leaving the lights or a TV on at night, or a radio playing in the background.
- What "spiritual remedies" work best?
- Are there times when running away from what you fear is wisdom?
- How about the other times? Has fear ever backed you into a corner?
- What fears have you fought through to final victory?
- What fear has paralyzed you?
- How could you prepare if you were to meet it again?
- Have you ever applied the Steps to Freedom in Chapter 7?
- Ever thought to apply them? Why not?

MAIN POINTS

- Fear in any of its forms is the cause of many illnesses.
- Fear is sin (confess it as such) and fear is an evil spirit (resist it).
- Fear blocks power, love and a sound mind. You can't have it both ways!
- Fear and faith are opposites—both are "magnets" for what we focus upon.
- Fear is rooted in distrust of God and unbelief in His Word.
- Fear actually works to bring what you fear upon you!
- The best time to defeat fear is the first moment you discern it.
- Faith in the perfect love of the Father casts out fear and establishes our heart as we trust His promises to us.

DIGGING DEEPER

Study and then confess these affirmations concerning fear, proclaiming them out loud if you need to:

Fears are liars and bullies, and they are very deceptive at how they are lying to me. If I believe them a little, I get anxious; if I believe them a lot, I am tormented. When I believe a lie about God or myself, I lose the peace. When I begin believing the truth again, the peace returns. My feelings are the biggest liars in my life about God and myself. I only half believe what others tell me, but all too often, I believe my feelings—no matter what they say. If I believed only the truth about God and myself, I would never fall into fear.

"And you will know the truth, and the truth will set you free." John 8:32

If I only believed the truth about God and myself I would be full of peace and joy.

May the God of hope fill you with all joy and peace in believing, so that by the power of the Holy Spirit you may abound in hope. Romans 15:13

My feelings lie to me by mixing falsehoods with truth and by not telling the whole truth. From now on I am going to bet my life on believing the truth, the whole truth and nothing but the truth!

SWORD AND SHIELD

Scriptures greatly help us to counter fear. Saying scripture over and over has power to slowly push back the attack of fear. Believing scripture has awesome and immediate power once it becomes a living and life-giving Word to you. Truth must be touching your heart and your spirit to really bring release and freedom. Take your stand on the truth as Jesus did—and stoutly resist the temptation to fear (see also Ps 27:3; Ps 118:6; Pr 29:25; Isa 12:2; Isa 43:1; Lk 12:32; Ro 8:15).

Lord is my light and my salvation; whom shall I fear? The Lord is the stronghold of my life; of whom shall I be afraid? Fear not, for I am with you. Psalm 27:1

"Be not dismayed, for I am your God; I will strengthen you, I will help you, I will uphold you with my righteous right hand." Isaiah 41:10

"Look to me, and be you saved, all the ends of the earth; for I am God, and there is none else." Isaiah 45:22 WEB

"Why, even the hairs of your head are all numbered. Fear not; you are of more value than many sparrows." Luke 12:7

So we can confidently say, "The Lord is my helper; I will not fear; what can man do to me?" Hebrews 13:6

Humble yourselves, therefore, under the mighty hand of God so that at the proper time he may exalt you, casting all your anxieties on him, because he cares for you. 1 Peter 5:6-7

PRAYER FOCUS

It is actually an act of faith-fullness to confess our fears as unbelief and sin. Our Father loves an honest conversation, even if it is about our failings. Naming fear as sin begins the process of repentance and restoration to trust. As we do we enter into fellowship with the Father about the truth of our situation.

The problem is not with God in what He has allowed — it is with our inability or unwillingness to trust Him with it. Now that we are talking it over with Him, we can draw strength from our relationship. So let us go boldly to the throne of grace and obtain mercy, then re-discover and receive His grace to help us in our time of need (He 4:16).

Father, help me to remember to come running home to You whenever I fall into the arms of my enemy and find myself in the pigsty of fear in the future. I pray that You will grant me boldness to always know that I can come into Your presence no matter how fear-filled I happen to be. Help me to draw my strength from believing in Your love and power.

The following is a sample prayer for resisting an attack of fear. Don't panic if you can't remember it the way it is here — He knows your heart! Pray it the way the Holy Spirit helps you to remember.

Father, forgive me for falling into fear again. Thank You that I can come boldly into Your presence and ask You to cleanse me of this iniquity. Thank You that You love me and want to fellowship with me even now. Thank You that You have made great plans for how to help me and that even this situation will be made to work for my good. I ask You to send Jesus for my deliverance and to meet me with peace and power by Your Spirit right where I am, as I am, and lead me forward. Strengthen me to hold on to You as I resist fear and watch for Your final victory to arrive.

RENUNCIATIONS AND AFFIRMATIONS

Renounce any agreements with untruth; believe Jesus' *truth* as your new *way of life*.[72]

Father, I renounce ___ (Fears about death, Fear of man...) in the generations of my fathers and I repent of having walked in it myself. I repent of my own sin of ___ (Fear of death, dying...). Forgive me and break its power over me and off my generations.

Fears about death	Fear of man	Fears related to religion
Fear of death, dying	Fear of rejection	Afraid of God
Fear of not going to heaven	Fear of public speaking	Fear of punishment
	Self-consciousness	Fear of losing salvation
Fear of dying prematurely	Shyness	Superstitions
	Inferiority, insecurity	Dread of obedience
Fear of losing loved ones	Fear of inadequacy	Fear of deliverance
Fear of loss of relationships	Fear of humiliation	Fear of evil spirits
	Fear of success/failure	Fear of final judgment
Fear of abandonment	Fear of responsibility	

---

[72] Renunciation list is modified from Be In Health® teaching and materials, Dr. Henry W. Wright, Thomaston, Georgia, seminar notes, October 2000.

Fears about the future	Fear of dependency	Other fears
Panic attacks	Perfectionism	Nightmares, evil visions
Fear of tomorrow, future	Driven-ness	Fears related to nature
Worry and anxiety	Suspicious of others	Fear of poverty, lack
Dread (expecting evil)	Controlling of others	Fear of enclosed spaces
Fear of change	Fear of people in authority	Fear of allergens
Fear of unknown	Fear of abandonment	Phobias
		Fears related to illness

PUTTING FEET TO YOUR PRAYERS: STRETCH YOURSELF!

Do it afraid! Do it anyway! Whatever your fears are, don't let them back you into a corner. Fears are bullies who want to rob you of peace and then block your path into the future. Don't let them!

Things fear tries to stop me from doing   **My strategy for counteracting fear will be**

_____   _____
_____   _____
_____   _____
_____   _____
_____   _____

CHAPTER 22

NO MORE IDOLS!

The Stronghold of Addiction

In the previous chapters on strongholds we examined each one in its uniqueness. With this lesson we will explore the common elements that constitute their binding power. Although this is a lesson focused upon addictions, it actually applies to anything in life that we can't "just say no" to. That is because the ground beneath the cross is level. People with addictions are not a special class of sinners. All of us have been badly broken by the Fall and need to be saved and mended by the love and mercy of God. The root issues are the same for all of us. The path of redemption and restoration is also the same: We are all saved *by grace through faith*.

> People with addictions are not a special class of sinners.

> **For by grace you have been saved through faith. And this is not your own doing; it is the gift of God.** Ephesians 2:8

Understanding Addictions

Narrowly defined addictions have to do with substance abuse; a wider term for addictions, one that is Biblical, is *a besetting sin*. The besetting sin is the sin that "besets" us—assails us and hems us in—whenever the temptation for it comes along. Certainly this scripture applies to those who are beset with substance abuse issues, but it applies equally well to those who can't seem to give up being judgmental or jealous or worried. Carefully study this passage from Hebrews. These are deeply instructive of our freedom. For instance, AA says when you are Hungry, Angry, Lonely or Tired, it is time to HALT—lay aside that weight, then get your focus back before trying to go on. Where should our focus be? On the Lord. Looking to Him we prevail!

> **Wherefore <u>seeing we also are compassed about</u> with so great a cloud of witnesses, let us <u>lay aside every weight</u>, and the sin which doth so easily beset us, and let us <u>run with patience</u> the race that is set before us, <u>looking unto Jesus</u> the author and finisher of our faith; who for the joy that was set before him <u>endured the cross</u>, despising the shame, and is set down at the right hand of the throne of God.** Hebrews 12:1-2 KJV

What is an addiction? An addiction is anything that controls us and holds us in bondage. That which controls us, rules us, and whenever it gets triggered, God is not our master—sin is.

> **The Lord said to Cain, "Why are you angry, and why has your face fallen? If you do well, will you not be accepted? And if you do not do well, sin is crouching at the door. Its desire is for you, but you must rule over it."** Genesis 4:6-7

Whatever we cannot just say no to (that which is not of God) holds us in its power. It seeks to enslave us (Romans 6:6), then destroy us and in the process, destroy as many others as it can (John 10:10). Some things that are good can become an addiction when moderation is exceeded. Some things are no good to begin with. There are many forms that addictions can take:

Legal and illegal drugs	Alcohol	Eating disorders
Foul language	Sexual sins	Pornography
Relationships	"Workaholism"	Gambling
Shopping	Entertainment	Compulsive behaviors
The love of money	Obsessions	Worry, anxiety, panic

Combating Addictions

Learn the "want to want to" prayer: "Lord, help me want to want what You want and hate what You hate." This enlists the Lord to work with your emotional life and honestly admits to God that deep down *in this moment* a large part of you doesn't want His will. Like Esau you are being strongly tempted to trade your inheritance for a bowl of porridge (Genesis 25:29-34). Remember the teaching on who we are in Christ (Chapter 9)? No matter how much we may crave the wrong thing, that desire is still not who we really are now as New Creations. The real you truly does want what He wants. The real you already has the nature of Jesus joined to you by the Spirit. Even so, all you may "see" of the new you is a tiny wish that you weren't so weak against the temptation. That's the "David" in you wanting to take down your "Goliath" side. Don't get in his way!

The number one way of escape is running to God (1 Corinthians 10:13). Many run *from* God, instead of *to* God. Many run from their troubles, their weaknesses, their failings, rather than face them, winding up in even worse predicaments. Hear this life-saving promise: We are absolutely, unconditionally promised that *everyone* who calls on the Name of the Lord *will* be saved (rescued, delivered, restored).

The same Lord is Lord of all, bestowing his riches on all who call on him. For "<u>everyone</u> who calls on the name of the Lord <u>will</u> be saved." Romans 10:12-13

To get free of any besetting sin we have to learn to call and keep on calling on the Lord—learning how to lean hard on Him and draw on His saving help, casting *all* our hope on Him and hanging on for dear life. How much do you have to call? As much as it takes, as often as it takes, as long as it takes. Our full recovery requires becoming 100% surrendered to and committed to God. There is no peace, no victory without surrender. We cannot be 90% surrendered to the Lord and still gain lasting victory over any besetting sin. Since we will never be more committed to God than we believe *deep down* that God is committed to us, believing the truth about our Father's love is truly a life and death issue. It was for Jesus—He was willing to die to reveal the Father to us (John 14:9-11 and 17:1-5). Believing the truth about your Father's unflinching and amazing love for you is the cure for backsliding—once it is believed in enough for you to run to Him, rather than from Him.

Three Powerful Lies

There are three deadly deceptions of the enemy. These lies must be recognized and cast down (see Ecclesiastes 4:12 for the metaphor of a threefold cord's strength).

Lie #1) The Lie of the Idol: The spirit behind the idol promises to give life to those it seeks to capture. The strong grip of addiction upon the soon-to-be enslaved one comes from a spiritual power working through the idol to steal, kill or destroy. Remember that an idol is anything that we place *above* God, anything that we want *more* than God.

> What am I saying then? That a thing sacrificed to idols is anything, or that an idol is anything? But I say that the things which the Gentiles sacrifice, they sacrifice to demons, and not to God, and I don't desire that you would have communion with demons. 1 Corinthians 10:20 WEB

Demons still offer a "fix" in exchange for worship. Worship means "to ascribe worth to." It also translates as "to serve." How have you been serving them? What are they saying to you? Does it sound anything like this?

1 ADDICTION FROM 3 LIES

Satan's convincing lies can form powerful strongholds within us. Renounce and resist any lies coming to you from the idol, the wounded places in your heart and any distorted image of the Father you may have.

> *Come to me and I will give you power to mend your life. Give yourself to me and I will satisfy you. I will ease the pain and give you gain.*

Lie #2) The Lie of the Wounded Heart: This keeps the one bound looking in the wrong direction, but the problem is not "out there" (in the world of things to get or people to blame) and can't be fixed out there. The problem lies within—in a heart so broken that it desperately needs a great love to heal it. The root cause of addiction is pain where love should have been. It has been famously observed that "the young man who rings the bell at the brothel is unconsciously looking for God." [73] All such attempts to fill the "God void" the wrong way are

---

[73] Bruce Marshall, *The World, the Flesh and Father Smith* (Boston, MA: Houghton Mifflin Company, 1945), p. 108. Often mistakenly attributed to G. K. Chesterton.

doomed to failure, often resulting in bondage. Being disgusted with one's self over the besetting sin doesn't help; it actually increases sin's bondage through self-hatred and self-rejection (Chapter 18).

Lie #3) The Lie of the Distorted Image: Only the revelation of the Father's great love can mend such a broken heart, but a distorted image of the Father keeps the one bound running *from* God, rather than *to* Him—the root cause of backsliding. A distorted image of self binds the pain of self-rejection in the heart (Chapters 8-10). Both images need thorough cleansing and mending in order to liberate the heart from these deep roots of the besetting sin.

Satan is a liar from the beginning. His lies are very convincing and once they have had a chance to impact our feeling system, they become powerful strongholds within us. Our task is to recognize and renounce those lies, carry them captive to Christ and then come into agreement with God's truths (2 Corinthians 10:4-6). This is war so be prepared to go to battle stations at a moment's notice. Don't tarry in the pig pen like the prodigal did—race to your Father at the first sign of weakness. Take that Hebrews 4:16 "elevator" straight to His throne of grace. As quickly as you can, obtain the mercy and find the grace He so freely wants to give you. Learn to let your place of disgrace reveal your Father's greater grace!

We are clearly instructed that we are saved "by grace through faith" (Ephesians 2:8). Therefore, in order to overcome our besetting sins, compulsions and addictions we will need to grow a great faith in the greatness of the saving grace of God. Staying well-connected with the Lord is not an option!

1) We will need to call on the Name of the Lord for rescue (Romans 10:12-13).

2) We will need a "love of the truth that we may be saved"—so that we will stay determined to fight to the death against believing the three lies in our moments of doubt and pain (2 Thessalonians 2:10).

3) We will need balance concerning our struggle with the flesh.

    a) The flesh is crucified for us. Because the sinful nature has already been crucified by Christ, at times all we will have to do is simply turn away from it and entrust ourselves to God. In this way the flesh remains in its crucified state (accomplished by His Hand) and we live the new life in the Spirit (Romans 6:6; 7:5-6; 8:10-11; Galatians 2:19-21).

    b) We must crucify the flesh. At other times, when the flesh rises up with too much power for us to easily turn back to trusting God, we are called to crucify the flesh in order to deal with the stronghold it now has over us. These are the times of battle, exertion and endurance (Romans 8:13; 13:12-14; Galatians 5:22-25; Ephesians 4:20-24; Colossians 3:1-5). They require prayer, patience (with ourselves) and perseverance (against the enemy).

4) We will need wisdom in discerning when to fight and how to trust.

a) We fight *as if* it all depends on us (Matthew 11:12; Ephesians 6:13).

b) We trust our victory depends upon Him (Exodus 14:13; Zechariah 4:6).

5) We will need a willingness to fight to the death. Depending upon the power of the stronghold that has grown in us from habitual past sins, we will need a holy resolve and determination to choose to die fighting for our freedom (if it comes to that), rather than give in to the old bondage and become slaves to sin again (Luke 9:23-25; Revelation 12:11).

> **Consider him who endured from sinners such hostility against himself, so that you may not grow weary or fainthearted. In your struggle against sin you have not yet resisted to the point of shedding your blood.** Hebrews 12:3-4

Don't let your trials be wasted! Don't try to get out of your trials so quickly that you don't take the time to look up to the Father and make sure your heart believes that even while you are "at your worst," even when your weaknesses are in your face, even when you seem filled with wrong desire or shameful emotions, *even in those moments* He is loving you, covering you with immense mercy and grace, cheering for you, and desiring your conversation and fellowship—over the sins or temptations you are struggling with! Get a good look by faith at the beautiful God who loves us even in our places of disgrace. This breaks the deep grip of shame over our fallenness that came in through Adam's nature. But don't try to feel these things, just refresh your heart by saying to Him what His Word says is true about Him.

The Way to Freedom

The self-blinding barrier of denial must be broken through before any addiction can be recognized for what it is and honestly resisted. Assuming that has already happened, then the following steps can be doggedly pursued. Victory rarely comes easily.

1) Take full responsibility for every aspect of the addiction you have recognized: Repent, renounce making it an idol you worshiped and served so whole-heartedly.

2) Carry every area of disobedience and rebellion captive to Christ until you see something in Him that restores your trust and confidence in God's love and mercy for you and His power to help you.

3) Turn to the Father and release gratitude to Him that even in your worst places of disgrace He covers you with His grace! Pray for a passion to worship and serve Him instead of the idol.

4) Be prepared to call on His Name at a moment's notice!

NOTES/JOURNAL

_____
_____
_____
_____
_____
_____
_____
_____
_____
_____

EXERCISE

Revelation is God turning on the lights so that we can see something that was formerly hidden to us. The enemy hides much in plain sight—hence, what is obvious to others about us, may not be something we "see" at all. This is called denial by some, but from the Bible's point of view it is usually not a conscious refusal to see truth, but a self blinding work by the deceiver (2Ti 2:24-26; Re 4:12:9). Ask the Holy Spirit to reveal truth. As you go over this list, place a check mark beside areas where you are frequently beset (harassed or besieged).

__ Legal and illegal drugs	__ Workaholism	__ Envy or jealousy
__ Alcohol	__ Compulsive behaviors	__ Fear or anxiety
__ Eating disorders	__ Shopping	__ Guilt and shame
__ Foul language	__ Entertainment	__ Judging others
__ Sexual sins	__ Gambling	__ Depression
__ Pornography	__ Anger/unforgiveness	__ Self hatred
__ Relationships	__ Rejection	__ Television

Now review the three powerful lies that bind besetting sins to us, making it hard for anyone to "just say no" and walk in freedom. Write down the reasons why these lies might have gained a foothold in your heart and life. Take those reasons to the trauma teaching (Lesson 16) and pray through the issues that each one raises guided by the five ways that God mends trauma.

1) The lie of the idol

_____
_____

2) The lie of the wounded heart

_____
_____

3) The lie of the distorted image

_____

_____

DISCUSSION QUESTIONS

The author of Hebrews says that the enemy was defeated by the Blood of the Lamb and the word of testimony (Rv 12:11). Personal testimony is a powerful bondage breaker. It increases freedom and grace to the one who shares (Mt 10:32) and it provides faith and insight to others for gaining their own breakthroughs.

1) Praise Reports: With this in mind ask the group to look over the above Exercise section and share (where they feel wiling) about areas of former struggle where God helped them gain real and lasting freedom. In sharing these Praise Reports ask people to stay on the glory side (focusing on what the Lord did for them or revealed to them that brought victory) and not on the "gory" side (rehashing the tales of bondage and failure). Look especially for how one or all of the three lies were overcome in their belief system as victory was won.

2) Prayer Requests: Ask the group to briefly mention for prayer the areas where they are still struggling. Break into small groups to pray for (not counsel) one another. Pray for the three lies to be exposed to the light and overturned. Pray also for the graced ability to call and keep calling on the Lord, to more fully surrender to Him and to persevere until final victory comes.

MAIN POINTS

- A "besetting" sin is a Biblical word for things we can't "just say no" to.
- It takes being 100% surrendered to God to get free of an addiction.
- Freedom is primarily a truth issue. We fight to believe truth.
- The binding power of addiction comes from three powerful lies: of the idol (#1), of the wounded heart (#2) and of the distorted image (#3).
- Behind addiction is a demon seeking to be worshipped and served.
- Lie #1 tells you the object of your craving will satisfy you or heal you.
- The root cause of all addictions is the inability to receive love.
- Lie #2 has you looking for love in all the wrong places—in the world.
- Receiving the Father's perfect love is an ongoing necessity of life.
- Lie #3 has you running from the Father rather than to Him.
- In your times of testing learn to get grace into every place of disgrace.

DIGGING DEEPER

Compare the 12 steps of AA to Christian truths that we all need to walk in if we want to be free of besetting sins of any kind. While AA does not recognize Jesus as Lord, the 12 steps are disciple-making steps such as Jesus commanded the church to teach (Mt 28:19) and will transform the lives of believing Christians who practice them. Simply replace "alcohol" with the name of your besetting sin and replace "God as we understood Him" with the Name that is above every name—Jesus! Then see if there are any steps you have been missing in your walk with the Lord.[74]

> 1) We admitted we were powerless over *alcohol*—that our lives had become unmanageable.
> 2) Came to believe that a Power greater than ourselves could restore us to sanity.
> 3) Made a decision to turn our will and our lives over to the care of God *as we understood Him*.
> 4) Made a searching and fearless moral inventory of ourselves.
> 5) Admitted to God, to ourselves and to another human being the exact nature of our wrongs.
> 6) Were entirely ready to have God remove all these defects of character.
> 7) Humbly asked Him to remove our shortcomings.
> 8) Made a list of all persons we had harmed and became willing to make amends to them all.
> 9) Made direct amends to such people wherever possible, except when to do so would injure them or others.
> 10) Continued to take personal inventory and when we were wrong promptly admitted it.
> 11) Sought through prayer and meditation to improve our conscious contact with God, *as we understood Him*, praying only for knowledge of His will for us and the power to carry that out.
> 12) Having had a spiritual awakening as the result of these steps, we tried to carry this message to *alcoholics*, and to practice these principles in all our affairs.

SWORD AND SHIELD

To meditate in scripture means to chew on truth like a cow chewing its cud. Chew on these scriptures—meditatively—until you are fully convinced that you have received every bit of life strengthening power they have for you.

> **Wherefore seeing we also are compassed about with so great a cloud of witnesses, let us lay aside every weight, and the sin which doth so easily beset us, and let us run with patience the race that is set before us, looking unto Jesus the author and finisher of our faith; who for the joy that was set before him endured the cross, despising the shame, and is set down at the right hand of the throne of God.** Hebrews 12:1-2 KJV

---

[74] A.A. *Alcoholics Anonymous* (New York: Alcoholics Anonymous World Services, Inc. 2001) 59-60.

For there is no distinction between Jew and Greek; the same Lord is Lord of all, bestowing his riches on all who call on him. For "everyone who calls on the name of the Lord will be saved." Romans 10:12-13

For by grace you have been saved through faith. And this is not your own doing; it is the gift of God, not a result of works, so that no one may boast. For we are his workmanship, created in Christ Jesus for good works, which God prepared beforehand, that we should walk in them. Ephesians 2:8-10

PRAYER FOCUS

Every fresh struggle with temptation is actually the best place to gain eyes of faith to see that your loving Father is steadfast and true to His Word. Take the Hebrews 4:16 "elevator" to His throne of grace and get a good look at the God of Mercy who is every ready to receive you! This will establish your heart (Heb 13:9).

Father, You are loving me with perfect, unconditional love even now, even in times of great trial and temptation. You are not holding my weaknesses against me. What an amazing God you are! Your gentleness is making me great and giving me strength. Your strength is even now being made perfect in my weakness! Your perfect love is casting out my fears! You are at work even through this for my good. I am truly finding Your grace in my place of dis-grace! Keep coming to my rescue as I call on Your Name.

RENUNCIATIONS AND AFFIRMATIONS

Renounce any agreements with untruth; believe Jesus' *truth* as your new *way* of *life*.

Father, I renounce these addictive patterns in the generations of my fathers and I repent of having walked in it myself. I repent of my own sin of ___ (Deceitful, lying…). Forgive me and break its power over me and off my generations.

Deceitful, lying, thieving	Sexual immorality	Self-pity, victimization
Blame shifting, irresponsible	Angry, defiant	Domineering, controlling
Abusing others, violent	Self-destructive	Disrespectful of authority
Reckless, foolish, lazy	Stubborn, rebellious	Distrustful of God

PUTTING FEET TO YOUR PRAYERS: STRETCH YOURSELF!

Pray over the root issues! If you have things in your life you can't just say "no" to that are not of God, then there has been mental and emotional "programming" by the enemy to make his lies seem more believable than God's truth. It may take some serious "re-programming" in truth to undo the damage. But be encouraged:

Whatever got in can be gotten out—if you persevere in believing the truth the way your heart once persevered in believing the lie. Keep sowing these prayers!

Lie #1: the lie of the idol.

Father, I confess that I have wanted and craved _____ (substance, wrong behavior, compulsion, negative emotion). It has become an idol to me and in my heart of hearts I keep believing that I need it. And yet the truth is that through it I have not only fellowshipped with demons, I have served them and been enslaved by them to do their will. Forgive me and break its power over me. I fully acknowledge that these desires and behaviors are wrong. Help me to see that they are also untrue. Expose the lies of the idol to me: I do not need it for me to be mended or to be fulfilled. I only need You and what You show me is right for me. I cast down all of my previous beliefs in the lies this idol represents. Thank you for telling me the truth and giving me grace to be able to turn from darkness to light.

Lie #2: the lie of the wounded heart.

Father, I confess and renounce my pattern(s) of putting the blame for my besetting sins and messed up emotional life on others. These are my sinful reactions and I am taking total responsibility for why I chose in my heart to respond to the conditions of my life in these ways. No one held a gun to my head and made me choose fear and un-forgiveness or substances or any other deeply held sinful state as a way of life. By taking responsibility for all of my choices, I am taking back authority over my heart and life. I am now giving my life to my God (Father, Son and Holy Spirit) as You have always wanted me to—in complete trust and surrender and genuine willingness to obey You and walk in Your ways. You will help me learn how to deal with my emotions because You are the best Teacher on earth and Your love cannot fail. You will help me get my life back so that I am the head and not the tail where my emotional reactions are concerned. By retaking responsibility for all of my thoughts, emotions and reactions, I am retaking freedom of my will to exercise authority over my life.

Lie #3: the lie of the distorted image.

Father, I confess that I have run to idols, rather than to You. I have tried to find an answer to my pain and my longing in lesser things and it has been to my ruin. Thank You for loving me even while I was turning away from You. I now see that You really are the joy-filled, all-loving Father that my heart has been aching to know. Your love really is the answer to my wounded heart. And so I confess that I have not fully believed in Your love. I have let the enemy and my own life experiences build up false images about You that have kept me from running to You. But those days are ending now! From now on I will fight to believe in the truth about You that Jesus is revealing to me. I will fight to run to You when I am beset. I will seek Your grace even in my places of deepest disgrace. Let Your perfect love cast out all of my fears!

SECTION FOUR

The Journey Forward

*"How narrow is the gate,
and restricted is the way that leads to life!
Few are those who find it."*
Matthew 7:14 WEB

CHAPTER 23

SPIRITUAL WARFARE 101

The New Stronghold of Surrender

Now that we have worked our way through the many strongholds that typically afflict and hinder our life in Christ, these lessons could seem overwhelming. "It's too complicated!" is the legitimate cry of a heart yearning for freedom as well as transformation. We surely need a principle of simplicity or we may quickly fall again into bondage. Jesus said, "How narrow is the gate and restricted is the way that leads to life" (Matthew 7:14 WEB). His way seems "restricted" at times, but it is always simple. Children live in the Kingdom far better than we do (Luke 18:16). The really hard part is re-learning how to stay surrendered to the Giver of Life, something we could all do as children. An old hymn summarizes the walk nicely: "Trust and obey for there's no other way to be happy in Jesus, but to trust and obey."[75] This chapter is about the warfare around trusting (the "narrow gate"); the next chapter will be about guidance—learning to walk in the sometimes "difficult way" of obedience to the Spirit.

Our Number One Assignment

Spiritual Warfare 101 points us to the elementary battle of our daily life in Christ. Our job as "soldiers" is to make sure that our hearts stay surrendered to the Lord throughout the day—keeping us willing and able to trust and obey our Master and Commander (who is also our best Friend). This is our number one assignment in life given to us by Jesus Himself as the "first and great" commandment (Matthew 22:38). Loving God with our whole hearts certainly entails giving the whole of our life over to Him in full submission to His leadership. Such surrender and centering of our life in Him is not possible without the gift of faith; living un-surrendered and un-centered in Him is unthinkable once true faith has come. Indeed a *living faith* always carries us into this position of humble, trusting dependence and willingness to follow the One who has revealed such love to us (Galatians 2:20).

Either our hearts are moving towards surrender or they are drifting into the Great Rebellion. This not Star Trek: There is no Neutral Zone. There are only two spiritual principles at work in our universe and they are *always* at work upon us. This is why the keeping of the first and great commandment is so critical to our life mission: We cannot fulfill our secondary purpose in the lives of others if we do not learn to stay united to His life (our primary purpose). The level of peace and confidence we have in God will declare the issue all day long—that's God's way of giving us feedback moment by moment on how well we are doing with the most

---

[75] John H. Sammis (1846-1919), lyrics: *Trust and Obey*.

important thing we need to be doing—trusting and obeying Him (Colossians 3:15). This is the battle for one's own life—and it is waged in the heart (Proverbs 4:23).

In boot camp all new recruits are issued rifles and taught to protect their lives and the lives of their comrades. In the "battle" of daily life our rifle is our heart! The enemy wants to get his finger on the trigger of our heart and start firing it off at ourselves and others. Such "misfires" are almost irresistible when we don't keep our heart clean and clear in the Lord (of negative emotions and stronghold issues). But suppose the Lord gets His finger on your heart, then He can use you to give mercy, peace and patience where it is needed as you go through your day. That's much better isn't it? So our heart is a powerful weapon for advancing either the Kingdom of God or the kingdom of darkness. We need to get this Spiritual Warfare 101 lesson under our belts!

Trusting His Hands; Seeking His Face

Here is another principle of simplicity that companions with trust and obey: No matter what the enemy is doing, God is also at work to accomplish His good purposes. This is especially true of the dynamics of transformation taking place every moment of every day. Since the great battle of daily life is for our heart, we need to learn to trust His Hands and seek His Face.

1) His Hands: God is at work on *all things* in our lives with one great purpose in mind. We need to know, understand and be in agreement with that purpose, or our lives will not make sense, nor will we realize the focal point of the enemy's attacks. God's Hands are always at work to conform you to Christ—shaping you from the outside in. Picture the Lord reaching through

> *His Hands conform us.*
> *His Face transforms us.*

and working through all of the outward circumstances of your life, seeking to "center you" on the Potter's Wheel. What is His goal in each and every moment? To draw out of you a Christlike response, or (if you can't yet do that) to prepare you to be able to respond as the New Creation you are at some point down the road. The ultimate good that God has in mind is not just His blessings being poured into our lives, though that is certainly a part of it, but the incomparable blessing of actually becoming more like Jesus in all of our ways *in this life.*

> **And we know that for those who love God <u>all things</u> work together for good, for those who are called according to his purpose. For those whom he foreknew he also predestined to be <u>conformed</u> to the image of his Son. Romans 8:28-29**

2) His Face: What is God's work on our interior? His primary purpose is to transform us into the Image of His Son from the inside out—by revealing His Image to us. The Father reveals the Son; the Son reveals the Father (Matthew 11:27). Whenever we get our spiritual eyes back on Jesus, we experience a shift

> *The work of His Hands helps us seek His Face.*

from being self-centered to becoming Christ-centered. This interior transformation happens as we "see" by faith some offering of grace in Jesus that enables us to fully surrender to whatever He has allowed or is asking of us in His sovereignty. Once we again become centered and surrendered, submitted and committed, the good fruit of His Spirit flows into us and through us. In this way His Face transforms us into His Image (Chapter 8).

> **But we all, with unveiled face beholding as in a mirror the glory of the Lord, are <u>transformed</u> into the same image from glory to glory, even as from the Lord, the Spirit.** 2 Corinthians 3:18 WEB

> **For God, who said, "Let light shine out of darkness," has shone in our hearts to give the light of the knowledge of the glory of God in the face of Jesus Christ.** 2 Corinthians 4:6

These two great works of God are going on all of the time. Always the Father's Hands are upon us to raise up whatever we surrender to Him and to work through all things to increase our willingness to surrender all, even if we are fighting against what He is doing through our ignorance of His ways. At the same time the revelation of Jesus Christ is working within us at all times, however little we may be aware of it, to transform the way that we live and to enable us to surrender to the Father. But *this process can be greatly enhanced by our cooperation*. We can make it our goal to more frequently choose to surrender to the work of His Hands; we can also choose to more actively seek His Face and re-surrender at any moment. As you learn this you will discover that you are in the "driver's seat" where your spiritual growth is concerned!

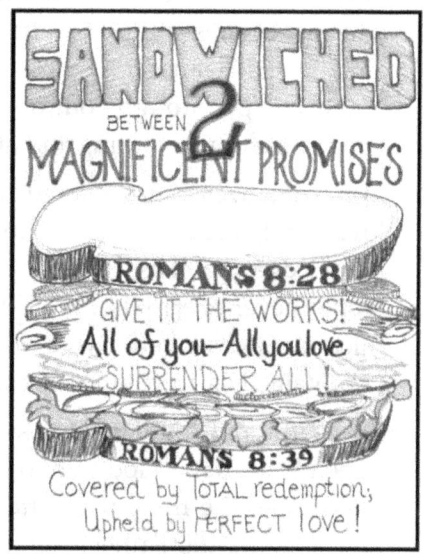

SANDWICHED!

Take all your life and all whom you love and put it between these two magnificent promises, then taste and see how good your God is as you live with an active faith "sandwiched" between His promises.

Let's see how this plays out. The Father has His Hands on our lives like a Master Potter working with absolutely everything (the good, the bad and the seemingly indifferent) to accomplish His great desire—to refashion us into children who display the nature of His Son. As a potter exerts great pressure with his hands to center clay on the wheel, the Father also works through the stress in our lives to bring us again and again to the place of inward surrender. Like uncentered clay we often try to fly off the wheel! But under the pressure ("humble yourselves under the mighty hand..." 1 Peter 5:6) we finally stretch our faith vision to see something in the Lord that helps us to yield our stubborn resistance and say, "Not my will, but Yours be done." *The work of His Hands helps us to seek His Face!* From this hallowed place of surrender the Father is able to raise us into new life—just as a potter raises the centered clay into the form he envisions (Romans 9:22-24).

Going through Our Day like Jesus

Since the Father is working 24/7 to conform us to Christ, it will certainly help us to cooperate with Him if we gain vision for what that looks like. Though outward works are important fruit to cultivate, for the purpose of this series, let's consider what it means to be conformed to Christ in terms of the inner life and your emotional state (Galatians 5:22). Would you like to go through your days the way Jesus did? No one alive has walked through daily life with more love, more peace, or more joy. Yet no one alive has ever had a tougher assignment to carry out or faced more opposition. Consider how your approach to daily life might change if you would follow Jesus in these ways:

1) Love and joy: Jesus walked through a world of sinful people who caused no end of problems and persecutions for Him, yet He was able to keep joy and love alive in His Heart because He was masterful at forgiving sinful people. Would you like to go through your day free of hurt and offense *like Jesus did*? You have Him inside of you willing and able to help you forgive.

2) Acceptance: Jesus suffered the unjust rejections of many people He deeply loved and cared about, yet He was able to live with His Heart secure in the knowledge that His Father's love for Him was perfect and that His Father would never reject Him. Would you like to go through your day protected and filled by God's love for you *like Jesus did*? You have the same Father devoted to you. Value His acceptance of you more than the opinions of other people.

3) Peace and guidance: Jesus was able to live in moment to moment dependence upon God's control of the world, not His, and yet He was peace-filled all of the time, no matter what the enemy was stirring up, because He kept trusting the Father *with* all things and was willing to obey *in* all things. Would you like to go through your day with peace and trust *like Jesus did*? You have a new nature in you that loves to live by trusting and obeying God.

4) Stress free: Jesus saw people who He completely loved all around Him that were carrying heavy burdens and living with great anguish and injustice, but He never got burned out, over-burdened, angry or depressed in trying to be God's instrument for helping them. Would you like to be able to care for others in your daily life *like Jesus did*? He is right beside you wanting to help you learn from Him how to let Him carry your burdens.

This is the way of life that Jesus wants to live in us by His Spirit, and our Father is so zealous for giving it to us that He is making *all things* serve this higher purpose. What's to stop us?

The Counter Feints of the Enemy

Certainly the enemy cannot stop us—he is a defeated foe. The enemy can do nothing to stop this work of the Father's Hands—for God absolutely hates every evil and has determined and declared that *all things* will be made to work for the good of the people He is redeeming. Meditate on this life-changing truth: *The enemy cannot make the evil he does through human sin stick to anyone.* God will overturn it all and make even the worst things the enemy does work for our good. So how does the enemy make evil stick? By getting us to bind the hurt, pain and injustice of the past to ourselves through bitterness of heart and by unbelief in God's promises. We are being manipulated into becoming our own captors! This is monstrous, outrageous and infernally ingenious all at the same time. Don't fall for it one moment longer.

If God is working upon us through all things by His Hands and working within us through all things by His Spirit to conform us to Christ, then the enemy (having read the Bible) is also working through everything to oppose God's work by a) tempting us to doubt that all things are working for our good (thus trying to counter the work of His Hands) and b) by drawing us away from the revelation of Jesus Christ (thus trying to counter the work of His Face). As Dr. Jack Deere once said, "The enemy has WMD's of his own—Weapons of Mass Distraction."[76]

But each one is tempted, when he is drawn away by his own lust, and enticed.
James 1:14 WEB

Once we are no longer beholding our God with a heart of confident faith, we are prey to the enemy and of little threat to his kingdom. Even worse, we are unwittingly being re-shaped into the image of the ultimate fallen one, Satan, who is the most un-forgiving and anxious being in the universe. Have you been tempted to doubt the work of God's Hands? Have you been distracted from keeping your focus on Jesus? Then be prepared to fight! You get to choose what you want to believe and whose image you want to focus on and live by. If something in you doesn't want to trust in, surrender to and rely upon your God you have just met the enemy's handiwork—don't let it reign over you. Carry it captive to Christ instead.

---

[76] Jack Deere, from notes taken during a MorningStar Ministry conference, Charlotte, NC, 2005.

Recruited into God's All Volunteer Army

Perhaps this is as good a time as any to enlist in this God's army (if you haven't already done so). By nature most of us would rather be wheat farmers, or wine tasters, or minstrels only. Few desire to fight the battles. Like those who rebuilt the walls of Jerusalem, we have to learn to do the work of the Kingdom with our sword and shield at our side if we want to see the old stronghold walls of self-protection come down and the new, glorious walls of His salvation go up (Nehemiah 4:17-18; Isaiah 60:18). How long will that campaign take? Only He knows. But we can be sure of this: It will be well worth the effort it takes to fully enter His Kingdom in this life. Fight the good fight of faith!

> **Fight the good fight of the faith. Take hold of the eternal life to which you were called and about which you made the good confession in the presence of many witnesses.** 1 Timothy 6:12
>
> **I have fought the good fight, I have finished the race, I have kept the faith. Henceforth there is laid up for me the crown of righteousness.** 2 Timothy 4:7-8

NOTES/JOURNAL

_____
_____
_____
_____
_____
_____
_____
_____
_____

EXERCISE

Fill in the blanks with a situation where the enemy isn't firing "blanks" at you—he is scoring direct hits! Then match it with scriptures or insights that will shield your heart. This is war! Prepare for the assaults to come and then beat the weapons of the enemy into plowshares (Mic 4:3) to cultivate a greater capacity to hold faith.

The work of His Hands

Circumstances that are hardest for me to believe that they can work for my good.

_____

Scriptures and insights that will help me activate my faith.

_____

The revelation of His Face

Times when I find it hardest to believe that He really does love me.

_____

Scriptures and insights that will help me activate my faith.

_____

DISCUSSION QUESTIONS

God's promise of redemption (Ro 8:28) is so strong that everyone gives it a head bob. But many of the same folks shake their heads in utter disbelief when something disastrous happens to them, absolutely convinced "permanent damage" is being done. This exercise is not meant to minimize the suffering and harm sin does, but to magnify the goodness, love and power of our God in overturning evil. Let it grow eyes to see the Father's Hands. Ask the group to review what they know of the following events. What good things eventually came about as (largely unforeseen) outcomes?

The crucifixion of Jesus (this is easy!)	The NYC garment district fire
British oppression of the Am. Colonies	Bombing of Pearl Harbor
The cruelty of slavery in the Am. South	Hitler's attempt to destroy the Jews

Yes, not everyone knows enough about the past to be able to trace the outline of redemption in history. Much is forgotten. That is also the point. We tend to remember only the tragedy. Years later, as the overturning work of God begins to manifest on the earth, few are they who connect the dots and give God credit. Let's be ones who do: Redemption is *His*-story in the midst of our history.

MAIN POINTS

- Your heart is a "weapon" both God and the devil want submitted to them.
- Our Father is working 24/7 to help you learn how to go through your day the way Jesus went through His.
- His Hands are working for good *in all things*—no evil can stick to you.

- His Face is always available to be "seen" by you to give you joy and peace.
- The enemy can *only* make evil stick to us by our own unbelief and unforgiveness—by deceiving us into sticking it to ourselves.
- The enemy can't steal your joy and peace unless he gets you to "look away" from Jesus to focus on the problem instead.
- Basic training in spiritual warfare is learning to diligently guard your heart by keeping it surrendered to the Lord!

DIGGING DEEPER

Romans 8:28 says God works all things together for our good. There are "generic" good things that He is always "working" through experiences of brokenness, weakness and pain. This is a partial list intended to expand your vision to see your life from heaven's perspective. Pray for God to move upon your heart and will so that you can deeply agree with Him that these good things are worth the suffering, the "pain of passage" into His higher life (2Co 4:17).

1) Our brokenness humbles us.
2) Our brokenness helps us realize our dependence upon God.
3) In our brokenness God draws near.
4) Our brokenness enables us to have compassion on others.
5) His strength is made perfect in places of our weakness.
6) In our weakness we discover that His grace is sufficient.
7) He comforts us.
8) With the comfort we learn to receive from Him, we learn to comfort others.
9) He grieves with us—and we learn to enter into His sufferings.
10) We learn (in our hearts—not just heads) He is not the author of evil or of suffering.
11) We grow a stronger prayer life.
12) We really begin to search for God's love and hope and help.
13) We really begin to search His Word for understanding.
14) We cling to His Word and learn to trust it.
15) We cling to His Word and learn to obey it.
16) We see His salvation as He delivers us.
17) We learn to love the world less and God more.
18) We learn to mistrust what is in us.
19) We learn to mistrust what is in others.
20) We learn to open ourselves to the help and encouragement of others.
21) We learn to discern whom to trust and when.
22) We learn to discern true good and true evil (not what we call good and evil).
23) We learn to forgive and so become more like Him in His way of loving us.
24) We learn to receive His forgiveness and so become more aware of His love.
25) God develops a track record with us and this establishes us in trusting Him.

SWORD AND SHIELD

We apply Romans 8:28 like jam on toast, but it is only one of the ways that this saving work is described in scripture. Drink deeply of these powerful promises of restoration (see also Ps 51:10-13, 80:3-7, 130:7-8; Isa 49:8-9, 57:17-18; Jer 30:17; Na 2:2; Gal 6:1-2; Ac 3:9, 14:21-22).

> "As for you, you meant evil against me, but God meant it for good, to bring to pass, as it is this day, to save many people alive." Genesis 50:20 WEB

> O Israel, hope in the Lord! For with the Lord there is steadfast love, and with him is plentiful redemption. And he will redeem Israel from all his iniquities. Psalm 130:7-8

> Men don't despise a thief, if he steals to satisfy himself when he is hungry: But if he is found, he shall restore seven times. He shall give all the wealth of his house. Proverbs 6:30-31 WEB

> "And he went on backsliding in the way of his heart. I have seen his ways, and will heal him: I will lead him also, and restore comforts to him and to his mourners." Isaiah 57:17-18 WEB

> "Return to your stronghold, O prisoners of hope; today I declare that I will restore to you double." Zechariah 9:12

> "I will restore to you the years that the swarming locust has eaten, the hopper, the destroyer, and the cutter, my great army, which I sent among you." Joel 2:25

> "Repent therefore, and turn again, that your sins may be blotted out, that times of refreshing may come from the presence of the Lord." Acts 3:19-20

> For this slight momentary affliction is preparing for us an eternal weight of glory beyond all comparison, as we look not to the things that are seen but to the things that are unseen. For the things that are seen are transient, but the things that are unseen are eternal. 2 Corinthians 4:17-18

> Consequently, he is able to save to the uttermost those who draw near to God through him, since he always lives to make intercession for them. Hebrews 7:25

PRAYER FOCUS

Perhaps this is as good a time as any to enlist in this God's army (if you haven't already done so). By nature most of us would rather be farmers, or wine tasters, or minstrels *only*. Few desire to fight the battles! But like those who rebuilt the walls of Jerusalem under Nehemiah, we have to learn to do the work of the Kingdom with our sword and shield at our side (Ne 4:17-18). Consider offering this prayer:

Father, You know that part of me would prefer not to have to fight these battles of the spiritual life. Whenever it is possible take this cup from me. Nevertheless, may Your will be done. I ask for every grace that You supply—especially courage and patient perseverance! Thank You for all of the ways that You are training my hands and my heart for those conflicts with the enemy that cannot be avoided. May I ever trust that

You are also fighting with me and for me. I fully accept this calling upon my life—to fight the good fight of faith—and I realize that the first battle is always for my own heart—to keep it surrendered to You. Make me willing to be made willing to surrender everything to You, each and every day.

RENUNCIATIONS AND AFFIRMATIONS

Renounce any agreements with untruth; believe Jesus' *truth* as your new *way* of *life*.

Repent and renounce any disbelief in the work of His Hands:

Father, I confess that in many ways I have not believed the Magnificent Promise of redemption. Forgive my unbelief and break its power over me. I utterly renounce that view of my world and Your universe and I choose by an act of my will to believe that the truth really is that a greater good will always come out of everything that goes wrong—because You love us enough to promise it. I rest my heart upon Your Word and turn in hope filled expectations of good things to come. Make me alert to run to You and reach for this sword whenever the devil tries to tempt me to doubt the work of Your Hands!

Repent and renounce any disbelief in the revelation of His Face:

Father, I confess that in many ways I have not believed that You are as loving and merciful as Jesus. Like Adam I have hidden in shame. Like the prodigal I have been slow to return, fearing I would have to work my way back into Your good graces. Thank You for never being angry with me even over my unbelief in You. Thank You that whenever I look to Jesus and see what He is like, I can also look through Him to see You smiling my way. Forgive me and break the power of unbelief and anything else that is keeping me from running home to You. I rest my heart fully on the love I see in Yours. Alert me whenever I begin to lose sight of Your Face.

PUTTING FEET TO YOUR PRAYERS: STRETCH YOURSELF!

Start keeping a mental journal of your moments of complete surrender. Notice first of all how good it feels to release every care and concern to Him. Know that to live in a flow of moments like this is your true, new life—your inheritance. Your Father is working through everything to restore you to this when you lose it. It is that important to Him! But your enemy will seek to rob you of it. Be vigilant!

Notice whatever takes you away from this place of inward surrender. It is never the outward thing. It is always a letting go of trust or love. Watch to see from this what the main temptations are that the enemy is using against you. Then take the six steps of Chapter 7 into those stronghold areas and do some holy demolition!

CHAPTER 24

WALKING IN THE SPIRIT

The New Stronghold of Submission

It would hardly be fair or right, having given so much attention to the enemy's ways of distracting us, mis-leading us, and hindering us with strongholds, to finish this series without giving time to the Lord and His ways of leading us in new life. After all, the point is not to pull the emotional strongholds down (either of the past or of the present) just so that we can be free of them—as good as that is. Rather, our quest is to become free so that we can now follow Jesus in everything! The truly healed and restored life is one that is continually given over to the Lord, seeking to walk with Him as He leads the way. For that we will need to learn how to walk in the Spirit He supplies.

If we live by the Spirit, let us also walk by the Spirit. Galatians 5:25

Let us begin by acknowledging that as great as His Word is—He even set it above His Name (Psalm 138:2)—God speaks to us in many more ways than scripture alone. We are guided by His example (Jesus' life is a *visible* word—a word *shown* to us), His voice (a word *spoken* to us, however we may receive it), and His Spirit (a word *living* in us, however He may inspire us). It is easy to see from this that there is a progression of increasing intimacy from following the written Word of scripture to imitating Jesus' example to listening for His voice to yielding the whole flow of our daily life to His Spirit. Jesus gave us— His Bride on earth—more than a book when He pledged Himself to us as our Husband. He gave *Himself* to us.

> *If we live by the Spirit, let us also walk by the Spirit.*
> Galatians 5:25

Our new life in Christ comes through the forgiveness of our sins (by the Blood of Jesus) and through the gift of the Holy Spirit now joined to us (1 Corinthians 6:17; Ephesians 1:13). Just as Jesus died our death for us, so now He desires to live His life in us and through us. This happens beautifully whenever we yield ourselves to the Holy Spirit and walk in the steps He shows us. Whenever we are released to trust and obey, Jesus "comes to life" in us!

> **I have been crucified with Christ** [in Him I have shared His crucifixion]; **it is no longer I who live, but Christ (the Messiah) lives in me; and the life I now live in the body I live by faith in (by adherence to and reliance on and complete trust in) the Son of God, Who loved me and gave Himself up for me.** Galatians 2:20 AMP

Walking in the Spirit has two dimensions: conscious and unconscious. Though this may be a strange way of phrasing it, the truth is that we have been "sleep walking" with the Lord all of our lives. That is, He has been guiding us in countless ways all along, but we have not been consciously aware of the many specific ways by which He has done so. Our first task, therefore, is to identify and understand these hidden ways of *un-self-conscious* guidance. The Holy Spirit is like the perfect waiter who doesn't make His service to us obvious. It is up to us to seek to acknowledge Him so that He can more intimately direct our paths.

> **Lean on, trust in,** *and* **be confident in the Lord with all your heart** *and* **mind and do not rely on your own insight** *or* **understanding. In all your ways know, recognize,** *and* **acknowledge Him, and He will direct** *and* **make straight** *and* **plain your paths.** Proverbs 3:5-6 AMP

Dimension One: Unselfconscious Guidance

Walking in the Spirit is like breathing which is hardly surprising since He is called the "breath of the Almighty" and He is the "breath" of life imparted to us both in creation and in the new birth. This Spirit-empowered walk, therefore, is easy and natural—literally child's play! In fact it was the Spirit, the great Teacher and Giver of life, who "secretly" taught us how to suckle, to eat, to speak, to walk, even to play. Every good thing about us including childhood is His gift to us, or will we have some "work" of our own apart from God to boast about? Not according to scripture, which says that we are saved *by grace* through faith and that not of ourselves, *not of our works*, "lest anyone should boast" (Ephesians 2:8). So let us acknowledge then that this Spirit-empowered walk has been going on since birth *as His gift to us*. God said that even the "infancy" of Israel, the forty years of their wilderness journey, was a time when He "carried Israel" as a child: He led them through it all and then explained it to them later, so that they could understand and acknowledge what He had done (Isaiah 46:3-4).

We are guided by:
1) His Word
2) His example
3) His voice
4) His Spirit
...a progression of increasing intimacy and surrender!

> **And in the wilderness, where you have seen how the Lord your God carried you, as a man carries his son, all the way that you went until you came to this place.** Deuteronomy 1:31

To this day the greatest exemplars of what it is like to walk in the Spirit and display the fruit of the Spirit are little children (Matthew 18:2-4). Their sparkling qualities are His gift of grace to them and through them to us! Children are simply more open and trusting than we are, which makes them such splendid receivers of grace that they are masters at living in the Kingdom, showing us the way to go.

> **But Jesus called them to him, saying, "Let the children come to me, and do not hinder them, for to such belongs the kingdom of God. Truly, I say to you, whoever does not receive the kingdom of God like a child shall not enter it."** Luke 18:16-17

The Holy Spirit has been with us all along. He is always teaching us and leading us into life. He is the Giver and Sustainer of life (Isaiah 42:5). Jesus told His disciples *before* the events of Easter and Pentecost that they already "knew" the Holy Spirit He would be sending because the Spirit had been dwelling "with" them and would soon be "in" them (John 14:16-18). This same Spirit has been continually with you in your journey, helping you, guiding you, teaching you and comforting you, even before you became a Christian, even from before birth!

> **Now the word of the Lord came to me, saying, "Before I formed you in the womb I knew you, and before you were born I consecrated you; I appointed you a prophet to the nations."** Jeremiah 1:4-5

> **In him was life, and the life was the light of men... The true light, which enlightens everyone, was coming into the world.** John 1:4, 9

St. Augustine put it this way: "Love God and do as you please."[77] He means of course that once we "love God" by surrendering to Him everything about our lives and loved ones and are willing to do His will above our own, *then* He begins to draw us by desires that please Him as well as us. Only fully yielded Christians can live the way Augustine recommends. However, even before we knew Him, God was already drawing us into to doing things that pleased us as well as Him. Examples of this are eating, sleeping, befriending, parenting, working, loving and laughing (Galatians 2:20). No one needs conscious guidance from the Lord to do good things which come to us with such natural grace attached.

> [Not in your own strength] **for it is God Who is all the while effectually at work in you** [energizing and creating in you the power and desire], **both to will and to work for His good pleasure** *and* **satisfaction** *and* **delight.** Philippians 2:13 AMP

Trusting is, therefore, essential to these everyday ways of Spirit-empowered guidance, since any interference by negative emotions disturbs the childlike manner of our walk. Proverbs 3:5-6 calls us to acknowledge Him and to *trust* Him, that He may "direct our paths." Guidance happens naturally for trusting hearts as Hannah Whitall Smith wrote in *The Christian's Secret of a Happy Life*.[78]

> *Above all else trust Him...God cannot guide the souls who never trust Him enough to believe that He is doing it.*

Dimension Two: Christ-Conscious Guidance

The Spirit-empowered walk described above is childlike and free. Not even being aware that it is happening is *almost* one of its requirements! On the other hand, the Spirit-led walk actually does require conscious and conscientious diligence and care in seeking it. It is harder work at first, but it is the way of the wise.

> **Therefore do not be foolish, but understand what the will of the Lord is.**
> Ephesians 5:17

---

[77] Saint Augustine of Hippo (354-430), Seventh Homily on 1st John
[78] Hannah Whitall Smith, *The Christian's Secret of a Happy Life* (New York, NY: Ballantine Books, 1986), 81.

The first principle of seeking this kind of "awake and aware" guidance is: "Don't ask, if you don't really want to know." The Lord is not out to satisfy our intellectual *curiosity* about His will! He is interested in leading us through our *obedience* to His will. The likelihood exists that He may not tell you what you want to hear, so be prepared to yield to His will and avoid the pitfall of poor King Ahab who didn't want his plans disturbed by a contrary word from the Lord (1 Kings 22:7-8). As Hannah Whitall Smith advises, "An immediate obedience is the safest and easiest course."[79] There are five "voices" that should harmonize: scripture, conscience, inward impressions, wise counsel and providential circumstances. Tread softly in this area—guidance is an art, not a science.[80]

First Voice: Scripture

In His Word, God provides boundaries and guidelines (see Psalm 119—all of it) so that we can know right and wrong with clarity on many issues and see the general outline of a right path for our lives. We, therefore, need to take the scriptures to heart so that the Holy Spirit may use them to direct us and keep us from error, just as we would study a map to navigate our way through dangerous and unfamiliar terrain (John 17:17). This guidance takes precedence over all else. Hence there is a real need to search the scriptures and keep things in balance. Some general guidelines to follow are "whatever is plainly taught must be obeyed"; "adhere to principles, not isolated texts"; and "keep the main thing, the main thing." The "main thing" is keeping love for Jesus and submission to Him as our first and foremost consideration! At times the Lord will even "quicken" His written Word, making it come alive with guidance about specific steps to take. Remember, though, that in Biblical times they didn't have airport searchlights! The lamp that lit their path on a dark night barely showed more than a few steps ahead at a time. He says His Word is like that kind of lamp (Psalms 119:105).

Rule of Thumb: Don't expect to "hear" a word spoken if it has already been written.

Negative Guidance: The Lord will never lead us contrary to His written Word.

Positive Guidance: General principles of scripture point the way—but not all is made plain.

Consider this progression: *Good* is the wide range of what He permits by His Word; *better* is trying to find the path of His specific will for you; *best* is actually walking in the center of it!

---

[79] Ibid., p. 79.
[80] Ibid., p. 72. The "voices" of guidance are expanded from the chapter "Difficulties Concerning Guidance." The consensus of wise counsel has been added to the four "voices" listed in The Christian's Secret.

Second Voice: Conscience

Thought not infallible, "Do the next right thing" is a handy way of expressing that aspect of the Spirit-led walk which is a steady succession of "right" ideas to follow supplied by the Spirit to our minds. We are meant to cultivate practical wisdom and right understanding as one means of being guided by the Lord (Proverbs 4:5-7). We have been given the ability to make right judgments and are expected to use it: "Common sense" is a gift of God; its counterfeit is the natural mind. We have a duty to educate our consciences, renewing our minds by His Word (Romans 12:2; 2 Thessalonians 2:13). At the same time we are told not to lean on our understanding at those times when we should be trusting (Proverbs 3:5-6). How do you know it is time to trust? Whenever something happens that you don't understand! Curiously, it is not as hard to "get" wisdom as one might suppose. It's free for the asking, but the catch is you have to have a) the humility to realize you don't have wisdom and b) some basic confidence in His ability to send it your way (James 1:5-6). There are three divine guides that common sense and a reasonably renewed understanding can judge fairly easily:

Right Desire: Heart and feelings can safely lead if no moral law contradicts the direction they would take.

Obvious Necessity: Intellect and observation leave no room for doubt about the action that is needed in the moment.

Genuine Duty: The moral call is clear, even if it is undesired, and there is a sense that it would be dishonorable not to do it.

Third Voice: Inward Impressions

Movements of the Holy Spirit upon us, especially when we are "at rest" in the Lord, help to show us how to move in step with the Spirit (Hebrews 5:14). Only the Lord can teach you this way of "continual guidance" (Isaiah 58:11). Because leadings are often so faint, it really is a process of trial and error. But take heart, He loves it that we are seeking to be led and, after all, He *is* the best Teacher on earth! For instance He instructs us to "walk humbly with our God" (Micah 6:8). Humility is not just the *only* appropriate posture, it actually positions us to receive the wisdom necessary for guidance (James 4-6)). Don't be too eager to proclaim that you've heard from the Lord, even if you have. Let events unfold by themselves. His wisdom will become evident to all (Matthew 11:19).

> **He has showed you, O man, what is good. And what does the Lord require of you but to do justly, and to love kindness *and* mercy, and to humble yourself *and* walk humbly with your God? Micah 6:8 AMP**

He speaks ever quieter, so we have to learn to become still, if we don't want to miss anything. Quieting our own interior landscape may seem daunting, but it truly is something that we can do (Psalm 131:1-3). Picture a pond surrounded by trees with the wind blowing and rain pelting the surface. A pebble tossed into it wouldn't be heard or noticed. Then see the pond on a totally calm day: The splash can be heard and every ripple followed to the shore. Now you be that pond and listen for His "pebbles"!

As with our speech, both the Lord and the enemy have a message (words) and an impression (tone of voice). Learn to recognize the ripple effect of their voice upon your soul. The enemy's voice often makes "a splash" that disrupts your inward sense of peace and well-being. The Lord's ripple effect is peace-filled. Listen in quietness for the "still, small voice" and you will catch His gentle whispers (1 Kings 19:12). Be patient. Wait patiently upon Him. It is better to wait for the light to come than to proceed in the dark, but the moment you are sure, yield a complete obedience.

Rule of Thumb: When in doubt, wait it out; if you feel led, go ahead. Negative impressions (checking, grieving, restraining) caution us to stop, look and listen. Positive impressions (prompting, leading, impelling, calling) lead us forth.

Warning: Inward impressions may come from wrong spirits or from un-renewed areas of our souls (unhealed wounds, wrong desires, unmet needs, etc.). Proceed with caution! The heart of the old nature is very deceptive (Jeremiah 17:9). Hannah Whitall Smith cautions, "It is not enough... for the leading to be very remarkable or the coincidences to be very striking, to stamp it as being surely from God."[4]

Fourth Voice: Consensus of Wise Counsel

The counsel of others is not meant to be a substitute for one's own judgment, since every choice we face is an opportunity for the Lord to grow us in the proper use of the free will He has given us. God will use others to confirm, but rarely to give direction. Agreement of counselors *may* be a sign of God's leading. It needs to be heeded, but not followed slavishly (Proverbs 15:22). Who are the wise ones whose walk with the Lord you admire and who God has placed in your life? Make sure you seek them out—not people who will molly-coddle you (Proverbs 13:14). Even so, keep in mind that His ultimate purpose is for us to be able to listen for ourselves. It is good to go to others for counsel, but we are not to lean on them— we are to learn to lean on the Lord.

"And no longer shall each one teach his neighbor and each his brother, saying, 'Know the Lord,' for they shall all know me, from the least of them to the greatest, declares the Lord." Jeremiah 31:34

Fifth Voice: Providential Circumstances

Reading providential signs is for confirmation only. Even open and closed doors are not a sign in themselves: Closed doors need to be respected, but they are not always of the Lord; neither are open doors. As a rule don't force your way past a closed door or turn from it in despair. Learn to wait upon the Lord to open what needs to be opened (Revelation 3:7-8). However, don't race through every open door you see—it could be a snare. We are meant to let the Shepherd (not signs) go before us, leading us in the way. He *is* the way: Sticking close to Him is the secret of guidance (John 14:6). We are also meant to mature to the point where we can hear and discern His voice. By Jesus' own description "lambs" may not hear His voice, but His "sheep"—those who have matured—certainly do (John 10:3-4).

Slow Down Signs: Closed doors, hindrances, disturbances "in the flow" of peace.

Proceed With Caution Signs: Open doors, a peaceful flow of events, coincidences; a river of joy and peace.

Willingness is the coin of the realm where guidance is concerned. Have you ever seen someone trying to get a resistant dog on a leash to walk obediently in the direction and at the pace they desire? Some dogs are rebellious and dig their paws in; some are easily distracted by cats or other dogs. Such dogs may not be taken out beyond necessity and then only under great restraint! Then there are other dogs who don't even need a leash, who go everywhere with their masters. That is our goal—to become so captivated by Jesus in our hearts that we no longer need the sometimes unpleasant discipline of being constrained by Him through our circumstances!

I will instruct you and teach you in the way you should go; I will counsel you with my eye upon you. Be not like a horse or a mule, without understanding, which must be curbed with bit and bridle, or it will not stay near you. Psalm 32:8-9

Sweet Surrender

If you would love to be readily and frequently guided, then the issue of living with a surrendered heart and a willing spirit is paramount. When Isaiah *saw* the Lord, he fully surrendered and became willing for anything (Isaiah 6:1-8). So would we all! So let's be alert to our innermost thoughts: Even a twinge of unwillingness to surrender is a step towards the Great Rebellion. If you see it in you, you have met the enemy. Carry that thought captive to Christ. Then keep checking to make sure your surrender and willingness stay intact. Let the acronym S.A.A.W. remind you to look to Him.

Father, according to Your love and wisdom,

S. Send: *Send whatever You desire to send*
(He is the Giver of blessings, never the curse)

A. Allow: *Allow whatever You have to allow*
(Of free will and its consequences)

A. Ask: *Ask of me whatever You desire or require*
(Of inward and outward obedience)

W. Withhold: *Withhold me from and Withhold from me*
(Whatever is necessary to fulfill Your plans)

Make me willing to be made willing to surrender everything to You.

The River of Peace

The River of Peace is worth all the battles. There is a vision in Ezekiel of water flowing from the Temple that begins as a shallow stream and eventually becomes a river which no one can cross (Ezekiel 47:1-5). This gives us a picture of our life of faith flowing from the place of consecration and surrender, signified by the Temple and its Altar—the place where lives are offered in devotion to the Lord. There is peace as we trust and obey, but at first it is all too easy to step out of the flow of His Spirit's gentle guidance.

With practice we can learn to live in the peace Jesus supplies—a peace for our hearts (as we trust Him) and a peace for our feet (as we follow Him). The Holy Spirit is a river of life to all who learn to live in Him and walk by Him. With practice, determined effort, childlike faith and tons of grace this flow of peace and divine purpose, which once was so hard to find (only ankle deep), will become a mighty river that lifts and carries you into great adventures in the Lord. *So what are you waiting for? Go ahead—jump in with both feet!*

For thus says the Lord: "Behold, I will extend peace to her like a river." Isaiah 66:12

NOTES/JOURNAL

_____
_____
_____
_____
_____
_____
_____
_____
_____
_____

EXERCISE

Recognize and acknowledge what God has already been doing in your life. Don't be "sheepish" about admitting the truth that the Lord has been speaking to you and showing you things all along. Wise King Solomon advises us to learn to acknowledge the Lord—give Him credit for what He is already doing—and He will direct our paths (Pr 3:5-6). One meaning of this is that if we will learn to see the ways He has been guiding us all along (by Hand and voice), we will be that much better prepared to recognize, acknowledge and follow Him in the future. Mark this check list if you have encountered God in these ways, even without realizing it at the time, and then add some of your own to it.

- __ A little bird whispered in my ear…
- __ It's just a hunch, but have you tried…
- __ The thought just dropped in out of the blue!
- __ That same idea just occurred to me too!
- __ This idea just stays on my mind…
- __ That gave me chills and goose bumps!
- __ I have a gut feeling this will work…
- __ Something just doesn't seem right…
- __ I've got a bad feeling about this…
- __ All of a sudden I remembered…
- __ It's a feeling I just can't shake off…
- __ What an incredible coincidence!
- __ _____
- __ _____
- __ _____
- __ _____

DISCUSSION QUESTIONS

Since guidance is an art, not a science, it really helps to share stories of guidance. This enables us to "listen in" on the ways God has been speaking to and guiding others and the ways they have been listening to and observing His directions. So go ahead—testify. Share your stories of how the great God of heaven has been guiding you on earth into fun, into fruitfulness, or out of trouble. Celebrate that you are heaven-directed people!

1) How do you usually "hear" from the Lord?

2) What are some things He has spoken to you? How did you hear it?

3) What are some things He has shown you to do? How did He show you?

4) What enabled you to receive guidance: was it your quietness or desperation, or what?

5) When you know you need guidance how do you seek to receive it?

MAIN POINTS

- God has been guiding you all along by Hand and voice—often without your noticing it.
- Acknowledging past ways He guided you helps you notice present ways.
- He guides us directly by His Word, His example, His voice and His Spirit.
- Five "voices" will harmonize: scripture, conscience, inward impressions, wise counsel, providential circumstances.

- Scripture is the most powerful voice: It must be heeded above all others.
- In major decisions listen for agreement of all five voices. Never force it!
- "Heart" peace comes by trusting; "foot" peace comes by obeying. Get both.
- The path of trusting obedience eventually becomes a mighty river of peace!

DIGGING DEEPER

Guidance is different than obedience. With obedience it is "trust Him and *do it*" (the command is clear); with guidance it is "trust Him and *try it*" (a "hunch" is tentative).

Trying to be guided is like trying to be good. If you try too hard, you will foul it up by not trusting. Just as His goodness is already there for you to abide in, so is His guidance! Being overly self-conscious is disastrous in anything especially when graceful execution is required. Trust, trust, trust and "row your boat" gently down the stream…

Requirements for effective listening:

Willingness to hear and obey	Honesty	Time with Him	Time with Him
Willingness to wait (patience)	Quiet spirit	Time with Him	Time with Him

SWORD AND SHIELD

Study the following scripture looking for "tips" on how the Lord may be seeking to speak to you and lead you more closely.

I will instruct you and teach you in the way which you shall go. I will counsel you with my eye on you. Don't be like the horse, or like the mule, which have no understanding, Who are controlled by bit and bridle, or else they will not come near to you. Psalm 32:8-9 WEB

For this God is our God forever and ever. He will be our guide even to death.
Psalm 48:14 WEB

Nevertheless, I am continually with you; you hold my right hand. You guide me with your counsel, and afterward you will receive me to glory. Psalm 73:23-24

Blessed is the one who finds wisdom, and the one who gets understanding… Her ways are ways of pleasantness, and all her paths are peace. Proverbs 3:13, 17

If you pour yourself out for the hungry and satisfy the desire of the afflicted, then shall your light rise in the darkness and your gloom be as the noonday. And the Lord will guide you continually and satisfy your desire in scorched places and make your bones strong; and you shall be like a watered garden, like a spring of water, whose waters do not fail. Isaiah 58:10-11

Will you not from this time cry to me, My Father, you are the guide of my youth?
Jeremiah 3:4 WEB

"Because of the tender mercy of our God, whereby the sunrise shall visit us from on high to give light to those who sit in darkness and in the shadow of death, to guide our feet into the way of peace." Luke 1:78-79

"When the Spirit of truth comes, he will guide you into all the truth." John 16:13

PRAYER FOCUS

A surrendered heart receives guidance as gracefully and effortlessly as a flower that is opened by the sun receives the bees. So keep your spiritual eyes fastened on the "Son-shine" of the Father's love for you and make this prayer your own:

Father, according to Your love and wisdom, send whatever You desire to send of Your grace and blessings, allow whatever You have to allow of free will and its consequences, ask of me whatever You desire or require of inward and outward obedience, withhold me from and withhold from me whatever is necessary to fulfill Your plans. Help me to fully trust that you are working in and through all things for my good and Your glory. Make me willing to be made willing to surrender everything to You.

RENUNCIATIONS AND AFFIRMATIONS

Renounce any agreements with untruth; believe Jesus' *truth* as your new *way of life*.

Father, forgive me wherever I have thought or said that I have not heard Your voice or experienced Your guidance. I utterly renounce that false belief. The truth is that I am someone who knows how to be guided by You and who has been given ears to hear and eyes to see what You are speaking to me or showing me. I am learning how to listen for Your voice of wisdom through Your Word, through my inner life, and through other people. I am learning to recognize Your Hand—prompting, checking and guiding me. Thank You that You have been speaking to me and guiding me all of my life. Help me to recognize and acknowledge You in all of these ways, so that my eyes can open wider to give You credit and to more readily perceive Your ways of leading me.

PUTTING FEET TO YOUR PRAYERS: STRETCH YOURSELF!

Try these three steps in seeking guidance as you practice walking in the Spirit.

1) Consecrate: Take your present concerns to the Lord. Surrender all. Confess all that He shows you, and accept by faith that you are in the center of His will for you and that He is already working through you. Acknowledge and believe that He is governing everything in your life according to His good will for you, that nothing happens by accident. Tell Him you only want to know and obey

His voice. Ask Him to make it plain. Purpose to obey whatever He reveals. Then abide in simple trust, staying attentive to Him.

2) Wait: Look and listen as you go about your day. Include quiet times for seeking wisdom. Seek the counsel of others; ask for their prayers. Wait for clear light to come about matters of specific guidance. In the meantime accept by faith that you are now in the center of His will and that He is working through you "to will and to work for His good pleasure" (Php 2:13). Continue to abide in simple trust and obedience by doing the next right thing as you understand it. The peace of Christ is never static; it desires to move us—so learn to go as the peace leads you.

3) Act: Whenever you are reasonably sure about a step of specific guidance, yield an immediate obedience. Not to act, when guidance is received, darkens the path. Delays only make obedience more difficult later on. *Step out in faith!*

The Way of the Cross

*And those who belong to Christ Jesus
have crucified the flesh
with its passions and desires.*
Galatians 5:24

NEGATIVE EMOTIONS

By now you may be seeing that the negative emotions we live with on a daily basis are actually things that the Lord wants to help us live without. We cannot keep them from ever showing up, but we can certainly learn how to show them the door! Even though we were all issued hearts at birth, few of us were instructed in how to "guard them" with diligence (Proverbs 4:23). So let's explore more closely the realm of emotions. Your emotional state holds the key to:

Your enjoyment of daily life
Your ability to enjoy the Lord
Your relationships with others
Your ability to be guided by God

Your success in work
Your physical health
Your fruitfulness in ministry

Until fairly recently the intelligence quotient (IQ) was seen as the main indicator of a person's likelihood of success in life. Then EQ (emotional intelligence) gained prominence when it was discovered that the leaders of industry usually had moderate IQ, but high EQ—and the high IQ people were all working under them.[81] The good news for us is that unlike intellectual intelligence which rarely changes, emotional intelligence can be increased throughout life with proper cultivation. Emotional intelligence is defined as the ability to understand one's own emotions, empathize with those of others and act appropriately using those emotions, even under stress.[82] From the perspective of these lessons EQ includes the ability to exercise sovereignty over one's own emotional state, carrying every negative emotion that seeks dominance captive to Christ and being restored to confidence, trust and peace—*His emotional life*.

The ABC's of Emotions

Here are some of the ABC building blocks of healthy emotional intelligence. We may not have had them to play with as kids, but we can learn how to use them now.

A. We are sovereigns over our own hearts.

B. We can actually rule over our emotions, rather than be ruled by them—not as a tyrant, but as a listening, learning leader.

C. Left to itself your emotional state will tend to overrule your reason, will and desires—get to it before it gets to you.

D. No one can put an emotion in you and keep it there.

---

[81] Dr. Lance Wallnau during a Kingdom Business Assoc. conference at MorningStar Ministry, Charlotte, NC. January 2009.
[82] Daniel Coleman, *Working with Emotional Intelligence* (London: Bloomsbury Publishing, 1998) p. 7.

E. You alone get to decide what goes in, stays in and goes out—even though you may not "feel" like you have this ability.

F. All negative emotions are lying to you at *all* times.

G. Even positive emotions will lie to you at some times.

H. All emotions spring from what we actually believe to be true.

I. There is a thought/belief at the center of every emotion.

J. Find out what the emotion is telling you and deal with it.

K. Don't blame others for what you are feeling or you will never get free.

L. Others don't hold the key to what is in you—you do!

M. What you really believe and therefore what you feel is between you and God.

N. God made it that way so that no one can have power over your inner emotional state.

O. No one, not even God, can change your emotions or beliefs without your permission.

P. Your will is free. You are free.

This is truly good news: You are sovereign over your emotions! When it comes to your emotional state you are in charge (Pr 4:23). It may not feel that way at times, but no one else on the planet can force you to have a feeling or keep it in you if you don't want it. You get to choose what you are going to believe in mind and heart—and *what you deeply believe ultimately determines what you will feel*. Your present emotional reactions are the product of what your heart believes to be true—based on past experiences. These beliefs can be changed! You are actually created with an ability to rule over your emotions, though not by ignoring or overpowering them. The victory is not won by force of will, but by learning to agree deep down with what you know to be true that God is showing you. As new beliefs become rooted in you, your emotions begin to change.

Since ignoring negative emotions doesn't work, be honest about what emotions you are really feeling. Take a good look at them. Don't try to push them down, deny them, or hide them. You are not responsible for what goes off inside of you (so don't bother denying your feelings or feeling guilty for having them), but you are responsible for what you do in response to the feeling that just showed up. Will you let it rule over you or will you carry it captive to Christ so that He and you can begin to rule over that feeling (2 Co 10:4-6)?

In carrying your emotions to Christ, how quickly can an emotional state be shifted? In a heartbeat! How do you shift your emotional state? By getting your eyes back on something about the Lord that releases you and re-empowers you. Just imagine Jesus showing up *right now*. Would seeing His love for you shift your emotional state? Of course it would! Well... *active* faith enables us to see Him and get the shift *whenever* we exercise it.

Failing to master the art of getting our faith focus quickly restored guarantees that a lot of time will be spent in the company of negative emotions. That's not good company! Negative emotions are absolutely no good as spiritual guides. Our negative emotions in and of themselves will never help us to rightly understand other people, our self, God or the world we live in. They are no good at telling us about what is really real or really true from God's perspective—and His perspective is the only one that counts or that will be proven right in the end. Why keep holding on to an emotional life that will never be vindicated as truth? One has to wonder: Do they have *any* redemptive value?

Negative emotions are accurate indicators of our internal (usually hidden) belief system tucked away in the core of our hearts. This is the still unconverted part of us and it needs to hear and be taught to believe the gospel truths that we are beginning to believe (like trusting God, surrendering to God, forgiving others, accepting yourself, etc.). It is not enough to believe these things only in your head. Once your heart begins to believe them, your emotional response to people and situations will shift, but until then there will be a battle on the inside to believe truth. And that is because *negative emotions lie against the truth.*

Negative emotions lie to us and misdirect us. Why would an emotion do that? From the perspective of spiritual warfare, the negative emotion is like a glove; the evil spirit is like an invisible hand manipulating the glove, wanting to squeeze you and mislead you in the process. Think about what you have seen in your own life and that of others in terms of anger with God, fear, hopelessness, self-hatred and unforgiveness as you study these four lies that negative emotions promote.

1) The negative emotion wants to convince you that it has a right to stay as long as the problem exists.

2) It wants to focus you on something or someone else as the problem for why you are stuck with that emotion. It never says: "I'm the problem. Just get rid of me!"

3) It wants to make you think it is up to you to do something about it. It pressures you to be your own savior. It never reminds you to cast that care on the Lord.

4) It wants to get others to agree with it—that it has a right to be in you until the problem "out there" is fixed.

God has created you in such a way that no one and nothing on earth can control your emotional life but you! Whenever negative emotions or emotional pain come on you:

1) It is *always* coming from the enemy's sins against you—so learn to immediately recognize and get indignant at the enemy as the true source of your pain, not other people (2 Tim 2:24-26).

2) If it sticks to you beyond a day it is *always* your sin for holding on to it—so learn to recognize your responsibility and carry that negative emotion to Christ to be set free His way.

3) If you are having a hard time getting free, then the snag is likely coming from deceptive programming the enemy has worked into your innermost beliefs—*seek the Lord* (Chapter 7).

Negative programming comes out of past painful experiences of sins against us combined with our own wrong reactions based on false or ungodly beliefs from the fallen nature. These are the strongholds that we have built up over long periods and they still trap us at times in the mindset of the old nature. Review the lessons on the various strongholds that negative emotions form upon our flesh and pray your heart through the ways in God that these false systems of belief and feeling can be brought down. Where our emotional life is concerned, we really can be the head and not the tail (Dt 28:13-14). Let's go for mastery over these pesky invaders of our inner life with Christ!

THE DISCIPLE'S CROSS

Confronted with so much interior disarray, one could easily complain, "This is a lot of work!" True, it's hard dealing with strongholds, but it is harder still letting them rule over us unopposed. No one wants this battle. It is a genuine cross to bear, but because it is a cross, it is also the power of salvation. And that is because there are two crosses that save us. Was that *two* crosses?

Two Crosses that Save Us

Jesus Himself tells us in five separate passages of scripture about the second cross that brings His much needed salvation into our lives (Matthew 10:38, 16:24; Mark 8:34; Luke 9:23, 14:27). The cross of Jesus saves us by getting us to heaven and by "translating" us into the Kingdom of God on earth (Col 3:13). The disciple's cross "saves us" by getting us past the hidden barriers that block us from fully entering into His Kingdom's way of living. It is a major key! We need to understand the disciple's cross and why the Lord allows it—because forsaking the way of the cross will cause us to lose the very life we are trying to save. *How did we miss this?*

> **Then Jesus told his disciples, "If anyone would come after me, let him (1) deny himself and (2) take up his cross and (3) follow me. For whoever would save his life will lose it, but whoever loses his life for my sake will find it." Matthew 16:24-25**

We often stumble at accepting the cross, avoiding being "like our Teacher" (Lk 6:40). Notice the three steps outlined by Jesus which He says are necessary for all who would be His close followers:

1) "Deny himself": We are to trust and submit to Jesus letting Him be Lord—not Self. Self wants comfort and immediate gratification, no challenges, struggles or risks. Self wants to be in charge and be at the center. Self is our nemesis, the false god enthroned within us since the Fall. It is hard to give up living for Self if we have a poor image of Father God.

2) "Take up his cross": Derek Prince described the cross as that place "where your will and God's will cross."[83] The cross is never a person, but it may be a way about them that you don't like and can't easily live with. We "take up" the cross by fully accepting it and the pain that comes with it.

---

[83] Derek Prince, *The Christian Life Series: "The Grace of Yielding"*: (Ft. Lauderdale, FL: Messages by Derek Prince, 1982) Cassette teaching, message number 19.

3) "Follow Me": If we are not willing to do steps (1) and (2), how will we ever be able to do step (3)? How will we ever become close followers of Jesus without learning to embrace this cross?

The cross is by no means easy to embrace: It includes learning to endure grief, shame and rejection; it hovers between self-sacrifice and self-denial. Through the cross we learn to say no to Self (*deny yourself*) and yes to God (*take up your cross*) in order to keep walking with our God (*follow Me*). The cross looks like it is bringing death, but it really leads to life. The stakes are high, the onset is painful and the warfare is intense. No wonder the cross can be difficult to discern and hard to accept!

Two Death Dealing Agents

Did you know, for instance, that both the devil and the cross are trying to kill you? There is death by the enemy and death by the cross: The devil wants to kill all that is good and of God in us; the Lord wants to bring to death all that is wrong, all that is not of Christ in us. Furthermore, we are to *resist* the devil, yet we are to *submit* to the Lord (James 4:7-8). How do you know which is which? How do you know when to submit and when to resist? Here is the key: *We resist the devil in order to embrace the cross*. The enemy always wants us to resist the cross instead!

The cross identifies our places of unrecognized distrust and rebellion, coming out of self-love and self-will. By "blocking" the natural path of our desires, the disciple's cross raises up our "flesh" so that we can deal with it if we want to. The enemy will try to get us to go the wrong way, acting out of our fallen nature. Usually, the hidden side of our self-life just seems like common sense thinking in us, but the cross identifies it as *not of God* or *anti-God*. The Spirit shows us that *in this situation* we will have to deny Self in order to keep following Jesus. A struggle of wills ensues. Under the cross our spirit man still wants to fight Satan, even if we don't. Likewise, our flesh will often want to fight the Lord, even if we wish we could submit. Perhaps you can relate to the following excerpt from my own diary:

> *The cross reveals my pride, self-will, self-love, self-righteousness and self-protectiveness. So, I hate it. It is not much of a cross if I readily embrace it, not much of a cross if I don't truly want to spurn it at first—and all the more so because of what it makes me see in me.*

We may hate and fear the cross when it first "crosses" our path. We may hate and fear the struggle, pain, loss and risk that comes with it. It helps to know these two ways that God is using the cross:

1) He uses the cross to bring something good into our life we could not have received in any other way. If we could have recognized and crucified that part of our fallen nature on our own, we would have. The passage "through the

The Disciple's Cross

cross" produces a death to self in order for us to receive a resurrection into a new quality of life. All we are required to do is "hang in there."

2) In His Hands the cross also brings to death that side of us which hates and fears the cross because this too is a part of the self-life in us that doesn't trust the Father's love and wisdom. It needs to be exposed and brought to death for us to live free of those fears. We say "it's killing me," but the truth is that whatever it is in us that is resisting the cross *needs to die*.

Because the cross can be difficult to discern, here are a few ways to help you recognize the cross when it is working on you:

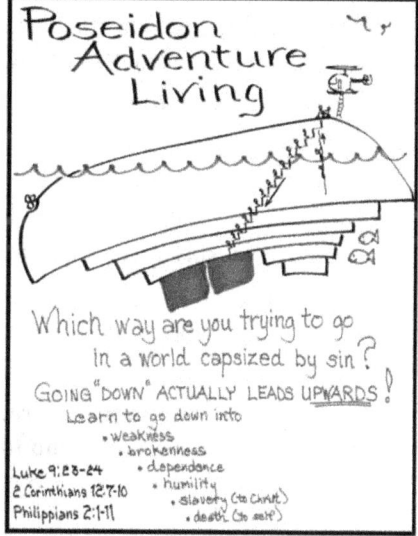

POSEIDON ADVENTURE LIFE

Like the stunned passengers on board the doomed ship Poseidon, there is a "dazed" tendency in us to go the wrong way. Under redemption, all former reliance upon Self has to be abandoned in favor of trusting Jesus.

- You can't get rid of it faithfully. You see no way to avoid it either legally in the law or honorably in the Lord.
- It seems to be killing you. You will actually hear yourself saying things like,"This is killing me!" or "I'll just die if..."
- You have to say, "Not my will, but Yours be done" in order to find any peace and freedom.
- There is often a restless search for a way out or around the problem, rather than an acceptance of what cannot be gracefully removed. "In the absence of something better" we have to accept what is presented to us.
- In the way of things, the cross will either be accepted (now) or repeated down the road (in a later trial).

There is great danger in refusing the cross. Jesus warns us that whoever tries to save His life by spurning the cross will lose it (Matthew 10:38). If we seek Self and Self's desires we will lose His kind of life. If we try to rescue our life we will lose it. If we try to protect our life from pain or from the call of God or from loving others or from risk and challenge, we will lose it. If we try to take control of our life (rather than trust God with it), we will lose it. Why are you here? What is your purpose in being here? To cater to Self? Or have you come to do God's will, as Jesus did? (Hebrews 10:9). True submission to the disciple's cross has been shown to us by the Lord in the way He accepted His own cross. The following is a prayer before the cross modeled on His.

Father, if it is Your will take this cup (the disciple's cross) from me. Nevertheless, not my will but Yours be done. I want to surrender to You in complete confidence and trust, willing to obey and follow Jesus in whatever He asks of me. Make me willing to be made willing.

We need both inner healing and the disciple's cross. Inner healing is often necessary, but it cannot take the place of the disciple's cross, nor remove the pain of it. No amount of inner healing will keep us from encountering the disciple's cross in small or large ways or remove our need for such crosses. However, the healing that comes to us helps restore our trust in the love of the Father, and that does make it easier to see the cross as life-giving, so that we can embrace it more readily. Even the things that we need healing of are themselves forms of the disciple's cross, which we learn to bear gracefully as we seek His healing.

Little crosses prepare us for larger ones. Every minor "crossing" of our will throughout the day prepares us for the larger crosses of life and keeps us in training at surrendering everything to Him. With wisdom we learn to accept our crosses for the same reason Jesus embraced and endured His—for the joy set before us!

> **Let us run with endurance the race that is set before us, looking to Jesus, the founder and perfecter of our faith, who for the joy that was set before him endured the cross, despising the shame, and is seated at the right hand of the throne of God.**
> Hebrews 12:1-2

Appendix

*To our God and Father be glory forever and ever. Amen.
The grace of the Lord Jesus Christ be with your spirit.*
Philippians 4:20, 23

BIBLIOGRAPHY

The Mind Body Connection and Inner Healing

Alexander Loyd, PhD with Ben Johnson, MD. *The Healing Code.*

Art Mathias. *In His Own Image.*

Don Colbert, MD. *Deadly Emotions.*

Henry Wright. *A More Excellent Way.*

John and Paula Sanford. *The Transformation of the Inner Man.*

Neil T. Anderson. *The Bondage Breaker; Victory over the Darkness.*

The Father's Heart

Gordon Dalbey. *Father and Son: The Wound, The Healing, The Call to Manhood.*

Hannah Whithall Smith. *The God of All Comfort.*

Henri J. M. Nouwen. *The Return of the Prodigal Son.*

Classics of the Spiritual Life

A. W. Tozer. *The Attributes of God; The Knowledge of the Holy; God's Pursuit of Man.*

Andrew Murray. *Humility; Abiding in Christ.*

Brother Lawrence. *The Practice of the Presence of God.*

C. S. Lewis. *Mere Chrisitianity.*

François Fénelon. *Spiritual Letters to Women; Mediations on the Heart of God.*

Hannah Whithall Smith. *The Christian's Secret of a Happy Life.*

Jeanne Guyon. *Experiencing the Depths of Jesus Christ; Intimacy with Christ.*

Roy and Revel Hession. *The Calvary Road; Our Nearest Kinsman.*

Watchman Nee. *Sit, Walk, Stand; The Release of the Spirit.*

Spiritual Warfare

Derek Prince. *Blessing or Curse*

Francis MacNutt. *Deliverance from Evil Spirits.*

Johanna Michaelsen. *The Beautiful Side of Evil.*

Rebecca Brown. *He Came to Set the Captives Free; Prepare for War.*

FORERUNNER MINISTRIES

*Which hope we have as an anchor of the soul,
both sure and steadfast, and which enters into that within the veil,
where the Forerunner has entered for us, even Jesus.*
Hebrews 6: 19-20a MKJV

THE eCOURSE FOR HEALING
www.HealingStreamsusa.org

Practically everyone needs recovery of their heart from some painful issues of the past or could readily benefit from gaining mastery over their emotional turbulence in the present. The peace of Christ is meant to be a river of life that we experience all day long—no matter what our circumstances may be. Let the 24 main healing lessons and workout sessions of our free eCourse for Healing take your heart on pilgrimage to a place called the Kingdom of God that is already right inside you.

SPIRIT FILLED LIVING IN CHRIST
www.Forerunners4Him.org

Whether you are a brand new recruit or a "seasoned veteran," if you find that your peace levels are slipping and your joy is not full, then everything on this site is designed to help you come into the fullness of what it truly means to be saved by grace through faith—in all of your days and all of your situations. For us a forerunner is anyone who receives salvation and begins a lifetime quest of "running" into the Heart of God for intimacy and "going before the Lord" to prepare His way into other lives. That's your heart too, isn't it? Come get the equipping you need to be a liberated lover of Jesus and a loving liberator of others.

SANE AND SENSIBLE PERSPECTIVES
www.TheLastDays.info

Many people these days have a God-given hunger to know more about the Last Days. You'll find a feast at this website! Savor the taste of these "sane and sensible perspectives" which are salted with humor and spiced with fresh insights. We have extensive sections devoted to Signs of His Coming, When Is the Rapture, Crucial Components, and Ways to Prepare along with free downloads, an Updates section and blog. Best of all, an entire six-hundred-page commentary on The Book of Revelation is available for free reading and chapter by chapter download.

BOOKS FROM FORERUNNER

If you enjoyed this book, you can purchase copies for friends and keep exploring the spiritual life through these other insightful books by Steve Evans, available in paperback and eBook at Amazon.com.

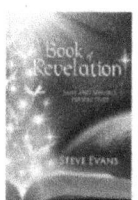
The Book of Revelation takes you on a verse-by-verse stroll through the most complex prophetic vision ever given. These "sane and sensible perspectives" are guaranteed to help you see what this amazing book is trying to show us. With this detailed overview, you'll have the insights you'll need for the days to come.
624 pages. Paperback: $22.00. Kindle: $3.99.

Matters of the Heart is a 24 lesson workbook designed to guide Christian believers through the basic understandings necessary for releasing emotional damage from the past and gaining a grace-based restoration to wholeness. Each chapter is filled with "tools" for practical application.
278 pages. Paperback: $20.00.

The Missing Peace includes all of the 24 lessons of the *Matters of the Heart* teaching series, but without the workbook's other material, focusing instead on a stream of scriptural revelation that will show you how to bring your heart to God and receive His Heart for you in return.
194 pages. Paperback: $15.00.

Rescued from Hell chronicles one man's journey into a ten year living nightmare and his astonishing true story of return. Was it an insane delusion or a satanic deception? This is a tale both incredible and terrible, yet studded with life affirming humor and hope-filled insights into the spiritual realities that surround us.
190 pages. Paperback: $12.50.

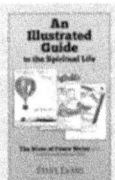
An Illustrated Guide to the Spiritual Life captures in living color with playful insights the otherwise elusive, invisible realities of our life in God. This "illustrated devotional" includes explanations, scriptures and prayers. It is written for the general reader, but is also a pictorial companion to ***The Missing Peace***.
126 pages. Paperback: $17.50.
The River of Peace Series, Vol. 1.

Good Grief is not for everyone, but for those who despite their pain have "set their hearts on pilgrimage", determined to make it to the other side of the Valley of Tears, allowing sorrow that is *rightly* carried to mend their hearts and guide their lives toward God's new beginning.
70 pages. Paperback: $10.00.
The River of Peace Series, Vol. 2.

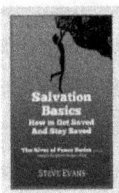
Salvation Basics provides easy to understand answers to life's most important questions: "What will happen to me when I die?" and "What can I do about it?" You will not only discover God's grace-filled way for getting you to heaven, but also His "secret" for living the heavenly life down here.
118 pages. Paperback: $10.00.
The River of Peace Series, Vol. 3.

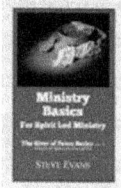
Ministry Basics will prepare you to launch into the sea of human need, lostness and misery which surrounds you, finding your place in the Rescue and your highest path of purpose at the Lord's side. Let these field-tested truths equip you for a joy-filled lifetime of Holy Spirit empowered ministry.
163 pages. Paperback: $10.00.
The River of Peace Series, Vol. 4.

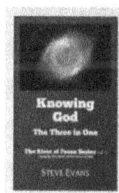
Knowing God may surprise you. The invisible God can be truly, intimately and delightfully known. But it gets even better because there are not just One of Him to get to know, but Three. Think of this as a guide book, not an encyclopedia. Three amazing Persons already know you and love you. What are you waiting for?
161 pages. Paperback: $10.00.
The River of Peace Series, Vol. 5.

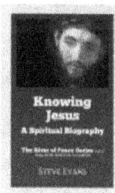
Knowing Jesus will introduce you to the God-Man. He is far and away the most wonderful Person in the universe to know. And He can be known! Simply opening one's heart to Him is all He needs for that life-long adventure to begin. Let this "Spiritual Biography" lead you into fresh revelations of key moments in His life.
159 pages. Paperback: $10.00.
The River of Peace Series, Vol. 6.

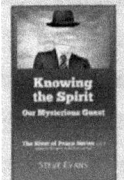
Knowing the Spirit will introduce you to the Mystery Person of the Trinity, help you recognize His ways and connect with His presence, so that you can live with greater delight in His guidance and power. Let this book give you eyes to see and ears to hear your inner Guest as He works with you each day.
149 pages. Paperback: $10.00.
The River of Peace Series, Vol. 7.

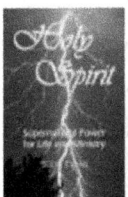
Holy Spirit explores practical ways of getting to know the One who supplies us with supernatural power for life and ministry. Why should the Person of the Trinity who lives within us be so mysterious to us? This book combines ***Knowing the Spirit*** with ***Ministry Basics*** in a single, sensational volume.
171 pages. Paperback: $15.00.

Jesus: An Intimate Portrait will give you fresh perspectives on His Story—the heroic story of the One who shapes all human history by His life and Word. Let these intimate insights reveal the living, breathing God-Man in ways you never encountered Him before. Seeing Him changes everything!
212 pages. Paperback: $15.00.

ABOUT THE AUTHOR

Steve Evans came to faith as one brought back from the dead after a decade of occult oppression and torment. His passion is to see people everywhere released from past brokenness and fully equipped for life and ministry. At HealingStreamsUSA.org he teaches believers how to recover their emotional freedom and master their inward state. At Forerunners4Him.org he shows how to live in the presence and power of the Spirit. His newest website, TheLastDays.info, gives "sane and sensible perspectives" on the events of the Last Days that are heading our way.

Steve has authored numerous books, including: *The Missing Peace, The Book of Revelation, Salvation Basics, Ministry Basics, Knowing the Spirit* and *Rescued from Hell* which tells the story of his own harrowing descent into inner darkness and ultimate restoration. Steve is an ordained minister and a former carpenter, craftsman and missionary.

www.ingramcontent.com/pod-product-compliance
Lightning Source LLC
Chambersburg PA
CBHW080333170426
43194CB00014B/2544